3 1336 00340 1156

D0098948

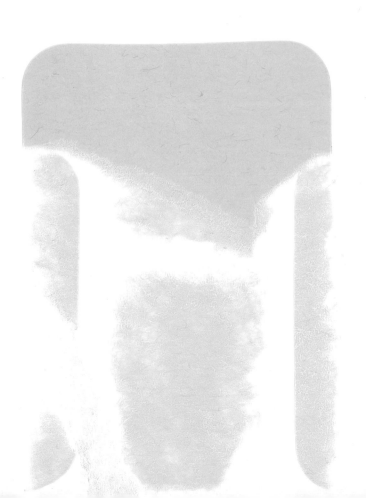

Also by LOUIS KRONENBERGER

THE CART AND THE HORSE

A MONTH OF SUNDAYS

MARLBOROUGH'S DUCHESS

THE REPUBLIC OF LETTERS

COMPANY MANNERS

THE THREAD OF LAUGHTER

GRAND RIGHT AND LEFT

KINGS AND DESPERATE MEN

Edited or translated by Louis Kronenberger

SELECTED WORKS OF
ALEXANDER POPE

THE VIKING BOOK OF APHORISMS
in collaboration with W. H. Auden

THE PORTABLE JOHNSON
AND BOSWELL

THE PLEASURE OF THEIR COMPANY

THE GREAT WORLD: FROM
GREVILLE'S MEMOIRS

THE MAXIMS OF LA ROCHEFOUCAULD

ANOUILH'S COLOMBE

THE POLISHED SURFACE

THE
POLISHED
SURFACE

Essays in the Literature
of Worldliness
by Louis Kronenberger

SAN DIEGO PUBLIC LIBRARY

ALFRED · A · KNOPF

New York 1969

THIS IS A BORZOI BOOK
PUBLISHED BY ALFRED A. KNOPF, INC.

First Edition
Copyright © 1965, 1966, 1967, 1969 by Louis Kronenberger
All rights reserved under International and Pan-American Copyright
Conventions. Published in the United States by Alfred A. Knopf, Inc.,
New York, and simultaneously in Canada by Random House of Canada
Limited, Toronto. Distributed by Random House, Inc., New York.
Library of Congress Catalog Card Number: 70–79350

"The Tribe of La Rochefoucauld" originally appeared as the Introduction
to *The Maxims of La Rochefoucauld*. Reprinted by permission of Random
House, Inc. Copyright © 1959 by Random House, Inc.

"Saint-Simon as Chronicler of Versailles" originally appeared as "Saint-
Simon, Chronicler of Versailles" in the March 1969 issue of *The Kenyon
Review*.

"Horace Walpole's Letters" originally appeared in the March 1965 issue
of *Encounter*.

"*Les Liaisons Dangereuses*" originally appeared in the October 1969 issue
of *The Michigan Quarterly Review*.

"*The Charterhouse of Parma*" originally appeared as "Stendhal's Charterhouse: Supreme Study of Worldliness" in the July 1966 issue of *The
Michigan Quarterly Review*.

"Edith Wharton: *The Age of Innocence* and *The House of Mirth*" originally
appeared as "Edith Wharton's New York: Two Period Pieces" in the
January 1965 issue of *The Michigan Quarterly Review*.

"The Letters and Life of Henry Adams" originally appeared as "The
Letters—and Life—of Henry Adams" in the March 1967 issue of *The
Atlantic Monthly*.

Manufactured in the United States of America

NOV 1969

CONTENTS

THE POLISHED SURFACE

INTRODUCTION

⚜ DURING THOSE YOUNGER STAGES OF OUR LIVES WHEN
the sense of discovery presses hardest upon us, we very
naturally tend to equate discovery with distance, with what
lies beyond the mountains rather than in our own backyard,
just as we equate truth with probing, with subterranean
chambers rather than drawing-room chairs. It is with a
Melville or a Dostoevsky that we would explore, with a
Spinoza or a Kant that we would excavate. We would know
about what we do not know about, as against knowing more
about what we do. We would go to Europe because we live
in America; we would investigate the darker, stranger,
more mystical sins and ecstasies because we ourselves in-
corporate the milder, less intoxicating ones. We crave mes-
sianic rages and apocalyptic visions because we know all
about merely losing one's temper or gazing out the window
at the house across the street. We yearn for the more
inflammatory lusts; we are caught up by the black pits of

guilt and temptation, by the white peaks of redemption and purity. We want great gates to open, we want great bells to peal, we want flourishes of trumpets to sound; we hanker after truths that give us goose flesh, whether in the sonorous foretellings of the prophets or in the harsh revelations of the Freuds; and we would have our light compacted of darkness, and our wisdom never prudential or facile—we would have it, at the least, after the fashion of Blake, "The road of excess leads to the palace of wisdom."

And it is *imaginatively* right to associate discovery with the "On! Sail on!" of Columbus, or truth with Archimedes' "Eureka!" and Newton's apple. Thus are the world's material limits extended or its natural laws made manifest. Thus indeed does man himself grow larger. Thus, too, all pride becomes satanic pride and none of it merely the silly kind; thus all unpleasantness becomes malignity or evil and none of it mere ill nature; thus all desire for a higher self takes on the nature of redemption and none of the quality of New Year resolutions. Taking that view, much of our lives may be unfortunate but nothing is trivial, much may be harrowing but nothing is sordid, we may all be apes, brutes, devils, gods, children of light or creatures of darkness, but we are not much like the man we nod to down the street or the face we catch sight of every morning in the mirror.

In celebrating these aspirations that transform us, I have myself, you will have observed, been a little carried away— and perhaps in the wrong direction, the direction of mockery. But it *is* true of our instincts and imaginations that those who care about the mind, and morality, and the whole lifelong problem of right and wrong and good and evil do find more provocative the distant, unchartable voyage than sticking close to home, do prefer dropping intellectual plumb lines to working with yardsticks and tape measures, and do desire that there be something heroic rather than just human, and black as ink rather than just sooty and drab, about what is wrong with the world. The villains are so much more fascinating than the nuisances; the damned so much more magnetic than the spotted.

But in life, as most of us experience it, many are spotted but few are damned. And though, even so, there is much in life that is heroic, most of it wears a rather homely, even suburban air; there is not much of the mountain peak or the abyss about it. In life, there is often less to be discovered than to be owned up to, and much less of wrongdoing that flatters us by its magnitude than that shames us by its pettiness. Also, in life as we personally experience it, we slowly come to know a great deal that is true—only such truths are far oftener chip diamonds than great blazing stones; and we even come to know, or suspect, a great deal that is true of ourselves. One such truth, indeed, may be that in our search for the great liberating verities there is an element of flight from the small and more ignominious ones.

But for most of us it is just the smaller truths, the less heroic crises, the more beclouded motives that play the largest role. And because, in literature, the worldly tradition constantly demonstrates how immediate and important all this is for us, we do well—both for how much of our actual experience it confirms and for how many of our evasions and self-deceptions it confronts us with—to examine it. It may often take us to unfamiliar milieus, to the world's far-flung capitals and to far-distant and long-vanished cultures; but extremely much of it involves the front lawn and the sitting-room chairs and the face in the mirror, the averted gaze rather than the uplifted vision, the social bore rather than the moral leper, mere dry cleaning rather than purification. Even about the tradition's finer moments there will probably be more of grace than of raptness or of good sense than of profound intuition. There will be, in such moments, the appeal of the best-bred French prose, of the neatest Georgian architecture, of the brightest talk and the best champagne; the appeal of what, I suppose, we call civilization. About all this at its best there is nothing stuffy, but neither is there anything nobly spacious; the right effect is of airiness. About it again there is nothing murky, but neither is there any deep inner glow; the right effect is of brilliance. About it, finally, there is nothing provincial, but neither is there anything inter-planetary; the right effect is of shapely human proportions. And in the literature of worldliness there is a much less distinguished, even a quite unseemly, side, where beneath the glove is discernible the claw, where behind the smile the countenance may show its teeth, where indeed the look is not even bland, the sneer not even veiled, where there is no glitter but only tarnish, no glove but only claw.

Much here, in other words, is disillusioning, skeptical, sharp-eyed, tight-lipped, and seems to contract rather than enlarge our sense of life. Yet not only in what it has produced does this seem to me a very remarkable literature; it seems also, from what it encompasses and signifies, an illuminating and important one. Worldliness is conceivably the most often snubbed of all philosophic attitudes toward life, for it is taxed with not having a soul, with regarding a *lack* of money as the root of all evil, with seeming amused where it ought to be shocked, or with shrugging its shoulders where it might better be unsheathing its sword. Such a tradition in literature may well seem to be pitched—a chic air-conditioned modern house with concealed plumbing and indirect lighting—near the very base of the slopes of Parnassus; while as one looks or clambers up those slopes, one advances from ivy-clad cottages to laurel-wreathed chalets to domed little observatories to severely perfect Doric temples. No doubt there is a certain incongruity about finding the Veuve Clicquot of worldliness beside the very springs of Helicon; enough in fact to provide a slightly embarrassing moral contrast. Yet, if hypocrisy is the homage that vice offers to virtue, doubtless such embarrassment is the homage that the drawing room offers to the cloister, that the twice-two-is-four of reality offers to the nth power of idealism. Yet, in another sense, the embarrassment itself is a *form* of worldliness, is a covert glance, a gesture, in the direction of public opinion.

Public opinion—even at its highest level, where it is sometimes known as human values or critical standards— is of course one of the great conditioners of life; a kind of police force in social matters, a kind of constabulary of culture. And, though born of constantly changing legislation, it is concerned with extremely rigid law enforcement. Public opinion can be peculiarly earnest and peculiarly hypocritical; in fact, the more it is the one, the more likely it will be the other. Yet worldliness, and in particular at the higher levels of public opinion, has sometimes occupied a very lustrous place. Thus, in the England of one of its own high priests, Charles II, worldliness was cock of the walk, and never gave the wall. Even in the England of a dowdy, churchy sovereign, the England of Queen Anne, it never had to give the wall; it had the entrée and very often took precedence. And in the England of the Yellow Nineties and the Green Carnation, worldliness, even absinthe glass in hand, got nicely about, though perhaps with a touch of bravado. And in the New York of the 1920's and the Green Hat, worldliness, even flask on hip, could call the tune,

though doubtless a jazz one. Rather unseemly ages, perhaps, but also quite stylish, and adventurous, and creative
ones.

By the same token they were not stuffy ages, not squeamish or self-righteous or Puritan. There were good men in
them, for all the free love and late hours, but few that were
unco guid. There were many lies told and deceptions practiced in terms of individual self-seeking but, perhaps all the
more, the truth was told about life itself. And very often the
lies were told with a certain humaneness, to save men's
feelings, as in more virtuous ages things are said with
malice or brutality, on the plea of saving men's souls. If
some great themes were missing from literature or art,
others, with a value and luster and piquancy of their own,
were not taboo. What Congreve or Halifax or Swift or Pope
had to say could not wholly have been said in an age of
stricter morals, which would have been one also of severer
censorship. Just so, how much more a Dickens or a Thackeray might have managed to say had their age been less
sanctimoniously upright. If all but the very best minds and
talents were a little coarsened and tarnished by a worldly
era, conversely were not all but the very best minds and
talents a little repressed and intimidated by holier-than-
thou ones? Swift and Dickens had more in common than
we might at first suspect: they both had memories of childhood that rankled deep; they had a feeling for the oppressed
that stoked the furnaces of their imagination; they had dark
and enraged visions of life; they had, each in his own way,
a tremendous sense of the comic and the grotesque. But if
Dickens, as a Victorian, avoids the curses and ravings of the
Yahoos, Swift as an Augustan spares us all the vapid, cloy-
ing sweetness of an Esther Summerson and all the deaths
of Little Nell. We know to what a mere children's classic a

mealy-mouthed age could by and large reduce such a great adult masterpiece as *Gulliver's Travels;* surely we can wonder in turn what a great adult masterpiece might have been written in a less inhibited age by Lewis Carroll.

In truth—and it is the kind of truth that worldly minds and contemplative minds can equally appreciate—the worldly, the social, the urbane tradition in literature brings into lively play all those ambivalences and dualities that are the razor strops for honing the moral intelligence, all those reverse sides of the coin wherewith the Emersonian law of compensation enjoys a continuing life and wherewith ethics becomes the bedfellow of relativism. If the tradition of worldliness has about it, for example, a certain distasteful hardness, it lacks what can be found in traditions with loftier aims: a certain squashy benevolence or hollow exaltedness. Or if the worldly tradition is the poorer for lacking the vox humana or the cello tone, it also lacks the falsetto notes of glibly uplifting traditions, the tremolo of sentimental ones. If the literature of worldliness is not often poetic, no more is it poetical, and in that connection it respects, unlike grander traditions, the firm genius of prose. I have no doubt that one can sometimes catch the worldly tradition sneering; on the other hand, I have never heard it sniffle. I have seen it walk away from human distress, I have seen it not react to social responsibility; but I have not seen it stand around busily and piously doing nothing.

What perhaps it comes down to is the danger that worldliness will descend to cynicism, as weightier philosophies induce hypocrisy and lip service. Or, taking a different view of both, the tradition of worldliness tends to attract and at times even create the snob, as more idealistic traditions foster and invite the prig. Even the greatest of writers—Shakespeare, I would suspect, and Congreve, Pope, Gibbon,

Goethe, Balzac, Proust, Henry James, I am sure—have been a little too much beguiled by the great world, by worldliness enthroned. And yet how much such men *learned* from their associations, profited from their involvements, in coming to understand the way of the world, the workings of society, the strengths and weaknesses of traditions and forms, not to mention all the small eloquent details that their era recorded or their eye caught sight of. And in none of them was the snobbish infatuation for the trappings so powerful as the artistic insistence on the truth. I have no wish to write, even with the playful precedent of an Erasmus, in analogous praise of snobbery; but from the point of view of literature snobbery is far more fruitful and rewarding than priggishness, for the snob tends to be preternaturally observant, and hence as a writer—and I am only concerned with him as a writer—to be extraordinarily enlightening. His orbit is society, his materials are concrete, specific, animate; and if he is something of a fool, he will impart more truth than he knows from being too blindly dazzled or misguidedly impressed. If, on the other hand, he is more than mere snob, if he is Proust, he will, along with imparting truth, bring higher values to bear; his scenes and characters will not just be presented, or even appraised, but enlarged.

Now the prig, though he may mine a richer ore and breathe a purer ether, is never in literature half so rewarding. For one thing, he goes about, nose in air, observing very little. Even were his eyes not turned upward, or inward, even were he in a position, or of an inclination, to observe, he would not much profit therefrom: your prig is not of a sort to judge by appearances. Your prig judges by general laws, or similitudes, or precedents. At his narrowest, unless what he finds coincides with what he is looking for, he won't find it, he will look right past it. Your literary prig is concerned, always, with proceeding from the particular to the general, from the small to the large, from the simple to the complex, from the factual to the symbolic. But for just that reason he tends to operate the other way round; he clamps a generalization onto the smallest fact, he girdles with symbolism the most obvious story. He sees all life in a grain of sand; and such a vision, with all due respect to Blake, must in anyone less than Blake be taken with a grain of salt. Unlike the worldling, for whom life is a genuine, if at times a dubious, education, the prig never learns anything unconsciously or instinctively. He learns only what he feels is worth learning; anything else he not only scorns but fears, or regards as compromise, contamination, deterioration. Your prig lives in a kind of many-windowed, not to say entirely glassed in, dwelling, bathed in a prim religious light; but the windows themselves he never opens, for fear that something may blow in from the street. He wants light without air, he prefers purity to humanity, in all too many cases the campus to the cosmos. He is the most complacent of men, where the snob will often be the most worried; and as he is not, like the snob, observant, so he is not, like the snob, adaptable. He is rigid equally by temperament and by training—rigid in all big ways, where the snob is only in small. For the snob, at his Proust-like task of studying the great world, there may be only one place to go for neckties; for the prig, there is only one way of going to heaven. Your prig is really a snob as well—a moral snob, trudging up holy mountains rather than clambering up social ladders, cutting you dead for not having the right opinions rather than for not knowing the right people. There are sometimes prigs of genius—Macaulay, for one; and so smug and assured that though he had a great genius for scene painting, and a great riveting style of a kind, and a marvelous gift for unrolling the past, he yet knew very little about life in any way he did not bring himself to know it, or about people either. Had he only, all those years that he held the floor at Holland House, orated a little less and examined the faces of men and women a little more, and brought to his unsurpassed memory for bookish things a finer eye for human ones, might he not have been among the very greatest of all historians and writers? As it is, he is very great but in another way very faulty: his knowledge shows a prejudiced cast, his enlightenment wears a period air. Indeed, it strikes me that the prig always ends up caught in the bear traps, encased in the ice of his age. Being inelastic, being dogmatic, he will treat the accepted values of his age, or clique, or caste, as absolutes; and as tastes change, or as standards alter, or knowledge transforms, they (and he with them) will be pushed to one side or swept away.

But it is time to show both prig and snob, both cynicism and cant, the door, and to assert the merits and enjoyments of our wares. Rather than cry the wonders of them, let me offer a kind of roll call of their makers. Taking a not too adventurous line, we may include, from far back, much of Lucian and Horace and Petronius; and, flying across the Dark Ages, resume with Chaucer and Boccaccio, journeying on to Erasmus and Montaigne; and thence to that extraordinary seventeenth century in England and France, when never were one kind of men so fanatical nor another so foppish, the century equally of bloodshed and the bagatelle, given to the most mystical visions and the most rapacious connivings—the century, on the one hand, of Vaughan and Herbert, Cromwell and Milton, Bossuet and Pascal, and, on the other, of Congreve and Halifax, Molière and La Rochefoucauld. And so to the century of worldliness and urbanity upraised—that much-titled period, the Augustan age, the Age of Reason, the Enlightenment, the century of Swift, Pope, Walpole, Gibbon, Hume in Britain, and preeminently Voltaire and the Encyclopedists in France. And now the modern novel is born, and our sense of worldliness widens: Fielding and Fanny Burney bring us to Jane Austen, and thence to Thackeray and Trollope; while in France, Laclos is followed by Stendhal; and we move, at length, to a prominent side of Henry James and to what is central in Edith Wharton; to a prominent side of Henry Adams, and to what is indispensable to Proust; while there is a whole minor tradition running, let us say, from Peacock to Max Beerbohm.

This is our great arterial road, our central region; though the greatest among our names, Molière and Stendhal, Henry James and Proust, are part of a wider domain. But the qualities that this literature most often manifests, the air it most happily breathes, would seem clear enough. This is the tradition of those who have observed and experienced, explored and exposed the way of the world; the wellsprings of conduct, the motives and movements of men and women in society, the commingling of its manners and morals and the more frequent clash, the extent to which its social forms embellish or asphyxiate. In view of the blandness, the sinuousness of so many of the principal actors—their need to pretend, disclaim, outwit; in view of how often this is a world where it is imperative to know every move in the game, much of it bespeaks a leisure class and a sophisticated way of life. Much here, in other words, possesses an acknowledged element of artifice. This at once distinguishes such a world and restricts it, the very artifice or manneredness putting out of bounds a whole literature that can, without question, prove extremely worldly—the literature of large-scale realism. Surely it would misrepresent some of the great masterpieces that deal much with worldly life—Balzac's, say, or Tolstoy's—to claim them for the worldly tradition, for again and again they shatter its mold, they dwarf its horizons.

There is a great region obviously contiguous to ours, the region of satire, which cannot but be involved at times with worldliness; and we encounter it, of course, along with other qualities in many writers we claim for our own. No conscious artist, indeed, can look upon the world's shams and surface behavior without making deductions or drawing conclusions in a satirical way; too much is pretentious, or fatuous, or amusingly self-revealing. But we must for the most part pass pure satire by. With comedy, on the other hand, we are constantly involved, for in any philosophic sense, from any long-term point of view, prescribed attitudes, social concerns, worldly considerations must acquire comic overtones. And even more we must find ourselves at the very side, indeed in the very midst of irony—being in a world of masks and ambiguities, of situations turning in upon themselves, of many things that are not what they seem.

Our habitat, as I said earlier, is on the lower slopes of Parnassus; our concern, we might say, is the fertile lowlands of wisdom. Yet even there we are within hailing distance of a greater tradition, one that also links man to society—the tradition of humanism. With that tradition, however, worldly concerns become a concomitant of human experience, a matter of growth and maturity. There society, though a great shaping force or guiding light, finds a partner in solitude. Of humanism Erasmus is, of course, one of the founding fathers or patron saints. I would from more modern times and an imposing list of names mention two writers, two great cultural and moral leaders who had much of the worldling outlook, but even more of what transcends it. And with such men, with Dr. Johnson and Matthew Arnold, we may grasp what is good about worldliness and yet often not sufficient. I call both these men humanists, though one of them was a devout and often tormented Christian, since their judgments were of a human sort and on a human plane. If they cannot be included here, they cannot quite be excluded either; for, though we may see what worldliness becomes when tarnished by something worse, they show us the kind of value it can acquire when imbued with something better.

I

THE TRIBE OF
LA ROCHEFOUCAULD

THE POINTED OBSERVATION OF ONE KIND OR AN-
other—whether an imaginative perception or an empirical
truth, an admonition to behave or an insight into behavior
—goes back to the beginnings of literature. It would almost
seem that men were distilling wisdom into short sayings
before they had time to be wise; what is more certain is that
from the dawn of letters they wished to father some kind of
text upon humanity or infuse some form of counsel or
exhortation into their writing—and one can only wonder
just how soon after the first maxim was circulated, the first
platitude was scorned. We know, at any rate, how very
ancient are certain sayings still in honorable use. Hippocra-
tes began his collection of medical aphorisms with "Art is
long, life short," as even earlier Heraclitus had proclaimed
what was to become the cornerstone—and in a sense the
touchstone—of his race's drama: Character is fate. And he
said too, in words that have always struck me as less Greek

than Chinese, that we cannot step twice into the same river.

And as with the Greeks, so with the Hebrews even earlier, and perhaps the actual Chinese earlier still; and as with the men of medicine, so with the men of law and the men of God; and so many kinds of truths and half-truths, and perceptions and admonitions, came to be circulated that all sorts of names soon existed for the things themselves—sayings, adages, axioms, maxims, laws, proverbs, aphorisms, apophthegms, gnomes, theorems, paradoxes, epigrams. And then came the names for the outmoded models and the broken-down forms—platitudes, commonplaces, truisms. Many of these sayings were extracted, of course, from longer works, from plays and poems and orations. They existed, very splendidly, in Homer; they appear thereafter throughout Greek drama; they abound in Plutarch, they punctuate Marcus Aurelius, they live on in Horace, they blaze up in Tacitus; and as we move into the modern world, they (often as quotations from the ancients) are the very marrow of Montaigne. The pregnant or witty saying was conceivably Oscar Wilde's most shining gift as a playwright, as it was Emerson's most valuable as an essayist, and Dr. Johnson's most vivid as a man. There is even that final fillip of aphoristic thought when, familiarity having bred contempt, clever—and occasionally more than clever —men turn ideas upside down, with a counter-truth or a bright wisecrack: Wilde's "Old enough to know worse," for example, or the celebrated "A gentleman is someone who is never unintentionally rude."

But as against those who, like Pascal or Blake, Goethe or Nietzsche or Emerson, have individually forged profound and pithy sayings, there developed in the life of politics and courts an almost royal line of aphorists whose particular view of the world, and attitude toward the world, not merely heightens what they write but wholly permeates it. They seem—La Rochefoucauld and Chamfort, Halifax and Chesterfield—often all of one mind, from being equally all of one party. In most cases they are united by the blueness of their blood, the silverness of their spoons; they represent, indeed they epitomize, the great world. They had access to it, they moved observantly about it, and not least of what they observed was how its members maneuvered to escape observation. The La Rochefoucaulds and Halifaxes and all their party took their angle of vision from their stance in the great world; we might even say that they spent their solitude reflecting upon society. The laws of God, the facts of nature, the manifestations of science were rarely a part of their thinking. So far as God affects their meditations, they might all be atheists; so far as nature colors their thoughts, they might all be blind men; so far as interplanetary matters touch their lives, they might all be cave dwellers. What they do, systematically and untiringly, is gaze back and forth from their fellow beings to themselves. From what they themselves are thinking, they postulate their neighbors' thoughts; from what they crave, they deduce their neighbors' desires; from what they themselves would conceal, they infer their neighbors' dissemblings. The province of this great line of aphorists is worldly existence; men and women; real-life masks and mummers; a way of life, moreover, that involves and that instructs the self.

Now one observation that these high-placed aphorists of the seventeenth and eighteenth centuries must very soon have made was how many of mankind's conceptions of itself, and of its beliefs and behavior, were already familiar; and how many of those that were familiar tended also to be flattering; and how many that tended to be flattering tended also to be false. Whether gazing about or peering within, they could not but wonder just how true was "*Amor omnia vincit*" or "*Labor omnia vincit*" or "Patience is a virtue" or "Poverty is a blessing." But even where our aphorists did not find such sayings too dubious for their purposes, they must have found them too worn—not perceptions any longer, but platitudes. Hence, equally a concern for truth and a contempt for triteness would have forced them farther afield. And noting that people most quickly conceal what is small and shameful and ignominious in their make-ups, that much of the truth about human nature is imbedded in man-made protective tissue, it was to such hidden motives of the human heart, such sly tactics of the human scene, that our aphorists addressed themselves. All the blessed isles, the "*Labor omnia vincits,*" in human geography having been discovered and overcolonized, it was toward the bleak, shunned, uninhabited cliffs, the dark and rocky coasts that our aphorists would set their course.

Accordingly, as they studied the human countenance, they would note something masklike or unduly bland about it, or too set about its smile; or, having the good luck to steal up on it unawares, they noted a look of hate or envy in the eyes, or of something bitter about the mouth. And as they peered into the human heart—not least their own— they would spy out much they had for a long time shunned, much else they had never suspected. They thus passed from the surface aspects of behavior to the hidden motives, from the polite assurances to the calculated aims. In promulgating what they had noted on a hundred occasions and then classified into a dozen attitudes, our aphorists displayed a certain sharpness, even acridness of tone; a certain skepticism, even cynicism of thought; and came themselves to seem sardonic, cold-hearted, on occasion misanthropic. And on this head their view of mankind has a less than universal relevance. For what they see is too much influenced by where they stand. Their view of the world, one might say, derives from their all too limited view of it; their verdict on humanity is too strongly colored by their own society. On the other hand, it can be argued that in concentrating on the seamy or undress aspects of their own world, when everything that gives it distinction is lacking, they often speak of faults that link it to human nature generally. When La Rochefoucauld comments that "We would rather run ourselves down than not speak of ourselves at all," it would be hard for the ordinary citizen to ascribe such feelings only to noblemen; when Chesterfield remarks that "It is not to be imagined by how many different ways vanity defeats its own purposes," it would be hard for an American today to make such words apply only to eighteenth-century English peers. All too often La Rochefoucauld's red-heeled slipper or Chesterfield's dancing pump fits us quite as snugly as any twentieth-century shoe.

All the same, in the leisure-class society whence these aphorists arose, there was greater license to be selfish, if only from the more privileged nature of one's upbringing. The social texture of such a world cannot but add to the human temptations; the primacy of manners must relax the potency of morals; it is less important to be a good friend than a good host or drinking companion, and less important to be a good man than not to be known as a bad one. From a desire to keep human intercourse smooth, to conceal the unsightly and ban the disruptive, must come the need to ignore what is open and honest. Can a world not prove deceitful when one of its foremost decrees is that men should go masked? Again, must not its worldlings often resort to shams and wiles less from the desire to shine in society than from the need to survive in it? So that, often as these upper-class verdicts apply to all classes generally, often too they fail to apply, or at least to an equal degree.

But it is not just an avoidance of platitude, or a place in a self-indulgent society, that dictates the coldly pessimistic findings of our line of aphorists. It is also that they are much less meditating philosophers than prying psychologists. Their objective is not the great truths of life but the painful, the all too human truths of living. They are doctors of sorts rather than preachers; scientists, not mentors; they work in laboratories and peer into microscopes—telescopes and observatories are for others. Rather than make flying leaps of the imagination, they probe, correlate, deduce; and less often at high altitudes or in far-off regions than in one another's drawing rooms. A La Rochefoucauld, watching those who have made an art of living, scrutinizes until, of their art of living, he in turn has found out all the hidden jets that water it. In the same way, of their efforts to succeed and their struggles to command, he has achieved a kind of document—a case history of an entire class, the secret confessions of a whole society.

As practicing psychologists, as students of manners and social critics, our line of aphorists are given to discovering how little men do that is altogether born of selfless thoughts and noble aims, of an unclouded benevolence or untainted generosity; and how much that seems good, and often accomplishes good, actually springs from a desire to be liked, or to be praised, or to seem impressive; or to curry favor, or gain benefits in return; or simply from fearing to act otherwise. Above all, our aphorists would tell us how, beyond acting from such motives, we are at the greatest pains to conceal *from ourselves* what those motives are. In our own day, from a quite different breed of investigators, we have come upon discoveries of the same kind; so that cynical as these aphorists may seem, or unscientific by modern standards their methods, none of them can be condemned as mere nay-sayers, mere conscienceless scoffers, least of all mere misanthropists.

Their province, as we have said, is human nature observed against a social background; their tone is sharp and even astringent; their method, the detached analytical method of psychology. It remains to speak for a moment of their form. An aphorism, that is to say, must *have* form, must seem not just shrewd but pointed, not just true but trenchant. The aphorist is the one practicing psychologist who resorts at his peril to longwindedness, who indulges to his ruin in jargon. He is the one sociologist who is forbidden those long cuts of meaning that are half the modern sociologist's writing technique. We are all familiar with that style, every ten words of which involve three that have been invented, three others that have been misapplied, and three others still that are wholly superfluous. At the same time, the true aphorist must be serious—his gift for polish must adorn something more than clever epigrams or flashy paradoxes; indeed, he must be not only serious but honestly investigative. He must be burrower, not borrower; he is to avoid "what oft was thought," be it never so well expressed. Traveling with the lightest baggage, he must offer at times the weightiest wares; cultivating the lapidary's art, he must hold fast to the practicing psychologist's objectives.

No one fulfills these conditions better than the Duc de la Rochefoucauld. The most famous of aphorists, he is no less —in a certain sense—the first of them. The statement holds even though from among men who had died long before La Rochefoucauld was born we might assemble enough aphorisms for a commodious and rewarding anthology. It holds, too, even though during La Rochefoucauld's own lifetime the making of moral maxims was one of the diversions of the salon, the pastimes of the great. But before La Rochefoucauld, only rarely was the moral warp crossed with a psychological woof; only rarely were aphorisms not concerned with definitions and distinctions, or absorbed in generalities. The publication of La Rochefoucauld's *Maxims* in 1665 brought before the world, in the very dawn of modern psychology, a determined and tireless psychologist and a largely empirical one who, while long a participant in worldly life—in politics and military affairs no less than courts and salons—had also been an instinctive observer. More, he had been, as it were, a collector of observations, as he might have been of swords or precious stones, and a collector who would in the same way arrange and display his possessions, and take them up and examine them. There was, Sainte-Beuve remarked of him, "an *arrière-pensée* in all his undertakings, namely to reflect on them when they were past." Moreover, the undertakings themselves—the part he played in the Fronde, his espousal of Anne of Austria's cause, only for her to pass him by when she became Queen Mother—helped shape his attitude. As they first involved him in danger, so they presently plunged him in disappointment and brought him at length to all lack of illusion. It was in this final spirit that La Rochefoucauld sat down to write; with that spirit much of what he wrote is strongly imbued; that element of disillusion is indeed the most pungent one in La Rochefoucauld's outlook upon life. As judge or lawmaker, he is very much a Doubting Thomas who grants no one the benefit of the doubt: La Rochefoucauld's law is France's criminal law, that men are guilty till proved innocent. Worse still, he constantly suggests that men are never guiltier than when they seem innocent; at times he even asserts that few men can *be* innocent, if we mean by that of stainless motive or selfless aim. Beneath all the appearances of benignity and virtue there persists for La Rochefoucauld, whether or not it protrudes, there continues to stir though it may seem to be sleeping or dead, the insatiable ego, the insistent omnivorous self.

Thus, in part from the dark view he takes of the world, in part from the distrustful view the world in turn has taken of him, La Rochefoucauld is regarded, or denounced, or disregarded, as a cynic. Up to a point, there is good reason for such distrust. There is a side to La Rochefoucauld where the judgments seem too cynically harsh or in any case not generally applicable. The courtier society he dissected was not just extremely worldly in its ambitions; it was outrageously privileged in its attitudes, it was treacherous and even conspiratorial in its methods. Living in constant fear of deception, men came to be schooled in deceit. At one moment we feel that La Rochefoucauld is writing of too special a world; the next moment, that he is nothing less than obsessed with ugly motives and methods. The *Maxims* seem tarnished by this strain of misanthropy, this readiness to believe the worst; as they are also dulled in places through stating the obvious or seeming, really, to say nothing at all—witness "Men's dispositions, like most buildings, vary in appearance: some are attractive, some are distasteful." But having admitted that he can seem merely cynical, or eccentric or platitudinous or false, we can pass on to what is central in him, and very permanently rewarding.

Even La Rochefoucauld's excessively cynical streak was born of his conviction that men are almost wholly actuated by self-interest (or by that blood brother of self-interest, vanity). Almost every bad quality in man La Rochefoucauld traced back to these; and to these, in some disguised form, he traced almost every good quality as well. For him, all this is a law of life that not so much disparages human nature as merely defines it; everything, for him, comes finally to rest on the unceasing assertiveness, acquisitiveness, aggrandizement of the ego. Men, do you maintain, feel a love of justice? "Love of justice," maintains La Rochefoucauld, "in most men is only a fear of encountering injustice." Men are benevolent? "We often do good that we may do harm with impunity." Men possess self-control? "If we resist our passions, it is oftener because they are weak than because we are strong." Men love virtue? "Virtue would not go nearly so far if vanity did not keep her company." Men feel gratitude? "In most men, gratitude is only a secret longing for greater benefits." Men confess their faults? "We confess to small faults to create the impression that we have no great ones." Each of these sayings must give us qualms; has, at the least, an uncomfortable grain of truth. And wherever we resist La Rochefoucauld's contentions, are we not helping to corroborate them—in the sense that our vanity and our ego inspire the resistance? On the other hand, I think we are far more prone to cry *touché* to all this than our grandfathers would have been, seeing how much that emerged three hundred years ago from La Rochefoucauld's writing table has been confirmed today on the psychoanalyst's couch. Again and again, and very remarkably, La Rochefoucauld anticipated the Freudians.

His field of operations, however, is much more limited. It remains, need one say again, chiefly in the great world; even in terms of sex, it largely concerns itself with lovemaking as a game, with passion as a seasonal sport, with the desire to achieve conquests and the fear of inviting ridicule, with lovers and mistresses rather than husbands and wives.

The basis of that world was a constant use of masks—whether the masks by which men mislead and misapprehend others, or mislead and misjudge themselves. La Rochefoucauld dissected a society in which compliments were conjoined to rapiers, in which men bowed suavely to one another at two o'clock and ruthlessly betrayed one another at four; and having participated in so dishonest a spectacle no less than observed it, he presumably unmasked not just other people's hearts but his own. I say "presumably," because no one ever wrote with a more detached and impersonal air. Even where his meaning is foolish or wholly absurd, there is no personal taint in it; the tone remains judicial and even legal; the errors resemble errors of nature.

Allowing for his narrow field of operations and for his focusing on only one real target, certainly his hits are numerous and deadly, certainly his exposé—whether of personal motive or of worldly method—is consummate. "To establish oneself in the world, one does all one can to seem established there already"; "We often add to our pride what we manage to subtract from our other faults"; "It is a form of coquetry to emphasize the fact that you do not indulge in it"; "If we did not flatter ourselves, the flattery of others could do us no harm"; "Our worth wins us the regard of the worthy, our success the regard of the world"; one could go profitably through the entire alphabet of self-interest with La Rochefoucauld, for what it says about avarice or benefactors or calculation, about distrust or envy or favor. Time and again, La Rochefoucauld makes us face the ugly facts that we have averted our gaze from; and time and again, as a result, he gives our self-esteem a blow from which it never wholly recovers. He has ferreted out some of our truest feelings in such matters as envy, jealousy, love, gratitude, ambition, and some of our slyest attempts to achieve what we want, be it friends or advancement or flattery. He, in his way, has peered quite as sharply as modern specialists in theirs, into a dark realm of tangled and unsightly motives; and in his way has preached, quite as much as any modern moralist, a harsh sermon on how self-loving is man, and how self-seeking.

All in all, he stands forth the greatest aphorist—and in a certain sense perhaps the greatest analyst—of purely worldly behavior. In the matter of form and style, he is a lapidary indeed, very often a model of succinctness and polish. In the matter of approach, he is no more deflected into satire than into sentimentality, he is no more a contriver of situations than an exploiter of self. He has stripped his stage of scenery, his actors of costume, has smoked out the perfume, extinguished the fire, iced the flesh. Self-interest and vanity in men may come to seem obsessive with him; but they are always scientifically inspected in a test tube, clinically examined through a microscope.

Self-interest and vanity *are*, I think, obsessive with him; and once La Rochefoucauld had made them the mainspring of men's conduct, once, that is to say, he had formed so inflexible a theory of human nature, he could perhaps never again, with quite all the old sharpness, scrutinize the human scene. He at times, alas, is the steed and his theory the heel-grinding rider. He ignores at times things that chasten and restrain even the most self-centered of people —the sudden prick of conscience or sense of honor, the particular code such men live by or their derelict but never quite extinct sense of duty. And La Rochefoucauld could have known very little of what we today know all too much —of that tyrannical hidden dissuader, man's gnawing sense of guilt. All these are things that rout self-interest at times or keep it at bay. Long after La Rochefoucauld found in self-love man's sovereign impulsion, Balzac was to find it in money; and the Freudians, in their turn, were to find it in sex. The massive claims of all three of these impulsions must warn us against ascribing too great a primacy to any one of them. Yet of the three, if only because it accounts for so many of our feelings about the other two, it is La Roche-foucauld's vanity that seems to me the most insatiable of hungers and, by all odds, the most incessant.

II

SAINT-SIMON, CHRONICLER OF VERSAILLES

"OF THE TWO DUKES WHO HAVE GAINED IMMORTAL-ity by letters, one depicted the follies of mankind in almost the lengthiest of human masterpieces, the other in almost the briefest." So I once began an introduction to the gem-like maxims of La Rochefoucauld, and so in no better way can I now begin upon the oceanic memoirs of Saint-Simon. With Saint-Simon, indeed, mention of his dukedom before everything else is altogether appropriate, for the dukedom itself came before everything else in his life. It is the rubric, the refrain, the battle standard at every stage of his career, it is the insistent subject matter of far too much of the forty-odd volumes of the standard edition of the *Mémoires*. But Saint-Simon's indefatigable pen has greater claims on our attention than his all-too-wearisome peerage; though the pen too, and not simply in terms of the peerage, can become a solemn bore. Fortunately the memoirs are also, and very frequently, of extraordinary vividness and brilliance, setting before us every manner of incident at the greatest, the most populous, emulous, conscienceless of royal courts. Here is the Versailles of a king who at fantastic labor and expense gave it the magic of a fairy tale, the discipline of a fortress, the deviousness of a labyrinth. Here is that King himself, here is Louis XIV, whose boasts and claims to homage have become bywords and clichés; but who almost literally *was* the state, *was* the sun, and remains today the aptest synonym for majesty—for the grand style in demeanor and the gloved fist in despotism.

The chronicler of this court was a most remarkable courtier in whom were lodged such diverse traits as enabled him to probe the most subterranean maneuvers; as could make for sane views on large issues, and for antediluvian ones about trifles; a courtier whose mode of life was often as ceremonious as his writing could be slapdash, whose idle ducal existence resembled a detective's round-the-clock assignment, and whose foolish side quite possibly proved as watchful and as fruitful as his perceptive one. In the twenty years and more before Louis XIV's death that Saint-Simon spent at Versailles, he was to chronicle the history of its intrigues, blueprint the architecture of its ambitions, and make of its inhabitants one of the supreme portrait galleries in all literature. And somehow pervading, directing, embossing all this—like a huge monogram encountered in every corridor, on every staircase, above every doorway— was the presence and personality of the King. Indeed, had Louis XIV been an immodest man, it might have occurred to him to remark: *"Versailles, c'est moi."*

Louis XIV—this was essential for Saint-Simon's great achievement—led the most public life imaginable. He was in a very real sense on display, to be seen by a few, by many, by all, from early morning when the curtains of his bed were parted till, having said his prayers at night and gone to bed, a special few still might speak to him. His routine, whether at Versailles or elsewhere, did not vary much, except that on certain days he went stag hunting or picnicking, and on others took physic; nor did his schedule create difficulties, for early in the morning he would formally announce his appointments for the day. In addition to his being constantly on view there were occasions, such as his coming from Mass or strolling round the gardens, when he might be approached, when indeed he might even be accompanied. Happily, there awaits us Saint-Simon's detailed account of the King's day; my point here is how public it was, which in a sense means how prescribed. This public side of things is an aspect of the God the Father image which Louis XIV wished to project, wherein he became frighteningly awesome but at the same time very accessible; just as the public side of things demonstrates the importance to him of protocol and ceremony. As for the first of these objectives, Louis truly believed himself answerable only to God, and vice-versa—as when after a military disaster he cried out: "How could God do this to me after all I have done for Him?" As for the protocol side of things, there was for the King a powerful sense of rank and position, wherein human society resembled the steps of a stairway, as court activities evoked the hands of a clock. There was an exact time for everything, and for everyone an exact place. Thus, through which door you entered, and how far it was opened for you; with whom you walked, and when—and on what—you sat down; whether you were seen to the head of the stairs, to the foot of the stairs, or to your carriage; who, again, might see the King in bed, or the King being shaved, or the King feeding his dogs, or the King getting into his breeches, were minutiae of prerogative and rank, as they were also matters of ritual. It sounds deadly, but there is perhaps something to be said for making the most boring or exhausting or trifling of human activities into coveted privileges and exalted ceremonies.

In much of all this, moreover, gaffes and faux pas could have unpleasant consequences. Least unpleasant was the gossip they created; but they could also be turned into affronts, or seized on for self-advancement, or lead to small pitched battles; worse, they might provoke the King's terrifying reprimands or call forth his relentless anger. Of all that went on at Versailles the King was omnisciently aware. He insisted that the whole court—which, counting servants, meant some 15,000 people—attend him there, and he was a past master at taking attendance. To avoid seeing the King was in his eyes a form of high treason. He had lackeys and toadies, intelligencers and spies enough, but almost as alarmingly, he had a gimlet eye that swept the scene; and to be marked absent was to be put quakingly on probation. Yet to be marked present, to be noticeably on hand, could be a sufficient trial. For Versailles, while purporting to be a luxurious dream world, was a kind of palace tenement; and the more privileged its occupants, the less palatial, in many cases, were their quarters. As against living in comfort on their own estates or even in the town of Versailles, it was a social cachet to live huddled inside the palace in two or three small airless rooms.

Louis XIV was not, of course, anomalous in his seventeenth-century personification of divine right—many fellow monarchs also claimed his attributes. That he outshone the others, that he endowed his person with a kind of divine rightness, is due to how fervently he believed in his role and how flawlessly he read his lines. That he read more into them, that he squeezed more out of them than anyone else

was not, however, entirely his doing. As Professor Guigne-
bert put it, "It was with the complicity of his own subjects"
that his "Moi" became so overpowering. As King he was not
simply looked up to, or even bowed down to; he was set
apart, reverenced, deified. Intemperately flattered, he was
also inordinately vain; he believed what he wished to hear,
and the more he believed it, the more of it he heard, the
more autocratic he became, the more servile became most
of his courtiers.

Adulation had begun very early—Louis XIV became King
at the age of five (as did Louis XIII at the age of nine and
Louis XV at the age of seven). His earliest days, to be sure,
were often void of flattery, for during the Fronde he and his
mother, Anne of Austria, were more than once sufficiently
menaced to have to flee Paris, which explains his dislike of
Paris in later life and his abandoning it for Versailles. He
grew up under the Regency of his mother and of Cardinal
Mazarin, which he never contested; but when in 1661 Mazarin died, the twenty-three-year-old Louis assumed complete control, asserting that he would be his own Prime
Minister, and during the next two decades, with the help of
able generals and ministers, he made France the most
powerful nation in Europe. It was in these same decades
that he created Versailles, which was to proclaim his majesty while a flourishing France proclaimed his might. Louis
had some feeling for the arts, at any rate for the theater
and music; he had much feeling for visual grandeur, and
most feeling of all for self-aggrandizement, so that there
labored or performed or eulogized at Versailles Mansart and
Le Nôtre, Racine and Molière, Fénelon and Bossuet, Lully
and La Bruyère.

It was during the same two decades that Louis introduced into his household three ladies who have continued

to be household names: Mademoiselle de La Vallière, Madame de Montespan, Madame de Maintenon. By La Vallière he had one, and by the Montespan four of the royal bastards who outraged and obsessed Saint-Simon's thinking. After the death of his Queen, Louis secretly married the childless Maintenon. Thereafter the King's life became more domestic and a shade less public: he and his unacknowledged spouse would sit in her room at night, side by side in armchairs, until it came time for Louis' well-attended, ostentatious *coucher*. So he grew older, more uncharitably pious, more unchartably despotic; still France, though its glories had diminished; still the sun, though a stormily setting one; still—indeed, more than ever—terrifying; and all these years constantly stalked and studied by Louis de Rouvroy, duc de Saint-Simon (1675–1755).

Saint-Simon was first presented to the King in 1691; his father brought him to Versailles that he might begin his military service as a Musketeer. Two years later, when he acquired the command of a troop, and when his twice-married father died at the age of eighty-seven, Saint-Simon, himself now a duke, began living at Versailles. His career as a courtier preceded by very little his career as a diarist, though it was not till late in life that he revised, corrected, and consolidated his vast *Mémoires*. His ambitions as a courtier—one might better say his objectives—were at once wholly straightforward and exceedingly complicated. He was a kind of crusader, seeking not so much to have himself upraised as to have others brought low; and not so much thirsting for power as obsessed by rank. The great sore spot about the King's illegitimate children was his having set them *above* the dukes, in an intermediate position between them and the princes of the blood. It was this horrendous act that made the King an even more central figure to the

fuming duke than his kingliness itself did. Yet even without
this Saint-Simon must have been faintly maniacal about
genealogy, precedence, prerogative; must have seemed in
the King's eyes a nuisance and a crank, hence someone
who, the more he gained royal notice, the more certain he
was to forfeit royal favor.

Not too surprisingly, our young duke held title to a young
dukedom: His father, having won great favor with Louis
XIII, was made a *duc et pair;* and though Saint-Simon's an-
cestry was seignorial enough, it was neither feudal nor
grand. Yet the howling snob he was does not altogether
explain him. If he opposed the elevation of the bastards
with a lunatic intensity, he fought the cause of the dukes
for allowable as well as foolish reasons. Louis had not just
subordinated the dukes in rank; he had quite stripped them
of power. His ministers and men of affairs were in origin—
and by design—almost uniformly bourgeois. The dukes and
lesser nobility might have, by way of ribbons and medals
and titles, a good deal to boast of; but they had little of
importance to keep them occupied. Some of them presumably deserved power, and others legitimately enough desired
it: to this extent Saint-Simon was not wrong in his indigna-
tion, and not alone. Unfortunately he was equally outraged
by the most trivial violations of privilege or precedence:
vigilant in detecting them, vociferous in denouncing them,
pertinacious in rounding up his fellow dukes to protest
them, he could emerge not just a fanatic, but a pest. We
cannot for long escape Saint-Simon's alarums about the
Bourgeois Threat or the Bend-Sinister Peril. In a different
way, although Saint-Simon was often of divided mind about
Louis XIV—on the one hand awed by him and craving his
favor; on the other hand, given to perceptive animosity and
dislike—he brings the King wonderfully to life with small

telltale touches, so that Louis is one of those people, those actors we might say—Queen Victoria was another—who "hold" us in everything, however trifling, that they do. We shall find more of the truth about Louis XIV elsewhere, but nowhere more that seems truer to life.

Yet, Saint-Simon in any vital sense, did not see much of the King in all his years at court. He had of him, and then by request, only three or four solid audiences. Often over the years Saint-Simon was either out of favor with Louis or in actual disgrace—whether from choosing to resign his commission in the army, or from persuading duchesses not to pass the alms bag at Mass, or from making a tactless bet which was magnified into a species of treason. It was to justify himself in such matters that he obtained the audiences—long-winded recitations on his part, which come off as long-suffering indulgences on the King's. It is fairly clear that his dislike of the King derives from his being so seldom liked or favored in turn; had this sovereign rich in qualities that Saint-Simon admired—grace, dignity, self-control— smiled on him, he must have responded with delight. As it was, Saint-Simon was never at Versailles a well-placed participant: only an unequaled observer.

And what a world to observe! Here, in the twenty-two years before the King's death, were gathered his morganatic wife; his son the Dauphin, called Monseigneur; Louis' brother, called Monsieur, and Monsieur's German-princess wife; Monseigneur's three sons and the wives of two of them; Louis' favored bastards—the Duke du Maine, the Count of Toulouse, the Princess of Conti, and the Duchess of Orleans. Here were the King's ministers and advisers, here were those who had the less important, the more important, the most important *entrées*, here all the cliques and cabals that a great court is diseased with; the foreign princes who abided here and those arriving for visits; the generals and marshals returning from Louis' wars; the great ladies and the great ladies' men; the men of God, who might sometimes be rakes and sodomites; the doctors and tutors, the grooms and gardeners and chefs. And all this not at Versailles alone; for though the King hated Paris, he went at regular intervals to the smaller palace he had built on swampy ground at Marly, or to Fontainebleau or Meudon; and with him went those who craved the honor of being asked, or who obeyed the summons.

The thousands of courtiers at Versailles constituted a world unrivaled for numbers and unrivaled for rivalry. In all the annals of worldliness, or the memoirs of worldlings, there is perhaps nothing comparable in ostentatious display or surreptitious maneuvering. The full effect of such a multitude of participants, entering and exiting, appearing and vanishing, reappearing and re-exiting can only be experienced by reading thousands of pages and millions of words, at the cost of much dullness, repetitiousness, and triviality. Yet it does provide the equivalent of a vast fictional tetralogy, of a great human, and often inhuman, comedy, whose dullnesses culminate in indelibly vivid scenes, whose duchesses approximate the *grandes dames* and magnificent grotesques of the greatest novels.

But happily many scenes are immediately compelling, many characters quickly and quintessentially portrayed; much that is wildly eccentric, brutally realistic, fatuously comic is flung at us without warning. Happily, too, the royal family, whether got on the right or wrong side of the sheets, form a densely interrelated group which constitute the memoirs' natural center of interest and intrigue. These people create what resembles an outwardly spacious, inwardly turbulent family novel—the autocratic father; the son and heir cowed into nonentity; the respectful brother; the three grandsons, the eldest serious and thoughtful, married to a vivacious girl; the second given not just castles in Spain but its actual crown; and the youngest and liveliest making a controversial "family" marriage. Despite the great eminence of the family, and its grand way of life, it makes a rather melancholy story, in the course of which almost all the people die, often very young, or not on speaking terms, or under suspicous circumstances.

Besides so much sudden and early death, there were most of the other elements that endow a family chronicle with drama. There was a shadowy stepmother and step-grandmother; there were ambitious and greedy relations on all sides; there were feuds and infidelities, strange foibles and fashionable vices. There was a homosexual married brother; and along with poison pens, there were perhaps poisoned viands—the suggestion that those sitting above the salt were also not above a little strychnine. There was much, too, concerning the head of the family's will, and indeed a good many deathbed connivings.

Moreover, it is round the highest-placed figures that almost everyone else's fortunes revolve; it is upon them that everyone's gaze is fixed, thoughts are centered, dreams are dependent. Hence all the worldly arts of foresight, flattery, double-dealing, self-seeking, social climbing are seen to operate, and the words of our other, somewhat earlier duke again and again become flesh and blood. Saint-Simon himself restates La Rochefoucauld's remark that we find it harder to forgive those whom we injure than those who injure us; and our chronicle constantly bears out such other of La Rochefoucauld's comments as that "We are much harder on people who betray us in small ways than on people who betray others in great ones" or that "To establish oneself in the world, one does all one can to seem established there already."

In an excellent account of Saint-Simon's direct relations with the King, Louis Auchincloss speaks of his surprise at finding Saint-Simon's Versailles generally regarded as a "shrine of artificiality and hypocrisy" when the people in the memoirs behave with "a brutal frankness and a doglike rapacity that is appalling to behold." And if we equate artificiality with elegant manners and hypocrisy with empty forms, what we often find in Saint-Simon instead is physical coarseness and foulness on the one hand, and rude and ruthless behavior on the other. But in the sense that the courtier's *life* was artificial—full of calculated self-promoting endeavors, given to evasive and guarded responses, so as to become a perfect masked ball of motives if not of manners; and in the sense that hypocrisy dictated a pretense of friendship or loyalty or devotion—on such grounds the attributes which Mr. Auchincloss questions would seem to me essentially valid. What much of it comes down to is whom one could trust and how far oneself could afford to be honest. Beyond how devious and circuitous was the way to self-advancement, it must never be forgotten that Louis XIV was an absolute monarch, against whose judgments there was little if any appeal; and that all court rumor and gossip, all personal misbehavior and every inkling of disloyalty was brought to him. Hence with every man's sense of how far he might rise went his awareness of how catastrophically he could fall. The King's displeasure, his forbidding glance and crushing tone, could be pulverizing enough. But his actual decrees of temporary exile, permanent banishment, imprisonment in a fortress jail, not to speak of death on the scaffold, were by no means unusual. Toward those beneath them men could indeed make Mr. Auchincloss' bear garden of Versailles; but with those above, it became a form of masquerade.

It could not be otherwise, in the opinion of a far wiser courtier than Saint-Simon, at a far less frightening court. Lord Halifax has said of life under Charles II that "Malice may be sometimes out of breath; envy never"; that "State business is a cruel trade; good nature is a bungler in it"; that "Men are so unwilling to displease a prince that it is as dangerous to inform him right as to serve him wrong." And there was another reason for how gross and brutal the world of Versailles could be, and hence how rouged and varnished. There was the age itself, with its fleshly indulgences and the monstrous penalties they exacted—an age when aristocratic life was not just rife with illness, but the doctor often did more harm than the disease; when everyone at court overate, to suffer hideous belly pains and even filthy drawing-room disasters; and when, what with the gargantuan meals, everyone regularly took mammoth purges.

As for dalliance, we may wonder how many besides the syphilitic Duke of Vendôme went about with half a nose— Vendôme, whose social habits must have made most of his acquaintance wish they had no nose at all. During this age of magnificence and rankness, of insolence and obsequiousness, extremes meet everywhere, even in the same man. Extremes meet in Versailles itself, as both an opulent dream and a shivering nightmare, as gaudy as Hollywood, as blasted as Hell. Fever, smallpox, bloodpoisoning were guests at all its pageants and fêtes; at Versailles duplicity smiled, curtsied, knelt at every grandee's feet; a whole pedigreed homosexual society infiltrated the palace, with princes "scurrying through the night." When straitlaced Madame de Maintenon remonstrated about this with the King, "Am I," he answered, "to begin with my own brother?"

—Monsieur indeed being known as the King of Sodom. Louis XIV had superb social talents and royal endowments; except as vanity could mislead him, he was a shrewd judge of men. He had much good sense, often great forbearance, and in *politesse* and kingliness he could be incomparable, in how he moved or bowed or sat at supper. But he could be a petty taskmaster and a heartless tyrant; when it came time to go from Versailles to Marly or Fontainebleau, sickness saved no one who had been asked there from going—indeed, to feel sick, Saint-Simon tells us, was an unforgivable sin. In the King's coach, when he desired conversation, no one could fall silent; when he offered food, no one could refuse it; when he chose to be awake, no one could dream of napping—and this fell hardest on those he favored most, as being those he kept most often about him. To refuse an "honor" that the King proposed could mean ruin; and as Louis grew older, and then old, during Saint-Simon's years at court there there was ever less of Hollywood and more of Hell—what with Louis' remorse for his sins and visions of a Hell beyond the grave; what with his black hours of military and financial disaster; what with his sitting by the fire with his morganatic conscience, or his contemplating the death-beds of his brother and his son (he was on bad terms with both) and of his grandsons and his grandson's wife. An increase in piety brought none in charity, and Louis became at once more unaccountable in his behavior and more auto-cratic. During these last years, a sort of mortuary hush—counterpointing the sense of conspiratorial stealth—comes into the story, only to be shattered with the sudden resumptions of splendor and attendant reverberations of scandal. For Saint-Simon and countless others, every royal death augurs gain or loss, fresh obstacles or opportunities, new arrangements in strategy, new patterns of intrigue. Our subject being an all-too-well-known chapter of history, there can be no concealing how the plot comes out; but our memories, faced with so many twists and turns of plotting, are bound to be sometimes defective, often permitting the story a considerable suspense.

Versailles was resplendent and grand; Versailles was ugly and gross; Versailles could also be weird and grotesque. One of the more recurrent traits of high society, whether descended from immemorial chieftains or recent robber barons, is that it develops a crazy streak fast. In such a society, every seventh multimillionaire is a psychopathic miser; every sixth duke sleeps with a teddy bear or his niece; every "proper" family boasts a cousin who insists that her room is haunted, or that there are bombs under his bed, or that the butler attempted to rape her, or that he helped to build the Pyramids. And certainly Saint-Simon's memoirs are a splendid chronicle, nay catalogue, of delusions, fixations, obsessions, with the chronicler himself not altogether exempt. The French, so lucidly absurd, so logically mad, so long on wit and short on humor, hold on to family quirks as though they were heirlooms. "All the Matignons are batty," it was said to the Regent, "except the Marquis." "True," the Regent answered, "he is not—but you can tell that his father was." Not least diverting are the anecdotes of high-born buffoonery; the gossip in the memoirs about crotchets and oddities; the schoolboy hoaxes, the small-scale hallucinations, these often being the pigmentation of Saint-Simon's portraiture or the flavorer of his obituaries; these, too, being the marks of an age still riddled with superstition and of a court that, when not all too knowing, can be wonderfully credulous. Between the missteps that made tongues wag and might prove costly, and the gaffes that inspired laughter and went the rounds, life at court was a resonant whispering gallery having all the newsiness of a modern gossip column with none of the need. Although every scrap of chitchat was of interest to Saint-Simon, he was rather a gossip-historian of sorts than an outright gossip. For one thing, the memoirs were aimed at posterity, when Saint-Simon himself should be dead; for another, in writing the memoirs he had an end in view requiring the instincts of the novelist, the insights of the psychologist, and the thoroughness of the historian. He was an untiring ferret, but not a magpie. That the memoirs are yet a mine of gossip, a museum of grotesquerie, indicates how encyclopedic—however on occasion inaccurate, prejudiced, fragmentary, false—was his knowledge of the court.

The vagaries and eccentricities start very high up; indeed, they have royal blood. With Monsieur le Prince or the Duke of Mazarin they are outstanding; more often, they yield us a paragraph or simply a sentence or two. Thus, there is something more touching than odd about the Emperor Leopold, who on his deathbed, having taken the sacraments, sent for his band—his only real pleasure—and, while it was playing for him, died. Or there was M. de Navailles, the Duke of Orleans' tutor, who, when Monsieur le Prince wanted information about a tiny stream in Flanders not shown on his map, came to his assistance by bringing him a map of the world. Saint-Simon himself must laugh at a bishop of the Clermont-Tonnere family whose "whole house was covered with coats of arms, even to the ceilings and floors, along with two great family trees on the wall, one labeled "Descent of the most august House of Clermont-Tonnere from the Emperors of the East"; its companion, "Descent of the most august House of Clermont-Tonnere from the Emperors of the West."

A rather disappointing side of the *Mémoires* is that,

though Saint-Simon speaks of a great many people as extremely witty, he seldom offers samples of their wit, nor are those he does particularly impressive. The *mots* rarely exceed the Duke of Orleans' comment when Marshal Tallard gained a governorship after constant defeat as a general: "It's only fair to give something to a man who has lost everything." With the point reversed, Saint-Simon himself said of Marshal Marchin that "He was treated with indifference; since he had made no mistake, he wasn't considered worthy of any recompense." And of Monaco it was wisecracked then, as it might be now, that "from the center of it you can spit in any direction across the frontier."

With imbecilities, however, the text abounds, closely followed by horseplay and practical jokes, many of them puerile or scatological or both. The King himself was not above throwing bread pellets at people while dining, and at least once had a lady fling back the contents of a bowl of food in his face. The Duke of Lausun, Saint-Simon's brother-in-law, got double fun from a hoax: he told Marshal de Chateaurenard, an intolerable bore, that his relations the Cavoyes complained that they never saw him; and he urged the marshal to visit them regularly, and not be put off by their cold manner in receiving him, which was simply a well-known quirk of theirs. Chateaurenard called, and to the Cavoyes' consternation stayed all afternoon; next he came at dinner time and stayed even longer; day after day he came, time after time, no matter how glacially received, until the Cavoyes nearly went mad.

Almost matching the highborn hen-brained whims are the solemn farce and the spiky dilemmas called forth by vanity and protocol. Thus, when the Elector of Bavaria visited the Dauphin, the dread matter of who should go first through a door could not be solved. It was finally compromised: the two men met out-of-doors, where a carriage stood ready, into which they climbed simultaneously from opposite sides (but the Dauphin sat on the right). How gravely all this could be regarded, by many others than our Duke, provides one of the memoirs' better remarks. The Duke of Coislin was famous for never making the first advances, or even the first bow. When the new buildings at Trianon were finished, a friend asked him what he thought of them; he said he hadn't seen them. "Why, of course you haven't," said his friend, "they haven't called on *you* yet."

Despite the joking, the whole spectacle was a deadly serious one; the whole set of maneuvers was played for crucially high stakes. It meant a career of dissimulation, a lifetime of intrigue, of ups and downs, of smiles and smiles, of confronting glaciers for temperature and hidden depths alike; of living through earthquakes for tremors and displacements as well. It imposed a constant need to face— and outstare—those who were one's rivals, or one's enemies, or one's superiors. When we add to this how much of it was plausible which in our eyes seems wild, how much was routine which to our ears sounds lurid, we can begin to grasp how even the most distinguished people lived in constant danger. Thus, the King's nephew, the Duke of Orleans —who for all his faults emerges one of the more sympathetic and least power-mad of these figures—was doubly branded. It was loudly whispered that he had poisoned the Duke and Duchess of Burgundy, a chief proof of guilt being his interest in chemical experiments; and it was whispered no less loud that he had committed incest with his daughter. Both charges, it appears, were quite untrue; but what could give substance to them was how Borgiastic was life at Versailles, how many poisoners were within its ranks, how many overcordial family relationships there were said to be.

Moreover, devices existed for poisoning minds no less than bodies. The word "Jansenist," Saint-Simon remarks, was a very convenient way of smearing whomever one wished to ruin; it was as damning as "Communist" can be, and particularly damning (even without a particle of supporting evidence) with the King. Trickery was inevitable in a world that dared not be trustful. During the Marlborough wars, the darling of the King and the court, the young Duchess of Burgundy, was collecting information for her father the Duke of Savoy, who was France's enemy.

Haughtiness and snobbishness in such a world will surprise us less, and there seem indeed to have been stiffer necks and colder stares than any Saint-Simon himself might display. Actually, he could be very approving and affable toward anyone who knew his place, whether a peer or a parvenu; next to being an agitator for the rights of dukes, Saint-Simon was best known as an authority on etiquette, a kind of medieval Emily Post; and on genealogy, a walking Almanach de Gotha. Genealogy was by all odds the most esteemed branch of higher learning at Versailles, and the one with the largest enrollment. One court lady never ceased to tell Louis XIV, to his amusement and hence to his credit, how much better born she was than he; and perhaps half the court refused to give an inch, and it often hardly amounted to more, in maintaining their privileges. Yet even the Versailles of Louis XIV, it appears, was rather free and easy compared to the particularities and pedantries of rank and usage at some of the German courts with their tightly closed society. Long, long after at one of these courts the remark was overheard: "Princes like you walk after counts like me." At least under Louis XIV the bourgeois, though lacking a crest, had first call on a career: he might handle the King's finances, administer his business, promulgate his laws or occupy his sees. The newcomers who could drop to their knees with sufficient grace, or prove useful with sufficient deference, might climb, indeed climb high, at times climb over their betters. Saint-Simon tells us how Fleury—a nobody by birth who under Louis XV became a cardinal and prime minister—was earlier in his career invited about, but not quite as an equal: "before bells were invented," Saint-Simon adds, Fleury was often made use of to deliver messages. At Saint-Simon's Versailles, moreover, for all the stress on rank and lineage, there was constantly need enough, and craving enough, for money to antedate by two centuries the modern-style alliances of American heiresses with European titles; Saint-Simon's own mother-in-law had little if any blue in her blood. The way of the world, *chez* Louis XIV, was very much the way of the great world generally; and the Sun King himself, in showing a rich banker around Versailles, could put his pride in his pocket in hopes of putting something more there as well. And indeed this citadel of majesty which was also a maze of ambitions is perhaps most "modern" and in the end most instructive for expanding into a commodious world of many colors, a humanity as well as society of many kinds.

Among so much emulousness and cold-heartedness and corruption, was there, one cannot but ask, no better side, no finer clay? There was indeed, right in Saint-Simon's memoirs, and perhaps even more in what he left out of them for providing no scandal or furnishing no anecdotes. To his credit, he speaks with warmth and esteem of men and women who are virtuous, who are generous or kind, eulogizing Madame de Pontchertrain for performing endless acts of goodness "all with the greatest secrecy"; or dilating, rather *ad nauseam,* on the upright natures of the two brothers-in-law the Dukes of Beauvilliers and Chevreuse (in the *Mémoires* a sort of virtuous Rosencrantz and Guildenstern, with something of Polonius thrown in). And we may suppose, indeed we can sometimes deduce, that certain people, uninfected with ambition, unattracted by intrigue, risked royal displeasure by staying away whenever possible on their own estates.

Of the principal "good" figures we shall keep meeting, Louis' grandson the Duke of Burgundy, who for a brief time was Dauphin, emerges in Saint-Simon's view the great hope for reforming and reinvigorating a war-bled, vice-blackened, despot-ruled France. In the less than a year between his father's death and his own, the new Dauphin had taken increasing notice of Saint-Simon, and seems indeed to have made in a small way a secret counsellor of him. From having been given to violent outbursts of anger, the Dauphin grew reflective, pious, and far more mature, conscious of the responsibilities awaiting him. It must be admitted that part of Saint-Simon's admiration for him rested on his sympathy with the cause of the dukes; we in turn can admire him for patiently enduring Saint-Simon's harangues on the Great Subject.

Of much greater interest and historically greater importance is the Duke of Orleans, proclaimed Regent after Louis XIV's death and the one man of high position and real power to whom Saint-Simon was close. Orleans' was an interesting place, or lack of it, in the royal and political scheme of things—in his being made to marry the King's illegitimate daughter; in the vile charges against him that I have spoken of, which led to an ostracism that Saint-Simon tells us he alone defied; in his flaunted debaucheries while Duke, his difficulties on becoming Regent, and his fault-ridden regime thereafter. But of greater interest, perhaps, is what was engaging and at the same time self-damaging in his make-up. With the endowments of a man of action, he dawdled and shrugged as a man of inaction instead. Witty, good-natured, intellectually curious, he led a life of indolence and indulgence, presiding after sundown over a "court" of roués and ladies of pleasure. There is in him the stuff of a wonderful character in fiction, again and again failing of purpose, and frittering luck and opportunities away; a fritterer of everything, even, it might seem, his very destiny. His wife, so proud a woman that as the King's bastard she thought herself the grander party in marrying the King's nephew; so proud that she was called, and relished being called, Madame Lucifer—had yet to bear her husband's total neglect and open infidelity with his *maîtresse en titre*. This, together with the Duke's other failings, so menaced his relations with the King that, with great guile and effort, Saint-Simon got Orleans to cast off his mistress and return to his wife. The Duchess had, certainly, superb dignity and every right to feel abused; she had also the great fault, even after the reconciliation, of caring above all else for the advancement of her bastard brother, the Duke du Maine, an advancement in venomous conflict with her husband's.

Two other women play more vital roles in the memoirs, the young Duchess of Burgundy, briefly the Dauphiness, and Madame de Maintenon. Brought from Savoy to Versailles when a mere child, married to the Duke long before they could live together, the Duchess captivated the whole court and endeared herself as no one else to the King and the Maintenon alike. Her dancing gaiety, her skipping vivacity, her bubbling youthfulness stand forth unforgettably against the ordered movement and stiff formality of the court as a whole. At moments she seems just a little like

Natasha, Natasha at the ball, in *War and Peace*—and married, like Natasha finally, to a version of Pierre. The deeper we go, the shallower the Duchess becomes, being neither a loyal subject nor a faithful wife; and someone who, for being so well liked, is a spoiled darling. But we must like her too, for often being friendly and kind, and for being in real life a veritable princess of fiction, bringing fragrance to the story, and sunlight.

The Madame de Maintenon of the *Mémoires* comes off a rather shadowy figure, in part because we never see her clearly at first hand, in part because Saint-Simon portrays her as given to secrecy and guile. Thus presented, she acquires a certain fascination, if only for eluding us; but it is a presentation to be wary of, since with Madame de Maintenon Saint-Simon was no more sure-footed than open-minded. Beyond the fact that he came to Versailles well after she was established there—and hence relied on hearsay about her past—she was someone whom he never came to know, whom he always mistrusted and hence misjudged, except as he could sense her dislike of him. Wherever this dislike did not ignite his prejudices, her fondness for people *he* disliked served equally well. Saint-Simon saw Madame de Maintenon as not just a devious intrigante, he saw her, if not quite as the power behind the throne, then as the quiet, omnipresent prompter behind the scenes who, by cleverly putting ideas into the King's head, by ingeniously calling matters to his attention, gained her own ends or ruined other people's. Doubtless this straitlaced widow of the poet Scarron, who had been governess to the children of her predecessor, Madame de Montespan; this woman whom Louis XIV at first could not bear the sight of and in the end, it would seem, could only possess by a secret marriage— doubtless she made the King more pious at the cost of his becoming less tolerant, and more seemly through creating a gloomier court and more frightened courtiers. Doubtless, too, by being present when the King met his ministers, she could insinuate certain opinions both on the spot and afterward. But there seems to be no foundation for Saint-Simon's thinking that she either dominated the King through her maneuvers, or got her way through his devotion. She idolized him, it appears, and on occasion influenced him; the court, moreover, paid her tremendous deference; and she, by remaining inaccessible and making admittance to her circle a great achievement, left all those outside it filled with chagrin and conjecture. Left very much outside of it, Saint-Simon overflowed with conjecture. Some kind of accomplished actress she must have been, but Saint-Simon never saw her perform; and his spidery lady at the center of a sinister web was by no means the real one.

There is, finally, Saint-Simon himself, who plays so noticeable a role in the *Mémoires* as to be virtually an autobiographer and who produced a lifework with, indeed, almost the dimensions of a lifetime. We can understand how, retiring to his country place after the Regent's death in 1723, he worked during the rest of his eighty years on the diaries and the notes and memoranda he had accumulated: at Versailles he had been known for "constantly scribbling notes in notebooks." In his retirement he must have been immensely aided by a kind of malicious total recall toward those he disliked, disdained, distrusted, and by a kind of erudition he had amassed concerning what fascinated or agitated or obsessed him. Even so, during his long years at Versailles he was so busy being a duke, a detective, a diner-out, a collector of grievances, a night watchman of backstairs and grand staircases alike as to have, one would suppose, no time left for being a diarist. Furthermore, at the very hour of night when most diarists set to work, Saint-Simon was usually in attendance at the king's *coucher*. It is wonderful that he had any private life at all, concerned as he was with everyone else's; and despite all the sifters of rumor and retailers of gossip whom he relied on, he was himself an indefatigable legman. In footwork and handiwork alike, he far surpasses Boswell, who, centering on one person, concentrated on one group, and much of the time led a life independent of both. He much exceeds Greville, who in nineteenth-century England, though he endlessly dined out pen rather than fork in hand, and as Clerk of the Privy Council heard all the news and gossip going, avoided miscellaneous gossip mongering. Greville *could*, however, be as pertinacious on occasion as Saint-Simon, and shares with him a notable talent for obituaries.

As a man with a sharp tongue in his head, a strange light in his eye, a great bee in his bonnet, Saint-Simon can scarcely have been popular; despite how many people he maintains he was on an intimate footing with, we cannot help remembering all those he was likely to snub, or inclined to pester, or given to scold, or known to harangue. By his methods he must have bored or antagonized people, as often when he was making sense as when he was being silly. Disliked himself, Saint-Simon's own dislikes were more accurately hatreds often begotten of the malice, corruption, duplicity he penetrated to in men; but quite as often of their presumptions, ambitions, usurpations of power and place. Frequently—as with Dubois, an obscure priest who from having been the Regent's tutor became virtual prime minister under the Regent and in whom, Saint-Simon says, "all the vices strove for mastery"—he was by no means wrong. But together with his prejudices went a personality that could be ill-natured and boastful; and just

so, the memoirs can be historically untrustworthy and ton-
ally overwrought. In a lesser fashion, Saint-Simon's sleepless curiosity and eternal vigilance could make him comi-
cally prying, intrusive, unwelcome: when he saw a group of
courtiers talking, Harold Nicolson vividly phrases it, he
would "like a bright-eyed robin hop step by step closer to
them" to overhear as much as possible.

Yet, beyond the element of genius in the memoirist there
were very real virtues in the man. They were not of a
personally endearing or a socially engaging sort; his merits,
indeed, much less suggest Versailles and the grand style
than Queen Victoria and the good life. Saint-Simon was a
faithful husband, a relatively forthright courtier, a man
who never gambled or drank. His choice of a wife proved
remarkably sound and valuable, both in what she was—
sensible, tactful, loyal; and in where she stood—for she
achieved a far solider place at court than he. (Their two
sons, whom Versailles nicknamed "the dachshunds," seem
to have been far from impressive; and in the generation
after theirs, the dukedom expired.) Saint-Simon had also a
certain probity and courage, as in firmly befriending the
Duke of Orleans when he was an outcast; he could be, as
well, a sort of liberal in chain mail, protesting the dreadful
treatment and taxation of the poor, or excoriating the In-
quisition and denouncing the later persecution of Hugue-
nots. The fine glints of enlightenment, the piercing stabs of
perception, that rather frequently emerge in the *Mémoires*
are the nonconformist insights into men, the untainted
intuitions about mankind which, with his gift for phrase
and his individuality of style, set Saint-Simon among the
writers of creative distinction. His Vendôme, his Orleans,
his Duchess of Burgundy, his Madame des Ursins, his however ambivalently regarded Louis XIV are alive, unmistaka-

ble, *there;* we see them move, hear them speak, catch them out. And the master of scene gives us episodes—the greatest is the death of Monseigneur—that many a novelist, and most of all perhaps a Proust, could only bow down before, and that very few would ever surpass.

III

THE WAY OF THE WORLD

THERE HAS NEVER BEEN A BODY OF LITERATURE more notable—indeed, more notorious—for its worldly tone than Restoration comedy. Nor is this simply because its plots abound in sexual license, that over it there hovers a sense of dissoluteness; it is equally because its plots pivot on trickery and that over it there hangs a sense of deceit. Its recurrent butt, its endless dupe, is the cuckold, who far from being sympathized with is to be made sport of. Nor, as in earlier, as in Elizabethan literature, is sexual license a matter of lustiness, of warm-hearted gallants and wanton ladies: when we move on to the Restoration, though we advance to a higher social world, we descend to a baser moral one. There is much less a sense of lustiness than of laxness; of animal spirits than of animal cunning; of love as an end in itself than of love as a rung on a ladder. Infidelity springs much less from a warm or foolish heart than from a kind of heartlessness. Into all the era's brittle assignations, its loveless lovemaking, go those companion motives of worldliness—personal ambition, fortune hunting, money. It is no wonder that, in the form of Jeremy Collier's celebrated *Short View of the Immorality and Profaneness of the English Stage*, Restoration comedy should in its own day have been strongly condemned, or that in ages more moral thereafter it should have been roundly denounced.

All the same, it has in many ways been rather unfairly denounced, not just because those who have done so most loudly have often been mere lip-service moralists, and not just because they have quite lacked appreciation of its literary merits; but because to a marked degree it is an honest picture of the life it portrays; because, again, it possesses the particular virtues, as well as faults, that go with its subject matter; and finally, because it is a special body of work, created less by the usual sort of professional than by what we may call the gentleman author, who might well have participated by night in the activities and intrigues that he recorded next morning.

Now in every age there have been what can be called gentlemen authors: in English literature we have, among others, Sir Philip Sidney, Dryden, Fielding, Byron, Shelley, Swinburne, all of them wellborn and some of them clearly possessed of genius. But in every age the wellborn more often tend to write like Queen Victoria, who underlined hundreds of words that she had far better have left out. Nor has there been much incentive among the wellborn to write well; authorship was until recently looked askance at; and though society might not mind if its members wrote skillfully, it minded even less if they didn't. It was more pleased when its members talked wittily, but it seldom assumed that they would. Most of the greatest society wits—Chamfort and Sheridan, Sydney Smith and Oscar Wilde—have been outsiders.

But just here the Restoration was rather different. Any number of its wellborn people were witty; a large number, indeed, were truly talented. Society for once not only repeated all kinds of good remarks; it coined them. Society not only went, night after night, to the playhouse; it often wrote the plays. This means, moreover, the most dissipated sections of society—the very people who stayed up late breaking all the commandments, who gambled and drank when they might have been reading and writing. They led scandalous lives and sometimes wrote scandalous plays, but they equally led stylish lives and wrote stylish plays, and could be as witty when alone with their pens as in company over the wine. There is something remarkable about a group of wastrels who should have been almost as concerned with the portrayal of pleasure as with the pursuit of it. And as a result, if these gentlemen authors produced an indecorous literature, it was yet a real literature of a kind. Lord Rochester, Lord Dorset, Sir Charles Sedley, Sir George Etherege, the Duke of Buckingham—and Dryden, though so much more than a gentleman; and Congreve, though he came well after the others—never, certainly, have we been so forcibly reminded that the Poets' Corner is only a stone's throw from the House of Lords.

Now what these men produced is rightly called artificial comedy; artifice is what shapes it, starches it, forms its very essence. But though artificial in itself, it mirrors a good deal that is real. These men wrote, more than we may imagine, about the wantons they knew and the rakes they were and the childish brutal pranks they played; about their own frivolities and lack of feeling, about their desire to dazzle, their need to ridicule. Autobiographical in any strict sense their plays are not, but at times they perhaps come as close to autobiography as to fiction. Rochester and Etherege, for example, took part in a notorious prank that began with tossing some fiddlers in a blanket and ended with one of their victims dying of his wounds. The wonder is that in coming so close to autobiography, they yet managed on occasion to come equally close to art. But they did, and all the more remarkably for refusing to work hard, for insisting that they only worked at all when they had nothing better to do. Obviously, they posed in all this; but then they never plodded. The result, as we might suppose, is often careless, often capricious, tenuous, sometimes plagiarized; but often elegant, often witty and perceptive, and sometimes full of truth.

It is not my purpose to provide a conspectus of Restoration comedy, though in many ways a worldlier *body* of work would be hard to find. *The Way of the World,* as the crowning play of that literature, is a sufficiently key play as well. But this is in some sense true because only Congreve could have made it both. Others who were equally suited by temperament were endowed with less talent; others with equal, and indeed one with superior, talent were less fitted for stage writing. On Dryden, we feel, stage comedy never sat easily: despite a keen sense of the absurd and a mastery of satire, he lacked the ability to frisk and romp; besides, the Restoration stage has a striking indoors quality, at odds with Dryden's outdoor vigor. No one would make words march as he did; but words that should skip, and splash one another with water, and mock while they seem to caress, and elude while they seem to consent—these were not his forte. And where Dryden found his true worldly calling in a vigorous, striding, deep-chested satirical poetry, something at which he remains unmatched, so a Wycherley failed, as I venture to think, to find his proper role at all. He too had a vigorous talent, and had often violent emotions, so that *he* often cannot keep life inside a drawing room. His age and his place in society led him to write for the theater, and with too little restraint and often a wrong kind of coarseness; in a later age he would almost certainly have turned novelist, and been as comfortable a figure in the world of Fielding and Smollett as he can be a marginal one in that of Etherege and Congreve. His name and Dryden's alone stand as high as Congreve's in the Restoration theater; but Congreve's alone fully graces, fully fits the Restoration on its comic and worldly side.

Strictly speaking, Congreve is not of the true generation of Restoration playwrights; when he began writing plays, not Charles II or even James II occupied the English throne, but rather William and Mary. The Revolution of 1688 had intervened, and brought with it something of a social as well as political revolution. William of Orange was a brilliant but cold, sickly, boorish figure with no love for the theater and none for London. There was no considerable court life, no stir of frivolity and fashion. The world of fashion may itself not have changed its morals for the better, but at least it pretended to. It was this touch of gray in the moral landscape, this hint of chill in the moral air, that led to Jeremy Collier's attack on the theater. In that attack Congreve was not spared, and it would be idle to suggest that he worked on a morally higher plane than had most of his predecessors. He was as little shocked as they by what he saw, and on occasion could be almost as shocking. But because he was so much more delicate an artist, with the theater itself much less gross a bear garden, there emerges a greater refinement of tone. Burke said of the court of Marie Antoinette that "vice itself lost half its evil by losing all its grossness." There, it seems to me, Burke was rather dangerously suggesting that aesthetics can do the work of morality, was rather implying that it is only half as ill-behaved to poison your uncle artistically as to slice him up with a meat ax. Actually, in real life, the premeditation involved in well-wrought immorality makes not for lesser guilt but for greater; but in literature, an elegant depiction of vice does tend to have, for a time at least, a genuine lure.

Congreve, in any case, stands apart from the earlier generation of Restoration playwrights as much for tone as for talent. Etherege, notably in *The Man of Mode*, has admirable ease and airiness and a sort of fashionable rattle, a constant fizz; but he is not endowed with such style and breeding as we encounter in the best of Congreve, who is at once in the literary sense a patrician and in the temperamental sense an almost too urbane worldling. And just so, he much less represents a period than a tradition: he does not simply mirror Restoration manners, he embodies the civilized point of view. If anything, I think, we shall find that it is the Restoration that makes Congreve a little less than completely civilized, that it is the Restoration that tarnishes him with a certain period cynicism, a certain modish sophistication. Of the completely civilized man we require something that, in the final reckoning, Congreve never quite gives us. We do not expect him, from the seriousness of an occasion, to raise his voice; but we ask that he do more than raise his eyebrows. He need not be warmhearted, but it must not be mere indifference or imperturbability that he conveys, it must be a kind of serenity. On the other hand, in an ability to appraise life in the very act of savoring it, in a fine appreciation of tangible civilized virtues Congreve is beautifully a master. As that, he is a type it is not easy to do exact justice to—one that can be about equally overpraised and undervalued.

Congreve's claims to embody, in spirit no less than style, the civilized point of view derive chiefly from the last and by all odds most distinguished of his plays, *The Way of the World*, which is, indeed, the finest of Restoration comedies. In his three previous plays, Congreve had either done something inferior or something different. In his first play, *The Old Bachelor*, he had made plain that a witty new playwright had arrived on the scene, but also that nothing new in playwriting had arrived at all. He borrowed the plots, the characters, the situations, the general atmosphere, the interminable amorousness, exactly as he found them, offering not creation but brilliant rewrite. *The Old Bachelor* is like something in a child's drawing book, where the picture is printed beforehand and the child colors it as he sees fit; Congreve's coloring is brilliantly precocious, but the design is not his own. In his second play, *The Double Dealer*, he has stopped copying and begun to write, and at his best not just the wit and style are delightfully Congrevian, but the attitude is as well: the trouble here was that the main action is melodrama and only the subordinate part stylish and witty. Congreve's third play, *Love for Love*, is a genuine success, indeed by far his most successful theater piece, full of liveliness and sprinkled with true worldly wit: in it Congreve has plainly mastered his medium, has written creditably in terms of pleasing others. But it was only with *The Way of the World* that he came to write entirely to please himself; into *The Way of the World* he poured everything, we feel, that earlier—whether from craving commercial success or worrying over artistic failure—he had consciously or unconsciously withheld or watered down.

As a result, the difference between *The Way of the World*

and Congreve's earlier work is less a matter of degree than of kind. This becomes evident, I think, if we consider the quality which Congreve is best known for and which best conveys his worldliness—I mean his wit. Now, witty though *Love for Love* often is, it nowhere equals *The Way of the World*, whether in amount, or degree, or effect. But that there is much more wit, or even much better wit, in *The Way of the World* is not the final point. The final point is that wit, in *The Way of the World*, is not a mere ingredient but a kind of essence. The play is not, so to speak, witty; it is wit. We can speak of it as wit as we can speak of an ode of Keats' as poetry, or an oration of Burke's as eloquence. The wit of *The Way of the World* is a way of writing, so that a speech in the play is almost as hard to paraphrase as a stanza in the *Ode to a Nightingale*. The idea is completely married to the words, and if you kill them off, the idea will fling itself into the same grave.

I shall not try to define wit, in part because no definition can be altogether adequate, in part because none can be sufficiently alive. But wit, like poetry, demands (as it provides) a peculiar climate, a particular atmosphere. Like poetry, wit lives in a house without stairs, moving upward in a rush, in sudden dizzying leaps; though where poetry is a kind of bright creature with wings, wit is more like a witch on a broomstick. But a kind of lightning suddenness is part of the thing itself. And as important as there being something bright about them both, there must be something concentrated. We may think of them as brilliantly clothed, but must also see them as essentially naked. Such concentratedness, such speed, makes both true wit and true poetry, however else they differ, into something barer and more direct than other forms of expression. That is why they can prove fatiguing: we have so much to absorb in so little space. One reason why *The Way of the World* finds it hard to succeed in the theater is that, theatrically, it moves too slow, with talk where there might better be action. But a perhaps deeper reason is that verbally it moves too fast: the wit has us panting to keep up with it. Such writing is too concise for the stage.

Moreover, the pervasive and carpeting wit of *The Way of the World* depends on context, and even on character. Detached from the play, deprived of its atmosphere and attitudes, the wit loses immeasurably. For it is wit and only seldom witticism, purring so smoothly that we are not always aware of how sharply it bites. It would rather be well-bred than emphatic, it would rather chime like a clock than go off like a gun. With, say, an Oscar Wilde, wit is the lights and bells on a Christmas tree, where with Congreve it is the sap in a living tree trunk. Moreover, at its most characteristic and impressive, Congreve's wit is inseparable from his worldliness, is the very lens through which he surveys the world. Listen to Witwould telling what trouble Petulant took in order to make himself seem sought after:

> Why he would slip out of this chocolate-house, just when you had been talking to him. As soon as your back was turned—whip he was gone; then trip to his lodging, clap on a hood and a scarf and a mask, slap into a hackney-coach, and drive hither to the door again in a trice; where he would send in for himself—I mean, call for himself; wait for himself; nay, and what's more, not finding himself, sometimes leave a letter for himself.

The whole tone of the play is as worldly and urbane as one could ask for. Indeed, Congreve has so perfectly captured what might be called drawing-room elegance that we may not realize that he has exhibited its limitations as well as its luster. So brilliant at times is his brushwork and his coloring, so unified his tone, that we are in the midst of a fairyland of fine manners: this is how we might expect people to talk in Heaven. But these, at the same time, are people we must expect to find in Hell. Inwardly they can be as tarnished as they are polished without. The play is well named, for its concern is not with this person's follies or that one's vices, but with leisure-class society in general, its incentives of pleasure, its temptations to betray or misbehave. Indeed, it is the social scene as a whole that is of thematic importance in the play; the actual plot, the individual intrigues, are often tediously complicated, and are perhaps more of a drawback to the play's success than the talkiness of the dialogue and the fatiguing brightness of the wit. *The Way of the World* is the most distinguished product of the Restoration theater, but there is no use going into it at length as a play in the technical sense, because even if it is rather better than it is usually thought to be, as playwriting it is still not impressive; and to try to work up enthusiasm for *The Way of the World* on the basis of its stagecraft would be like trying to work up enthusiasm for Chartres Cathedral on the basis of its acoustics. We must judge it for what its characters represent as symbolic figures, and not as puppets of the plot. Nonetheless, the plot does often serve to point up not only how self-indulgent and inconstant these people are, but how frustrated and foiled. They cannot, many of them, have what they want in the way of a husband or a lover; they cannot dare believe in friendship or hope for love. They are trapped by the baseness of their own view of life and by the very selfishness of their own desires. Even in suffering they can find no salvation, for they do not know how to suffer; they can only, when they feel pain, try to inflict it elsewhere.

This is something apprehended amid the spin and sparkle of language and wit, something that is a matter of tone; the teaching of the play, so far as it does teach, is in the tone. Congreve is, on the one hand, too sensitive an artist to try to teach more overtly; but on the other hand, I would think, too baffled and skeptical and perhaps superficial a philosopher to know how. He has far too much taste and sensibility to acquiesce cynically in what he sees of life, yet too ingrained and pessimistic a sense of the way of the world—and doubtless too great an affinity for it—ever to protest very much. We must look elsewhere for writers with more severe and positive values, for writers who aspire beyond tone to something like vision. But *The Way of the World* furnishes, in its own aesthetic fashion, a sense of the melancholy in life, of the awful hell of life. There is here a kind of paradox: no tone could be more civilized than Congreve's, yet no story better suggests how little being civilized avails.

But how much it avails in art. No naturalistic approach could bring off a Millamant or contrive, beyond even the verbal merits of *The Way of the World*, its decisive sense of style. When at length, well into the second act, Millamant appears and Mirabel salutes her with his celebrated words —"Here she comes, i' faith, full sail, with her fan spread and streamers out, and a shoal of fools for tender"—with what a splash, with what an air of the great world, she enters. Mirabel so glorifies Millamant in those words, we are scarcely aware that he is also making fun of her. She enters, there is some give-and-take, and then comes the business of the letters:

MILLAMANT.   Mincing, what had I? Why was I so long?
MINCING.   O mem, your laship stayed to peruse a packet of letters.
MILLAMANT.   Oh, ay, letters—I had letters—I am perse-

cuted with letters—I hate letters. Nobody knows how to write letters; and yet one has 'em, one does not know why. They serve one to pin up one's hair.

WITWOUD. Is that the way? Pray, madam, do you pin up your hair with all your letters? I find I must keep copies.

MILLAMANT. Only with those in verse, Mr. Witwoud. I never pin up my hair with prose. I think I tried once, Mincing.

MINCING. O mem, I shall never forget it.

MILLAMANT. Ay, poor Mincing tift and tift all the morning.

MINCING. Till I had the cramp in my fingers, I'll vow, mem. And all to no purpose. But when your laship pins it up with poetry, it fits so pleasant the next day as anything, and is so pure and so crips.

WITWOUD. Indeed, so crips?

MINCING. You're such a critic, Mr. Witwoud.

Here again it is not just the language or the fancifulness, but a certain turn and heightening, an effect of style, that gives this trivial little scene distinction; the same style that gives the play the exact pitch, the sure mark of high comedy; that adds a kind of breeding to the brilliance. It is the decisive element in a prose of the best sort—a prose that for word choice, rhythm, movement, can equal fine poetry but is not, in any usual sense, the least poetic. Indeed, it never loses a certain low-pitched dryness and coolness, a certain colloquial ease. It remains domesticated. Sterne, in his own way, can be the same kind of prose writer, can keep the same kind of colloquial ease.

Such dry, cool, yet invincibly stylish prose perfectly fits Congreve's conveying to us that the way of the world is no passing fashion but an eternal fact. Rather than the struggle against defeat that we find in drama, we find in such high comedy as this a skepticism which is very nearly defeatism. One knows here, or suspects, or fears, what the world can be like, or life can be like, or love can be like. Millamant holds Mirabel off throughout most of the play, but this cannot be regarded simply as a conventional plot device or as the coy tactics of a "romantic" heroine. The point is that Millamant is not just choosing a man, or even choosing one man from many: she is deciding whether to marry. Now it is assumed in novels and plays that everyone wishes to marry; indeed, marriage is the only way an ordinary writer has for indicating that certain characters lived happily ever after. But the issue is not so simple; the idea of marriage, which is not the same thing as the idea of mating, could be very disquieting, very much of a dilemma, to a clever, high-mettled, attractive, much-sought-after girl who is as much her own mistress as Millamant.

The marriage-contract scene between Millamant and Mirabel is so witty and delightful as mere banter that we almost fail to notice the altogether realistic basis of the bargaining. We are so pleased with Millamant's remark about how she "may dwindle into a wife" that we may miss the point of her conditions, which are that the marriage may not dwindle into a farce or deteriorate into a failure. Congreve, like other masters of comedy, employs a kind of paradox: he suggests the tarnish of life through the glitter, the lees through the froth, the clouds and shadows through the all-too-passing moment of sunlight. The marriage-contract scene is in its way Mozartian: here are the shimmer and gaiety of those who apprehend how fugitive is pleasure, how fraudulent are so many well-intended vows, how touched with melancholy is life. Reading the scene, we may of course ignore everything but its charm, and will have been notably rewarded; but there is more to it than charm. All earnest souls, all people who judge things by mere size and weight, distrust and dismiss gaiety as minor and even frivolous. But we ought not to be deceived; there is not only more health in the moment of joyousness, but very likely more resonance and depth. What could be gayer than Natasha at the ball in *War and Peace*—or more beautifully memorable? What has more brilliance than the court scenes in *The Charterhouse of Parma* and yet, at bottom, more of the hard truth of life? And who, in a way, for all his celebrated dispiritedness is gayer, brisker, more playful, more full of spring and wit than Hamlet?

Millamant seems to me an extremely successful creation as much for what Congreve did not make her as for what he did. Thus, he did not make her lovable: there is nothing warm-hearted or self-effacing or innocently girlish about her; you cannot imagine her being terribly kind to people she has no interest in, or staying home from a ball to sit at a sick aunt's bedside. She is not in the least noble-minded, she is not even, by modern standards, very humane. She is spoiled, she is pert, she is given to airs and affectations, she is invincibly feminine, she is an incorrigible coquette. She makes light of most things, she makes fun of many. She is a very superior girl who knows her own worth; and like anybody who is honest about it, she loves being sought after and complimented and courted.

The point is that she is the very best product of a certain world; the point is, equally, that she does not rise above it. She is captivating rather than lovable, and easier to find fault with than to resist. She has taste and sensibility and perceptiveness, and at moments that incomparable hoity-toityness wherewith women always have, if not the last

word, then something like the last laugh. Nowhere has she
it more superbly than in commenting on the vanity and
fatuousness of "lovers" (we should say "suitors"):

> Lord, what is a lover that it can give? Why one makes lovers
> as fast as one pleases, and they live as long as one pleases,
> and they die as soon as one pleases; and then, if one pleases,
> one makes more.

One particular virtue about Millamant is that, though a
perfect character of artificial comedy—endowed with an air
too perfect for real life—her actual behavior and motivations are convincingly realistic. She is incomparable for her
graces, not for her good qualities. And it is a tribute to
Congreve's honesty that he made Millamant a radiant figure
without making her a romantic or entirely girlish one.

Set against Millamant, most of the other characters, including Mirabel, rather tend to pale. But as worldlings, and
worldling types, a number of them are effective, and something in particular might be said for Witwoud, the sort of
fellow who must be always in the know and never caught
napping, who never lacks a smart or clever answer or an
up-to-date bit of gossip or slang: a very good kind of sec-
ond-rater, really, whom we almost admire till we see him
come up against somebody better. I don't share the usual
opinion about how tragic Lady Wishfort is—pathetic, yes,
and a truly wretched figure, burning with sexual desire
while grown old and ugly. But she is too much a fool, too
shallow, too gullible, for us to care about *her;* what we feel
for is her situation, is that of anyone unloved and wanting
love. She is also, and I think wisely, made quite farcical:
were she not, she might, without becoming tragic, be too
uncomfortably realistic for artificial comedy. In this vein

Congreve, it seems to me, does better elsewhere, even with his villains Fainall and Mrs. Marwood. They have a rather remarkable scene together; I quote the end of it:

FAIN.   Your guilt, not your resentment, begets your rage. If yet you loved, you could forgive a jealousy: but you are stung to find you are discovered.

MRS. MAR.   It shall be all discovered. You too shall be discovered; be sure you shall. I can but be exposed.—If I do it myself I shall prevent your baseness.

FAIN.   Why, what will you do?

MRS. MAR.   Disclose it to your wife; own what has passed between us.

FAIN.   Frenzy!

MRS. MAR.   By all my wrongs I'll do't!—I'll publish to the world the injuries you have done me, both in my fame and fortune! With both I trusted you, you bankrupt in honour, as indigent of wealth.

FAIN.   Your fame I have preserved: your fortune has been bestowed as the prodigality of your love would have it, in pleasures which we both have shared. Yet, had not you been false, I had ere this repaid it—'tis true—had you permitted Mirabel with Millamant to have stolen their marriage, my lady had been incensed beyond all means of reconcilement: Millamant had forfeited the moiety of her fortune; which then would have descended to my wife;— and wherefore did I marry, but to make lawful prize of a rich widow's wealth, and squander it on love and you?

MRS. MAR.   Deceit and frivolous pretence!

FAIN.   Death, am I not married? What's pretence? Am I not imprisoned, fettered? Have I not a wife? nay a wife that was a widow, a young widow, a handsome widow; and would be again a widow, but that I have a heart of proof, and something of a constitution to bustle through the ways of wedlock and this world! Will you yet be reconciled to truth and me?

MRS. MAR.   Impossible. Truth and you are inconsistent:

I hate you, and shall forever.

FAIN.   For loving you?

MRS. MAR.   I loathe the name of love after such usage; and next to the guilt with which you would asperse me, I scorn you most. Farewell!

FAIN.   Nay, we must not part thus.

MRS. MAR.   Let me go.

FAIN.   Come, I'm sorry.

MRS. MAR.   I care not—let me go—break my hands, do— I'd leave 'em to get loose.

FAIN.   I would not hurt you for the world. Have I no other hold to keep you here?

MRS. MAR.   Well, I have deserved it all.

FAIN.   You know I love you.

MRS. MAR.   Poor dissembling!—O that—well, it is not yet—

FAIN.   What? what is it not? what is it not yet? It is not yet too late—

MRS. MAR.   No, it is not yet too late;—I have that comfort.

FAIN.   It is, to love another.

MRS. MAR.   But not to loathe, detest, abhor mankind, myself, and the whole treacherous world.

FAIN.   Nay, this is extravagance.—Come, I ask your pardon—no tears—I was to blame, I could not love you and be easy in my doubts. Pray forbear—I believe you; I'm convinced I've done you wrong; and any way, every way will make amends. I'll hate my wife yet more, damn her! I'll part with her, rob her of all she's worth, and we'll retire somewhere, anywhere, to another world. I'll marry thee—be pacified.—'Sdeath, they come, hide your face, your tears— you have a mask, wear it a moment. This way, this way—be persuaded.

Now this is a scene which those people who always speak of how exquisite everything is in Congreve, as though he were as dainty as a coffee spoon, must have a little trouble over. For it seems to me a scene of quite inexorable realism; or, since realism is only a method, it might better be called reality—some speeches exchanged between two suddenly very believable people who have been in a very real relationship. Here, perhaps, is a good place to take leave of Congreve and his masterpiece—where he gives us something a little unexpected and out of his usual run, something that brings home to us the lees beneath the froth and the tarnish that diminishes the glitter.

IV

THE SCHOOL FOR SCANDAL

SHERIDAN, WRITING THREE-QUARTERS OF A CENTURY after Congreve, is his inheritor and successor, but falls short of equal success. The reason is only partly a matter of talent; it is rather more a matter of temperament, and of the times into which each man was born. Simply in terms of his gifts, Sheridan was a born satirist and student of manners; he had a sharp eye, an inventive mind, and a witty tongue. Like Congreve before him, he was a thorough worldling—the difference being that Congreve was an incorruptible one, whose worldliness nothing outward could shake, whose attitude nothing else could discolor. Congreve does not fight for virtue's sake, but he does have a sort of hard cold integrity, and does recognize the obligation to tell the truth. Thus, though in his worldling's way he scarcely so much as lays a finger on vice, he gives fraud and pretense a merciless thrashing.

About Sheridan there is something much more romantic

and quixotic; he has quite as much the sense of society and quite as many of a worldling's tastes as Congreve, but much less of a worldling's *mind*. Thus Sheridan made a romantic elopement where Congreve never married at all. Thus Sheridan, while still young, abandoned the theater for the world of politics, where Congreve at much the same age went frostily into retirement. Sheridan, again, made the most brilliant parliamentary speech of England's most brilliant age of oratory; it is difficult to imagine Congreve making any public speech at all.

But what creates a wider gulf between the two men than any qualities that divide them in temperament is the seventy-five years that separate them in time. Where Congreve's chief concern was to attack appearances, Sheridan had himself some to keep up. Sheridan, writing for a considerably more genteel age, accepts a more genteel tradition. There are some things, now, that one can no longer talk about at all; there are a good many that one cannot talk about with the old frankness and freedom. Immorality can no longer go unpunished, and indecency must go veiled. The difference between the two ages is most clearly brought out by comparing Vanbrugh's *The Relapse*, written in the 1690's, with Sheridan's cleaned-up version of it, *A Trip to Scarborough*, written some eighty years later. Sheridan's is often the tidier play, but it is always—where truth or revelation is concerned—the tamer one. Indeed, it is this sense of tameness, of worldly considerations in terms of one's audience as against worldly *revelations* in terms of one's characters, that distinguishes Sheridan from Congreve, and that ultimately diminishes him.

Historically this is understandable enough: where a Congreve came on the heels of stage comedy so hard, scheming, and licentious that his greater refinement of tone is as much a virtue in him as his honest disclosure of motive, a Sheridan entered a theater as vitiated by weepsy sentimental comedy as was Congreve's by nasty lewdness. Only Goldsmith, and Goldsmith only a year or two earlier than Sheridan, had attempted to combat this sentimentalism; and Sheridan, following Goldsmith, was himself as much concerned with dislodging false sentiment as with delineating true manners. That is why his first play, *The Rivals*, never manages to achieve any sustained attitude or tone, but is a theatrical coat-of-many-colors, oftener whimsical than witty, sometimes ridiculing sentimental comedy, sometimes echoing it, and, all in all, too inoffensive and vanilla-flavored, too given to playing safe.

The Rivals is only marginally in the tradition of the comedy of manners; it is with *The School for Scandal* that Sheridan takes his true place there, and displays his true talents. *The School for Scandal* is indeed—whether in public fame or theatrical popularity—the most famous comedy of manners in the language. Here the man of the world in Sheridan fulfills himself, here he indeed restores to the stage the wit and polish of the Restoration. Moreover, as a work for the theater, as something that deftly mingles plot and theme, characterization and background, it offers, I think, a surer hand, a stronger theatrical instinct, than any that the Restoration itself can provide. Equally for verbal polish and theatrical craftsmanship, equally for colloquial ease and theatrical canniness, it deserves its great popular fame.

The play's characterizing theme—a theme of the utmost worldly interest—is set forth in its title: the audience is to be allowed to watch, as it were, the preparation and distribution of scandal all the way from manufacturer to consumer, from where it is hatched to where it is served up at the breakfast table. It should be mentioned that at the time *The School for Scandal* was written, Sheridan was dealing, not just with something of permanent interest, but with something also of topical concern. There had just emerged a new kind of slanderous journalism, what we still describe as the scandal sheet; and the *Town and Country* magazine and the *Morning Post* newspaper were making of tattle and innuendo at once an art and a thriving industry, so that every one in society was in a panic over his own reputation while gorging on the curdled reputation of others.

Such a situation must, in Sheridan's own time, have given an extra fillip to the opening scene of the play. Here we are shown scandalmongers who make great oaks from the smallest acorns, who contrive scandal from what they hear, what they overhear, what they conclude they overhear, and what they clearly hear wrong. On one occasion, we are shown scandal for scandal's sake—where the motive is purely artistic and "disinterested"; we are shown it, on another occasion, for the scandalmonger's sake, where the object is to cast suspicion on the wrong person. And such scandalmongers as Lady Sneerwell and Mr. Snake are true artists in their line. It is part of the fun that when they and Mrs. Candour meet, they go in for the same kind of shop talk, the same kind of trade secrets as so many booksellers or innkeepers might indulge in. The tone is set at once in the opening scene; and scenes like it recur all through the play. Such scenes constitute the play's thematic whalebone; they are at once an illustration of manners and a comment on society. They give the play spice; they can also give it a suggestion of glitter. And the theme of scandal does something further: it goes far toward solving a difficulty born of a genteel age. Scandal provides Sheridan with the *sense* of naughtiness, with the atmosphere of sinfulness, which Restoration comedy achieved through sin itself. Of sin itself there is absolutely nothing in the *action* of Sheridan's play; there is only the imputation of sinning. The age—or, at any rate, the stage—had grown too prissy to deal honestly with sin: not only could no maiden surrender her virtue and retain the title of heroine, no wife could any longer deceive her husband and be permitted to prosper; indeed, no widow could by sinful means make her way to the altar. But just because actual sinning was now forbidden in the theater, it enjoyed there all the lure of forbidden fruit; and though vice might not triumph, female virtue would again and again be tempted, would again and again quake and begin to totter. By making scandal the theme of his play, Sheridan could thus brilliantly capitalize on the appearance without the reality.

In a worldly view, all this takes on a certain peculiar interest. There is perhaps good reason why, whenever we find much sin *or* much scandal, we find not much of the other. For in communities that are habitually sinful, there cannot be anything very newsworthy about sin; moreover, in a community composed entirely of glass houses, everyone will think twice about throwing stones. Scandal is really a sort of amusement tax that virtue demands of indecorum. For scandal really to thrive, there must be well-behaved people as well as ill-behaved ones, be people who can purse their lips as well as who cover their faces. Mere gossip has a certain fellow-feeling about it: we talk rather idly about our neighbors, knowing that our neighbors talk rather idly about us. It is all a contribution, almost a benevolent contribution, to community life. By not keeping her house sufficiently clean, Mrs. Westley is doing her bit for sewing-circle conversation; by not being able to hold his liquor, Mr. Westley is doing his bit for his pals on commuter trains. But

scandal concerns people who are not just humanly fallible
—they must be socially vulnerable as well. Scandal, indeed,
is predicated of people who possess a certain amount of
position, who are the equals—better yet, the superiors—of
those whom the scandal delights. When a society woman's
housemaid gets herself into trouble, this may seem to her
employer an outrage or a misfortune, and it may prove
bothersome or unsettling; but it is not a scandal. This is not
to elevate scandal to a philosophical level, or to involve it in
scientific laws; but only to indicate that it *is* a genuine and
permanent social phenomenon, and worth thinking about
in any study of worldly life or of the comedy of manners.
Certainly it is worth thinking about here, in the most famous comedy of manners in the language—and the more
so since, by Sheridan's time, a devout interest in scandal
had superseded an earlier interest in vice. Nor, for being
more strait-laced, is Sheridan's audience any less worldly: it
is, if anything, more so, in the sense that hypocrisy is more
worldly than frankness.

There is also a kind of aesthetic consideration: Sheridan
is writing in an age when "taste" is not a matter of how you
deal with things, but rather of what things you may deal
with. And just because, in *The School for Scandal,* no one
sexually sins, sin now becomes much wickeder and more
important than it once was. Restoration comedy is a tedious
succession of ladies and gentlemen being thrust behind
screens, pushed into closets, hidden under beds, flung down
back stairways; such scrambling for cover gets to be as
commonplace and routine as closing a window or opening a
door. But *here,* in *The School for Scandal,* we have Lady
Teazle hiding behind a screen in what, without question, is
the most famous scene in all English social comedy, just as
the moment when the screen is knocked over constitutes

the most climactic moment in all English social comedy. Some of this is clearly due to Sheridan's expertness as a playwright, to his building up the scene to get the utmost from it. But some of it is due to its being, as similar scenes a century earlier never were, so zealously, so breathlessly, scandalous. We are back in an age when sex takes on glamour through being illicit.

Impropriety is thus the very essence of what goes on; except that nothing goes on. The story itself is a good one to the extent that we regard it as merely a story; and it is worked out by someone completely at home in his medium. But, of itself, the story is almost obstreperously fictional: the key point about Sheridan here is not his high comedy, but his strong theater sense, the way he can give, even to his scandalmongers, not the sheen of wit alone, but the deviousness of spiders; the way he can plot; the specific way he can unravel, or expose, or turn the tables. There is about it all the conciseness of an adroit theater mind. Maria is Sir Peter's ward; Sir Peter and Sir Oliver are old friends; Maria wants Charles for a husband; Lady Sneerwell wants Charles for a lover; Joseph wants Maria for a wife; Joseph wants Lady Teazle for a mistress. The story is thus both concentrated and complicated. The plot thickens, as a good plot should. The hero's future darkens, as a proper hero's must. With just two acts to go, Sheridan leaves himself a tremendous lot to work out and clear up.

Sheridan solved everything in the fourth act—not least the perennial success of the play. First Charles Surface's fortune is made in the picture scene, when he refuses to put up his uncle's portrait for auction. Then Joseph Surface cooks his goose in the screen scene, when Lady Teazle exposes and denounces him. Two such scenes coming one upon another are a triumph of stagecraft; they also make an exhilarating contrast, one scene showing how really good is the bad boy, the other how really bad is the good one.

They are not quite the same *kind* of scene, however. The screen scene, descending straightforwardly from the Restoration, is altogether part of the worldly comedy of manners. In classic style, it involves the husband, imperils the heroine, and unmasks the villain; in equally classic style, it maintains the tone of artificial comedy. Conversely, the picture scene—at least on Sheridan's terms—would be very unusual, indeed hardly possible, in Restoration comedy. Its appeal, to the audience no less than to Charles's uncle, is unabashedly sentimental; and though audiences in Sheridan's day and ever since have found the appeal irresistible, I rather wonder whether audiences would have done so in the age of Charles II. Perhaps I am too cynical myself, but I venture to think that had any Restoration playwright thought up the picture scene, *his* Charles would have refused to part with the portrait through being shrewd rather than warmhearted, and the audience would have less condemned Charles for his wiliness than Uncle Oliver for his vanity. Plainly, in all this, it is the Restoration and not Sheridan that is anomalous; the Restoration and not Sheridan that flouts popular appeal and shrugs at sentiment. With virtually every age except the Restoration, Charles Surface is an ideal conventional hero. And though the Restoration stage is as extreme in offering so little conventional virtue as other ages are suspect for offering so much, it is just for providing such an offset that the Restoration can arouse a kind of gratitude in us. Lack of feeling is at least better than fraudulent feeling.

Charles and Joseph Surface are themselves a case in point. The theme of the good and the bad brother is literally the oldest in the world, for it first turns up with Cain and Abel. But the contrast, in Restoration comedy, is usually less one of good and evil than of naïveté and sophistication, of gaucherie and grace. Charles and Joseph descend much less from the Restoration than from Tom and Blifil in *Tom Jones*. Fielding, a really humane and *not* really sentimental man, with his deep hatred of hypocrisy, felt a strong need to contrast a Tom with a Blifil, to insist that real goodness is a thing of the heart, that decorum is not virtue, nor animality vice. Even so, his contrast is too pat. Yet, though Fielding may be judged a little diagrammatic, he was not, like Sheridan, genteel. Tom's heart might be made of gold but his will power was made of tinfoil, and his moral scruples were scarcely sawdust. Tom goes so far as to let himself be kept by Lady Bellaston; Charles Surface, on the other hand, isn't even the lover of any fine lady. There is just enough wrong with him to make him endearing. He drinks, but presumably like a gentleman. He piles up debts, but as much from being goodhearted as extravagant. Though he needs money, he won't sell his uncle's picture; though he needs money, he gives much of what he gets to an impoverished kinsman.

It is from this, and other things like it, that we discern, behind the worldliest of façades, the most sentimental of interiors—or the hard candy with the gooey center. It is from this, and other things, that we discover how superior is the storytelling of *The School for Scandal* to the story. We must not undervalue the adroitness of the storytelling and all the graces that go with it—the play has a certain verbal polish and drawing room *ton;* has even a genuine *air* of worldliness. And with his scandalmongers at work— brewing, bottling, labeling, purveying their scandal—Sheridan catches the accent, achieves the enameling, of worldly high comedy. Here the prose, at once starched and infor-mal, enhances a tradition; and in manner as in merit Sheri-dan stands close to Congreve and, like Congreve, asserts the worldling's point of view.

But when we pass beyond manner to actual substance, we find that sound plotting and brisk movement are only had at a very steep price; that the story belongs wholly to the stage, with no overtones of real life. What I mean by this has nothing to do with surface realism. The comedy of manners has no use for surface realism; being, indeed, concerned with the shams and pretenses of human beings, it has every need of artifice. But since its very orbit is a world of masks, what it must always be moving toward is a general unmasking, so that we see at last the true faces that lurk beneath. When a Congreve, or even a lesser figure like Etherege, has brought matters to an end on the stage, we have a proper sense of what often discreditable instincts underlie such exquisite manners; we comprehend by how narrow a margin virtue tends to survive, and with what sleepless pertinacity vanity conspires; we watch the eyes of Innocence first widen and then contract; we note the pol-ished in process of becoming the tarnished, and how the heart, too, has need of rouge. Above all, since the real dra-matis personae of the comedy of manners are the practices of society, the way of the world itself, we see in what fashion they alter and contaminate and corrupt; and though wickedness certainly need not triumph, a sense, at least, of man's dark, divided nature must somehow obtrude. Artifice, when expertly applied, can be a great short cut to truth.

But between artifice and the mere staginess that we en-counter at times in *The School for Scandal* there is a crucial difference. Sheridan, we feel, heightens certain of his scenes not in the service of revelation but for the sake of effect. Partly from being too stagy and partly from being too sentimental, his is a real "fiction" plot where, rather than the audience finding out the truth in human nature, the characters find out, for fictional ends, the truth about one another. Even where Sheridan digs a little deeper, as with Lady Teazle's inclination toward sin, we are shown—and expected to believe—that she is now thoroughly sick of social pretense; there is not a hint that this may only be temporary repentance born of sheer fright, and that a month hence this blooming young wife of a man twice her age will be tempted once more. Maria, again, from an adherence to vapid stage conventions, becomes the dullest of ingénues: she, who might be the Millamant of the piece, is not allowed—as though the presence of wit bespoke the absence of virtue—to be pert or amusing at all.

The trouble with this whole side of the play is not that it is artificial but that it is tame, is not that it snaps its fingers at realistic truth but that it clicks its heels before conventional morality. A man who acquiesces in the common morality of his age may just escape with his life, provided he abjures the usual trumpery of his profession. He may escape rather better if, while making use of technical tricks, he sternly preserves his independence of mind. But a man who succumbs to both temptations, who gives in to stage effects and audience reaction alike, cannot get off scot-free. What Sheridan accordingly wrote in *The School for Scandal* was one of the most brilliant box-office comedies in the language. He was too worldly in his own calculations to become one of the great delineators of worldliness.

Thus we are in a world of set rewards and punishments, of old-fashioned—or perennial—heroes and heroines, of rich uncles who are won over and wicked brothers who are shown up. As popular theater, there may be nothing wrong with this; but there is something wrong with a man of Sheridan's gifts acquiescing in popular theater. Sheridan satirizes, here, almost nothing that the world in general does not condemn; he nowhere boldly challenges fashionable opinion or assaults fashionable complacency. A Wycherley may not have shocked his own generation, but he can still shock us. A Shaw may not shock us, but he did shock our grandparents. But Sheridan, if at times delightfully impudent, is never at all subversive. Nor, to be fair to the *man*, is this altogether calculating on his part; much of it, I suspect, he half believed in. There was a good deal of the pure romantic in the Sheridan who himself fought duels, himself eloped, himself was overdazzled by the great world. The gentility of his age clearly did him harm, but something beyond conformity enters in; actually, he often did not so much conform as concur. Sheridan's wit always tends to face south and toward the sun; in his portrayal of venom there is nothing personally venomous; he had worldly tastes but not, like Congreve or Molière or La Rochefoucauld, an inviolably worldly mind. His scandalmongers constitute a kind of Greek chorus in a play that Sheridan never really got round to writing on their terms. Their air of iniquity is a false front for the play's essential innocuousness. Indeed, in terms of Sheridan's mastery of his trade, perhaps the most brilliant thing about *The School for Scandal* is not the actual glitter of its dialogue but the seeming wickedness of its plot.

HORACE WALPOLE'S LETTERS

OSCAR WILDE SAID OF THE ENGLISH ARISTOCRACY that it was the best thing the English had done in the way of fiction. Certainly it has provided not only many characters that the most enterprising novelist would have been delighted to invent; it contains many others that no self-respecting novelist would have dared to. Consider that highborn Victorian lady who woke up one night to feel hands moving back and forth, back and forth, over her bed. Too terrified to scream, she held her breath; the motions ceased at last and, too terrified to move, she presently fell asleep. When she woke it was broad daylight and she discovered that her butler had been walking in his sleep and had laid the table for eight on her bed. Could even Dickens have imagined that? Yet people like that dart in and out of Horace Walpole's letters. The English aristocracy, however, is more than a field for anecdote, as the letters of Horace

Walpole are more than a fund of it. During the eighteenth century the aristocracy not only ruled Great Britain; it forged, if it sometimes fettered, taste; it commanded a style; it established an attitude; it constituted a way of life. Despite Wilde, it was not fiction but fact: a great fact; a great force; and in its composure, its skepticism, its arrogant freedoms, its tyrannical forms, it was a supreme embodiment of worldliness. And in Horace Walpole it found not at all a simple mirror: were he only that, however great he might be as a social historian, he would have no place in literature. That he has a very marked place is due to his possessing no less distinctive a temperament than an eye, is due to a certain ambivalence of approach in him, which must mock at what delights it and satirize what it succumbs to.

If you are the son of a prime minister, you can become many things yourself. Indeed, if you share some of your father's genius, like the younger Pitt, you can become prime minister yourself. If, on the other hand, you are as elegant as your father was bluff, as waspishly well-bred as your father was carelessly open-handed, you would best use your place in the world to observe rather than participate. Horace Walpole had the entrée; he had, very early, an eye; and very early, in Horace Mann at Florence and in a number of other correspondents, he had an attentive ear. Had all his other correspondents perished, Horace Mann alone would have given Walpole a posterity. But most of the other correspondents lived ample lives, while Walpole himself lived on until eighty—so that he presents us with a just sufficiently altering England under many rulers and regimes, and a just sufficiently altering Walpole during many decades.

A conscious artist, he remains detached in much that he

observes, but he is obsessed with observing. He makes light of things, but he does *not* make light of the business of making light of things. He is probably the greatest artist in gossip in English literature, yet that does not really characterize him or constitute a wholly sound unit of measurement. It would be like calling Pope no more than an artist in abuse. Walpole has a real place, a real value, from constituting the voice of his age and class, and yet very much possessing a voice of his own. To us he seems, as he essentially was, a notable member of the *ancien régime;* yet in his own time there was something unaccountably avant-garde about him too, something of the innovator, who invented his own fopperies, who adapted his own fiction from the medieval, who translated his own pleasures from the French. In a dilettante way he constantly adds something to what he embodies; as ultimately, in his dilettante way, he subtracts something too. Walpole's own social world, we can feel sure, treated him as a kind of pet eccentric, regarded him as a kind of privileged sniffer, and consulted him with a certain faintly contemptuous deference. As we almost always see something flowering in great worldly societies at the cost of something drying up, so within such a society, so with Horace Walpole, there is all the bloom of the hothouse and almost nothing of the fragrance of the field.

He had the eighteenth-century patrician's horror of being a professional, yet could say with much truth, in his amateur fashion, that "no profession comes amiss to me—from tribune of the people to a habit-maker." We, after two centuries, remember him as a printer, an adventurous house builder, an M.P., an antiquary, a historian, a novelist, a playwright, and above all a letter writer; and in his own age he must have seemed one of the very greatest of collectors —of bon-mots preeminently, but also of objets d'art. And it was important for his role in life that he should have a retinue of intelligencers, of eavesdroppers, of drawing-room spies; it was not enough that the supreme social historian of his age should be able to go everywhere or meet everyone; he had to have, as it were, an eighteenth-century tape recorder in a corner of every room, at each end of every dinner table. In his own high-styled way he ran a kind of factory of anecdote and gossip and news, with duchesses doing piecework and cabinet ministers tying up parcels and ambassadors acting as delivery boys. But it was all hand-made, as durably elegant as Sheraton sideboards or Lamerie silver: it was not just transferred, it was transformed in the end into great letter writing.

The letter writing was no accidental virtue, but an almost predestined medium. Though plainly aimed at posterity, it remained in its own time private, offered to an appreciative few. With the secrets of society never peddled to the outside world, there was no need, for the most part, to dot i's. And in all this the point of view has acted as a preservative. The immense amount of mere information which Walpole's letters provide would make them an incomparable source book, but only that. The cultivated reader does not, however, take up the letters for mere information; having taken them up for pleasure, he puts them down having been in contact with perhaps the greatest letter writer of his century and with certainly one of its most indelible personalities. A fine thing about the eighteenth century is how beautifully it mingles a form of tradition and the individual talent; how one eighteenth-century master of language after another equally evokes his century and leaves his own signature:

Proud to catch cold at a Venetian door

—that surely can only be Pope;

Solitude is dangerous to reason without being favorable to virtue;

—that can only be Johnson. And so with Walpole:

The first step toward being in fashion is to lose an eye or a tooth . . . Not that I complain; it is charming to totter into vogue.

"Totter into vogue": part of Walpole's gift for phrase lies in its conveying a certain temperament, in its imparting a sense of *town*. Rather than *rus in urbe* he represents *urbs in rure;* he represents artifice in nature, the hedge that is at once ornament and boundary. He stands, in a sense, for the green house, the bandbox, Marie-Antoinette's dairy. He has some of the quality of the best society verse, in which great things contract into small with wit and grace. The universe, with Walpole, suddenly turns into a ballroom, the Trojan War into a hair-pulling match, murals into miniatures. This small, myopic purview is one way—perhaps the only way —to see things steadily and see them whole; nor is this just a polite fancy. Being a century of consolidation, of putting humanity's house in order after all the discoveries and upheavals of the seventeenth century, the eighteenth century in England, by practicing a bit of sleight-of-hand, by blinkering its eyes, by slowing down its pace, could just frame life into something manageable and precise. But if all this is myopic, it is not *really* blinkered. If it is toylike and rococo in many of its effects, it is not entirely frivolous. At least it enables us to see a *way* of life steadily and to see it whole, while noting a great host of details. Walpole is in one way as thorough and exact a realist as Defoe is in another, and along similar lines. Again, because Walpole fights all the century's wars with tin soldiers, or fills England's Parliaments and administrations with puppets and marionettes, it is not to say he is a bad critic of them, or even a bad reporter. His mock-heroic approach must be allowed for, yet remains an offset to the all-too-heroic approach; and, under the aspect of eternity, it comes closer to the truth. Curiously enough, Horace Walpole's father, with just as disenchanted and worldly a view of things, became the greatest and most useful of English administrators. Sir Robert's administrations were decidedly made up of—or turned into—puppets; and tin soldiers or real ones, he would fight no wars at all. There is a certain irony in the fact that Sir Robert was as excessively philistine as Horace could be exquisite, but there is no real contradiction. Common sense governed the father's life as its twin brother, worldliness, governed the son's. And in both men, in the one by way of experience, in the other of temperament, a certain cynicism predominated.

Take from Horace Walpole what makes him an incomparable storehouse of gathered fact and a superb writer of letters, and he emerges a recurrent type of all cultivated societies, someone who is about equally at home in the social world and the artistic one, and who in the final sense is conceivably not *quite* at home in either. Leaving his genius as letter writer and social chronicler aside—or supposing him to have had only a pleasant knack for either— he stands forth a dilettante diner-out, an elegantly fussy bachelor, a delicately feline observer, dainty about food but greedy about gossip; very vain; a connoisseur of wit, and an even greater connoisseur of social oddities and human blemishes. Walpole carefully examined every ointment in hopes of finding a fly; painstakingly tested all available armor in hopes of discovering chinks; and, I venture to suppose, went constantly to parties not so much to have a good time as to unearth a good story. And yet in all this, he is not to be thought unpleasant; in all this there was less malice involved than sense of métier. As Beau Brummell dressed for future ages, or Lucullus dined, so Walpole, we may say, dined out. But he had his more creditable and laborious pursuits. From his house at Twickenham, from Strawberry Hill, we can almost date the Gothic Revival in English architecture; from his novel, *The Castle of Otranto,* we can almost date the Gothic Revival in English fiction. At Strawberry he set up a printing press whose productions are still collected; and his memoirs of the reign of George III, by quite lacking genius, possess very solid virtues of documentation.

At Strawberry, too—it is one reason why Walpole built it —he remained by himself or with a close friend or two for long periods; he rusticated and read, he received tidings by the incoming post and recast them for the outgoing one. It is necessary to note these withdrawals from society, these communings with the self; and as time passed he was, as he said, to find it pleasantest to pay all his visits by letter. He had that bachelor-breed characteristic, a good deal of delicate sensibility, which, when aroused, could make him exceedingly squeamish and, when ruffled, extremely ill-natured. He had also, of course, a good deal of the snob in him. With his taste for special sauces, his snobbery had a certain peculiar flavor of its own—he was rather snobbish about snobs. More to his credit, he had that eighteenth-century ideal of the aristocratic republican; though when the French Revolution threatened to make a republic of England, it vanished. For working people, even for workers on strike, he had much theoretical sympathy and even genuine feeling; on the other hand, for everything bourgeois, or that to him seemed bourgeois, for everyone with the slightest tradesman touch, or with even good professional standing, he had the utmost scorn and contempt.

Walpole runs true to type, again, in being—as a weathercock of taste—more gilded than dependable; in being often the dupe of fashion, the victim of too great a sensibility, and in having in the end no real qualities of *mind*. It is instructive, of course, to glance down the corridors of criticism and see how many responsive, even distinguished, critics lacked—in terms of their great contemporaries—perception or sympathy or even interest. Dr. Johnson thought *Tristram Shandy* would not last long; Matthew Arnold is scarcely inspiring on Tolstoy, nor Emerson on Dickens. And we ourselves always tend to think that our reversals of previous judgments, and our revivals of discarded favorites, end the matter—only to find that twenty years later it is all reversed again. But about the dislikes of a Horace Walpole we can establish a kind of pattern: it is not just that his tastes are not sufficiently masculine, or his sympathies sufficiently broad. It is that he forever cultivates a lesser thing at the expense of a greater; that his feeling for Gothic is in essence a love of rococo, that his sense of the visionary is in essence a taste for the lurid, that Heaven, for him, is hardly more than a garden and Hell hardly more than a grotto. He stands at that eighteenth-century point when solid good sense and quick natural feeling are involved in a trial marriage to produce that very eighteenth-century thing, sensibility; just as he stands at that moment when the classical and the romantic elegantly cohabit to produce that very eighteenth-century thing, the picturesque. Walpole was himself a matchmaker in such alliances, in the course of which he could be something of an offender, too—one who worshipped winking idols and followed wandering lights. Strawberry Hill becomes a footnote in the revival of Gothic by virtue of having been a bit of a travesty on it. And that Walpole could not abide Chaucer or Michelangelo, that he sniffed, or sniped, at half the most enduring of his contemporaries—at Johnson, at Sterne, at Boswell, and eventually at Gibbon—if all this is an object lesson in the vagaries of taste, it is, I think, much more pertinently something else. The Walpole type is in the end not so much wrong-headed as wholly unintellectual, not so much intolerant of what is complex as merely uninterested. There was, however, another—and very eighteenth-century —element involved. It was not so much that a Walpole couldn't get inside a Dr. Johnson's mind as that he couldn't get past his manners; not that he couldn't perceive a Gibbon's greatness as a writer, but that he pounced on his small vanities as a man.

Yet, before we come to what lifts Walpole high above mere type, to what he did with genius and a particular grace, we must note what there was of genuine character and feeling in him, and of a kind, moreover, to charm or touch us. When his cousin General Conway lost, for political reasons, his court and army posts, Walpole sat down immediately and wrote him a notably warm and generous letter putting half his fortune at Conway's disposal. Like so many touchy men, Walpole had a great need of friends and a certain gift for friendship. Sometimes his prickliness proved costly, but in the end he would assume the blame. How eighteenth-century a tone hovers over his years-after comment on the quarrel with Gray: "He loved me, and I did not think he did." Early and late, Gray and Bentley, George Montagu and John Chute, General Conway and Horace Mann were the objects of his interest and affection; as were a succession of great ladies, along with Walpole's nieces, who turned into great ladies; and as finally, late in life, were the Miss Berrys. Meanwhile, amid the rewards and consolations of friendship, there was his career—which is to say, his chronicling the life of his times. We pass with him from Ranelagh to the opera, from Houghton to Knole, now to a masquerade, now to a *fête champêtre;* to Oxford, Cambridge, Paris; to a great ball, a midnight fire, a dinner party where dinner is three times brought to the table, awaiting M.P.'s, and three times removed. We accompany Walpole to an auction of pictures, to Charles James Fox losing a fortune at Brooks's, to a conversation with Hogarth, a social call with Gibbon, a visit with Gray; now there is rioting over Wilkes, and now over Catholics; someone resigns, someone else elopes, someone else expires. It resembles a great one-man news chronicle, with a beruffled columnist flavor. Do we want military comment?—take the surrender at Yorktown:

> Well—there ends another volume of the American war. It looks a little as if the history of it would be all we should have for it, except forty millions of debts, and three other wars that have grown out of it.

Do we want theatrical comment?—Walpole went to Drury Lane, the play was *Cymbeline* and seemed, he says, "as long as if everybody in it went really to Italy in every act, and came back again." Do we want political comment?—

> The Duke of Dorset retires with a pension of £4000 a year, to make room for Lord Gower, that he may make room for Lord Temple. Lord Geo. Sackville forces out Lord Barrington from Secretary at War, who was going to resign with the rest, for fear Mr. Fox *should* . . . Lord Hardwicke, young disinterested creature, waits till something drops.

Do we relish a little comment on decor?—"Blenheim looks like the palace of an auctioneer who has been chosen King of Poland." Or Walpole will write about nothing at all with that touch that proclaims the born letter writer. "If you was dead," he tells Richard Bentley,

> to be sure you have got somebody to tell me so. If you was alive, to be sure in all this time you would have told me so yourself. If you are not dead, I can tell you who is: don't be alarmed, it's only the Queen-Dowager of Prussia.

Or take this, with its suggestion of Congreve:

> Soh! Madam . . . It is very hard one can't come into your house and commend anything, but you must recollect it and send it after one! I will never dine in your house again; and, when I do, I will like nothing; and when I do, I will commend nothing; and when I do, you shan't *remember* it . . . I wonder you are not ashamed—I wonder you are not ashamed. Do you think there is no such thing as gluttony of the memory?

But, in his letters, there are the great scenes too, the epistolary tapestries—the coronation of George II, the events of the Seven Years War or the Gordon Riots, or the beheading of the Jacobite lords:

> Then came old Balmerino, treading with the air of a general. As soon as he mounted the scaffold, he read the inscription on his coffin, as he did again afterwards. He then surveyed the spectators . . . and pulling out his spectacles, read a treasonable speech . . . He said, if he had not taken the sacrament the day before, he would have knocked down Williamson, the lieutenant of the Tower, for his ill usage of him . . . Then he lay down; but being told he was on the wrong side, vaulted round, and immediately gave the sign by tossing up his arm, as if he were giving the signal for battle.

In all this Walpole characterizes, or castigates, or approximates, the tone of his era or the way of his world.

How much of what we call civilization is needed to sum up what, in the end, is so little of what we call culture. For all this raillery or reporting of Walpole's is done *con amore;* is what, temperamentally, he basks in and thrives on and could scarcely live without. "I could not help reflecting," Walpole wrote once, after meeting a countrified baronet, "that living always in the world makes one as unfit for living out of it, as always living out of it does for living in it." Just so, Walpole had already written when still in his twenties: "I am more convinced every day, that there is not only no knowledge of the world out of a great city, but no decency, no practicable society—I had almost said, not a virtue." These two remarks we may regard as classic statements for the Walpole type, for the worldling temperament. For them, *urban* and *urbane* are one; culture and comfort are one; society is more fundamental than humanity. The ennui of the dinner party is for them a pretended affliction, quite unlike that form of solitary confinement called staying at home. Such worldlings as these may yawn over the essential sameness of things, but what a scent they have for novelty—for the new play, the lattest witticism, last night's gaffe, this morning's gossip. They may grumble about *plus ça change*, but what they grumble over is largely what they crave. They want the old reassuring faces quite as much as they enjoy the New Look; for them exists that familiar social paradox—life, to be exhilarating, must shift with the speed and color of a kaleidoscope, yet, where one's own comfort and self-assurance are concerned, it must not shift at all. These eighteenth-century people wanted, indeed, old pictures in new frames; wanted what simultaneously could be called the last word but would not have shocked the last generation.

This love of the bravura, of the bagatelle, of the fashionable frisson, this beginning as the jeunesse dorée, this becoming a petit-maître or a connoisseur—you will have noted that every word describing these things is a foreign word—it is in terms of such tastes and cravings and ambitions that we must adduce superior values to pass judgment. If nothing of what these people did pleases one, one has either an extremely lofty or a peculiarly narrow view of things. Walpole, surely, is an artist who depicts and at length defines what is itself a kind of art of living. Here, figuratively, is all but the best of eighteenth-century music, all but the finest of Gluck or Mozart; and, of eighteenth-century painting, all but the finest of Guardi or Watteau. Here is almost everything that we appreciate in eighteenth-century gardens, and domestic architecture, and elegant decor. In other words, here is that sense of style, at once careless and starched, at once frivolous and elegiac, at once formal and intimate that, if it went into curtsies and bows, and compliments and insults, and picknicking and dancing and duels, went also into the arts, and how men wrote and painted, and said goodbye to life. "I shall be quite content," said Walpole himself, by way of goodbye, "I shall be quite content with a sprig of rosemary thrown after me, when the parson of the parish commits my dust to dust."

And with all this, we, up to a point, should be content as well. Beyond that point, however, there are obviously larger and greater things, and even many things we must deprecate. There is more concern for humanity than society, for life itself than for a way of life. This is not simply a matter of different talents, this is not to reject a Horace Walpole for what he never could have written or been. It is to pass judgment on him for never attempting to write, let us say, a *Way of the World*. No, he preferred writing a *Castle of Otranto* and building a Strawberry Hill. But the truth, perhaps, is that he was not only turned into a dilettante by temperament, he was also forced into it by a certain deficiency of mind. Ideas either bored him, or failed to exist for him, or needed to be simplified or personalized. He was not, in either the deep or the jargon sense of the word, at all intellectual; nor was he of large or porous enough mind to assimilate the really new. For all this worldling's craving for new forms and fashions, for the last word in gardens or smart slang, for a new poetic twist or vocal trill or pictorial vista, for all his passion for new types of decor or duplicity, Walpole, to the genuine new voices of the age, in Rousseau or the Encyclopedists, to the new waves of religion that swept over England, or of feeling that swept over Europe, was quite blind, deaf, insensible, uninterested, alien. He cultivated his garden, indeed, and so beautifully that nowhere else, nowhere untidier, did he really feel at ease, or at home, or himself.

CANDIDE

CANDIDE IS ONE OF THE MOST CELEBRATED OF CLAS-
sics, one of the shortest, one of the simplest in structure,
one of the most incisive in effect. It is also, in its movement,
one of the most cinematic, rushing precipitously from one
episode to the next, shamelessly from one country or one
cataclysm to another, with twenty words in explanation or
six for transition; and yet into about a hundred pages it
crams half the geography of the world and half the history
of its own times. It seems like a digest of some vast enter-
prise, or a history of thought told in parables of action. And
it *is* a digest—at any rate, of Voltaire himself; it is an
almost literal *reductio ad absurdum* of a rational judgment
on life. Its jests, its reckless adventures, its extravagant
fantasticalities are epitaphs of man's follies and false no-
tions. But it careers to some purpose, and it concludes not
with an epitaph but with a guidepost, not with a judgment
but with an injunction. *Candide* is not least one of the most

celebrated of classics because it ends by offering an equally celebrated piece of advice.

When we recall the great storehouse of writings—the squibs, the satires, the pamphlets, the protests with which Voltaire flooded the Europe of his age; and again his histories, his dramas, his works of philosophy and dialectics, not to speak of the multiple volumes of letters published since his death—when we recall all this and are simultaneously aware that for the world at large Voltaire is today merely the author of *Candide,* we cannot but indulge in a variety of ironic reflections. Yet, if popularly speaking, all Voltaire's works dwindle to one slender volume, there are in it enough ironic situations and reflections of his own to blot ours out.

Candide is not, to be sure, a milestone in either philosophical or literary development; it does not open a door on a new world of thought or a new era in feeling, or even show us a new kind of man looking into a mirror. Books by Rousseau, Stendhal, Baudelaire, Rimbaud are milestones in French letters as *Candide* is not. Even less have we here anything new or striking in the way of form; Voltaire's philosophical testament is nonchalantly imbedded in a picaresque tale; and his hero, far from being some new kind of crusader or romantic or egoist, is one more unworldly naïve young man who not so much reflects upon life as reacts to it, who not so much even reacts as is a rolling stone, an unselective anthology of experiences. He is much less pen than blotting paper; he is much less, at times, a character in fiction than the moral of a cautionary tale. But of course the very point of *Candide* is that it should not be a milestone, that it should rather be a reminder that, for all the constantly changing scenery and madly accelerating pace, this is a kind of classic journey along a kind of ageless road.

The guide for this journey is not quite so traditional, but a skeleton-thin aging gentleman with mischief in his eye and mind who guides *us* by leading Candide astray, warns us by getting Candide in trouble, awakens us by allowing Candide his dreams, enlightens us by allowing other people their prejudices, and constantly challenges us by revealing the nature, the predicaments, and the fate of our fellow-men. Our guide is, in other words, a very particular sort of man, so sharp of tongue as to seem at times revolutionary in thought. He also cleverly dashes us along so fast as to give *us* no time to think at all. Into a paragraph or two Voltaire can fling more mishaps and events than Henry James desires for a novel; into a page or two, more horror than Tennessee Williams can introduce into a play. No one rattling along that ageless road has ever, so often as Candide, been pushed clean off it, and yet in so short a time traverses such tremendous distances.

Voltaire is not simply specializing in calamity because he has a happy gift or a cruel taste for it; there is method in his mischief. He is much less devising his own guidebook than discrediting another man's, much less articulating a philosophy than exploding one. In writing *Candide*, Voltaire's specific object, as we all know, was to pour scorn on the optimism of Leibnitz. The young Candide, in fact, was not just to be catapulted into life as one more callow, ignorant, errant, blundering, trusting youth, or even as a young man with a pocketful of clinking gold pieces and a head full of contradictory clichés. He was to have for his tutor Dr. Pangloss, who taught, we are told, "metaphysico-theologo-cosmonigology," and who taught Candide that this is the best of all possible worlds. Everything indeed is for the best purpose: "Note," says Pangloss, "that noses were made to wear spectacles; we therefore have spectacles. Legs were clearly devised to wear breeches; therefore we have breeches."

Voltaire, being both a great ad hoc pamphleteer and one of the supreme comic imps of all time, would not refute Leibnitz with logic; he would smother him in ridicule. Dr. Pangloss was to be made not just a fool, but a byword for foolishness. Optimism was not just to be trounced and stood in a corner; it was to be drawn and quartered and scattered to the winds. Actual events—the brutalities and earthquakes and wars of Voltaire's era—were to be mingled with imaginary ones; the leitmotif that this is the best of all possible worlds was to be chanted antiphonally against rumbles of gunfire and screams of pain; and all this, as I have said, Voltaire would chronicle with cinematic speed, offering such a succession of calamities, such a compilation of disasters, as even a predacious, bloodthirsty mankind had never contrived. Nothing, even among the classical torments of antiquity, can equal it for horror—never such butchery, bombardment, rapine, slaughter, ravishment, shipwreck, plague, earthquake, piracy, auto-da-fé, disfigurement. The horror is most continuous early in the book, when we may surmise that Voltaire, most intent on dismembering Leibnitz, made a shambles of Leibnitz's philosophy by virtually massacring the human race. Here Voltaire's imagination was unsparing, his sense of mischief totally unmuzzled; never, surely, has so much that is grim been celebrated with a zest so gleeful. Here is something fuller of woes than Aeneas' wanderings, than Job's long ordeal—relentless in its horror, no less relentless in its hilarity. For, no matter what our sympathies or our sense of compassion, they simply cannot keep pace with Voltaire's presentment of calamities; and suddenly winded, we collapse with laughter. Leibnitz has been both done to a turn and burnt to a crisp; ridicule has gone berserk, and scorn been dissolved in lunacy: to prove that this is scarcely the best of all possible worlds, Voltaire has contrived, surely, the worst of all impossible ones.

But, though *Candide* has, right on to the end, its convulsions of laughter, it is more than wild-eyed extravaganza: it manages to refute Leibnitz on realistic as well as surrealist terms; it even manages to neglect a chief theme which has proved so easy a target. Voltaire was not to rest content pulverizing another man's philosophy; he was to promulgate his own opinions and drive home his own point of view. Against optimism he set not just a fantastic pessimism but a reasoned one; against Dr. Pangloss a Martin; and, finally, against a reasoned pessimism a reasoned relativism, a making the best of whatever sort of world ours may be. In a certain sense this little novel, however unacademic its curriculum, however unorthodox its graduate studies, *is* an education. Candide is not simply delivered from absurd illusions, he is converted to sensible views; and in the process this well-meaning innocent is often a victim, is on occasion a hero, but also—before we are through— achieves a most impressive criminal record, however unpremeditated the crimes. There are real bloodstains amid the book's buckets and torrents of stage gore; there are real human voices amid all its falsettos and catcalls and shrieks; and real villains, besides leaping devils and sword-brandishing dummies.

The reasoned pessimism of the book—set against what we might call the riotous pessimism of its incidents—we encounter in the reflections of Martin, the philosopher; and so far as it expounds and iterates the theme of man's inhumanity to man, though the voice may be Martin's, the hand is Voltaire's. Yet Martin goes a little further by suggesting that man's inhumanity has become his occupation, his special study, his way of making a livelihood:

> I've almost never seen a town that didn't desire the ruin of some neighboring town, or a family that didn't want to exterminate some other family. Everywhere in the world the weak detest the strong and grovel before them, and the strong treat them like flocks of sheep to be sold for their meat and wool. A million regimented assassins sweep over Europe from one end to the other, murdering and robbing with discipline to earn their bread.

But beyond this pessimistic view of life, beyond this sense of how man must earn his bread, or how alone he can maintain his safety, runs the theme of how he can save his soul. And here enters Voltaire's own very special villain, his picture of man's inhumanity to man *in the name of God.*

Here enters, in other words, the Church, or, at any rate, those aspects of religion which Voltaire militantly opposed, as creating fanticism and furthering superstition, as imposing shackles on human thought and perpetrating falsehood in the name of truth, as enjoying the material good things of life under cover of spiritual behests about the life hereafter. Voltaire, with serious doubts about the life hereafter, was outraged by how organized religion legislated for the life on earth. To Voltaire all too much in religion was absurd, exploitative, tyrannical, and set rigid rules without setting virtuous examples. The gist of his conclusions, in respect of positive religion, is in his own words "to worship God and be an honorable man."

One whole side of Voltaire fits of course into the humanist feeling of his times and is part of its skeptical leanings and secular position. It is part of that deism which, so to speak, gives God the benefit of the doubt; it is part of that

Organized Irreligion which had infiltrated the world of cultivated society as well as of intellect; on this latter head in particular, we must remember that there had developed a worldly age of skepticism generally; that anyone given to disbelief about men's motives could not help thinking about their origins. The secularist position was, in any case, to have Voltaire as its trumpet voice. But Voltaire's, I take it, was not a theological quarrel narrowly viewed; it was a broad-beamed intellectual and moral attack on religion for requiring blind obedience to institutionalized beliefs. Sometimes as an exhortation, *"Ecrasons l'infame"*; sometimes as a direct injunction, *"Ecrasez l'infame,"* Voltaire's impassioned slogan was like a gigantic clenched fist shaken at the world. It is no overriding slogan in *Candide*, where the guns are trained on a different target, and where the pamphleteer gives way to the inspired satirist. But in *Candide* it is never for long absent. If given no star part, the attack on religion is a kind of character actor who keeps coming upon the scene, or at any rate crossing the stage—a character actor whose character is steadily villainous.

But it is Voltaire's knowledge of this world, not his doubts about the next, that dominates his masterpiece. Even his wildest spoofing can have its historical counterparts. Consider Cunegonde's brother, the Baron, after his impassioned reunion with Candide, after his calling him brother and savior: when Candide speaks of marrying Cunegonde, the Baron goes wild at such presumption; when Candide persists, the Baron strikes him with his sword, only for Candide to rip out his own sword and kill him. The situation (the Baron having miraculously not died) is repeated when Cunegonde has grown coarse and ugly: pride of rank could hardly seem more pathological, yet we have only to recall the author of a masterpiece as great as Voltaire's, the Duc de Saint-Simon, to know how little in kind Voltaire has exaggerated.

For Leibnitzian—or inherently Voltairean—reasons little is spared, certainly not the scientists and writers of the day, or the high life of Paris, or the playwrights, or the eternal pooh-poohers and belittlers; or the English. Candide's brief experience of England includes his witnessing the execution of Admiral Byng, a historical and unjust event, since the Admiral at worst displayed bad judgment while in command at Minorca, but yet no idle event: "In this country," Candide is told, "it's good to kill an admiral now and then, to encourage the others."

In these later chapters, we may note, Voltaire brings us into something like the actual social and intellectual climate of the Europe of his day, and so can't help moderating his pace and toning down his picture. Civilization, rather than natural instinct and predatory man, becomes the target, causing a certain drop in pressure, a certain loss of verve. But here, as earlier, we are listening again and again to the voice of experience in the midst of folly, as we are conversely confronted with the blunderings of mankind in the presence of wisdom. Nothing in the whole book, however—nothing in all its horrors and holocausts—seems so melancholy a reflection on human nature as Candide's decision to leave El Dorado. Here indeed is a real utopia, which he rejects for a romantic illusion; here, most impossibly, life is ample and luxurious, and mankind benevolent and upright; here *is* the best of all possible worlds. But, no—in his search for Cunegonde, Candide must leave it, must go blundering on, to suffer ills while searching, to feel men's whips and knouts while clutching his tutor's philosophy; but also to encounter, periodically, someone who speaks truth born of worldly experience, who strips off veils and

masks. As the story races on, it gathers substance for its
hero as well as speed for us. As against Pangloss with his
idiot's cheer and Martin with his embittered growls, the
life-blistered old woman may bring to us a life-fostered
cynicism, or Candide's valet Cacambo may speak with the
voice of practicality, with the wisdom of the streets. And at
the very end there is the Mussulman who provides Candide
with his valedictory formula, his testamentary wisdom, so
that, as Pangloss is giving one of his finest performances,
Candide breaks in with: "I also know that we must cultivate
our garden."

Candide's recipe has become Voltaire's great practical
bequest to the world, the acre or two of worldly wisdom that
he has made universally available from the whole large
domain of the Enlightenment. With it, Voltaire holds an
unfounded optimism in check, an unrelieved pessimism at
bay. By digging his own garden, man can be saved from all
the presumptions and perils by which he might dig his own
grave. By not fighting the world, he will be in most ways
relieved of fighting himself; by not seeking rapture, he will
avoid despair; by not yearning for triumphs, he will escape
defeat. It is the voice of sense in a world that but intermit-
tently hears and scarcely ever heeds the voice of reason, a
voice not at all heroic and sometimes thought to be cow-
ardly.

Yet the very sanity of Candide's decision, of Voltaire's
advice, has an irony of its own. *We* may reject the realism
of *Il nous faut cultiver notre jardin* as a little too philistine,
but for the world in general, even the philistines themselves, such realism seems too unromantic. Small-scale gar-
dening has never become the rage; it, to begin with, lacks
glamour; and it hopelessly defeat's man's craving for success, for celebrity, for power. The garden patch is pretty to

talk about, now as two centuries ago; but now, even more than then, outside the garden wall men are striding and rats are racing by. In ancient Italy, Horace sang of it; and a few decades before *Candide,* Voltaire's friend Pope:

> *Happy the man whose wish and care*
> *A few paternal acres bound—*

and though Pope with his Twickenham grotto might pair off with Candide and his Turkish garden, Pope elsewhere was hardly practicing what he preached: in all history, at any rate, no one has ever thrown so many stones, as Pope did, over the garden wall, or torn up so many flowers in other men's gardens. The garden patch is not popular; and when it does briefly content men, they have only to notice a larger patch next door, or a more fertile one down the road, to become dissatisfied. The irony persists—the pessimism that pervades *Candide* is lightened into sanguine good sense at the end, but it is good sense, good counsel, that is seldom heeded: no more than idealism is worldliness here a match for the egos, the strong-willed aggressions, the ambitions of mankind.

VII

LES LIAISONS DANGEREUSES

ONLY A NATION SUCH AS FRANCE, WHICH HAD MADE of society something ritualized and ceremonious, and of sex the most sinuous of arts and sophisticated of games, could have produced a *Les Liaisons Dangereuses*, where ceremonies become the basis for shams, and artfulness maneuvers toward unfeeling and cold-blooded ends. In Laclos's famous novel, worldly amorous pleasures are not simply pursued for themselves; they become the prey of wicked schemes. Love, in *Les Liaisons*, is not just far removed from lovemaking; lovemaking itself has thoughts far beyond skillful seduction; lovemaking would help to weave webs, set traps, ruin reputations, put an end to happiness. The civilized deteriorates here into something overcivilized, sophistication festers into decadence. In the operations of Mme de Merteuil and the Vicomte de Valmont the clever must be outwitted, the complacent discomfited, the innocent and virtuous tempted, worn down, undone. And if there are immediate self-interested objectives to all this—physical desires to be satisfied or personal resentments to be paid off —there yet persists a kind of sheer artistic satisfaction in performing every chord and run and trill on the entire keyboard of deceit.

Literature—very notably the literature of the theater— abounds in characters who, while furthering their own selfish ends, gloat over making dupes and fools of others. In *Volpone,* Ben Jonson's hero, himself a rich grandee, is less greedy for other men's gold than exultant at how their own greed can make them victims. In *The Country Wife,* Wycherley's Horner, by pretending impotence, not only acquires a whole harem of women, but does so with the condescending cooperation of husbands who think him harmless. With Horner, in other words, there is as much malicious pleasure as physical pleasure; with Volpone, as much malicious pleasure as material gain.

About each of these examples derived from the theater there is something more dramatic than psychological. Though in both plays there are remarkably vivid characters, in both we are very particularly held by the plot, with its ruses and stratagems. But a *single* motivating pretense— Volpone's to be dying without heirs, Horner's to be impotent —colors all their actions and coerces all their victims; there is a straightforward cause and effect. Volpone and Horner can grow formidable, even unforgettable, but less as human beings than as symbols of greed, or lust, or love of power. When in Mme de Merteuil and Valmont we encounter something like them as maneuverers, we encounter something quite unlike them as well. We are in a world perhaps as artificial as the age, yet the world of an actual society, with the tempo of life about it, indeed of formalized life, ceremonious intrigue, adroit amour. Sex here is less a game of pursuit than of entanglement, and for the image of the fox or stallion we must substitute the spider's. The measured pace of the story is sustained by the particular manner of the storytelling, which is in the then fashionable form of letters. The form has a real relevance to the subject matter, in that it permits scheming characters to directly reveal their motives and methods, their knowledge—but equally their ignorance—of persons and events.

The limitations of the letter-writing form in fiction can, of course, be great. Not only is the form at odds with the Jamesian concept of an adhered to "point of view," with its greater artistic unity; it can also make for something laborious and slow-moving, so that to learn a little we must read a great deal. The form can make as well for something cyclical rather than rhythmic—as we look, on the very same day, into a whole succession of houses and hearts, we lose the sense of movement, the cumulative power of an advancing narrative. And more, even, than such limitations can seem shackling, they can prove monotonous. Yet the form can also have great merits. If we *care* about the characters and their problems, it can be no less revealing than fascinating to see successively through each one's eyes, to note successively in each one's words how little or much they know about themselves, or one another, or the truth. Moreover, if the characters are truly worth caring about, the cumbrous means can conduct us to greatly illuminating ends. Insofar as the epistolary form makes us privy to secret desires and spidery maneuvers, it can have the constant lure of the novel of intrigue; insofar as it makes us privy to concealed motives, warring interests, curious self-deceptions, it can have the rich returns of the psychological novel. Beyond that, when as here it concerns people of one background, their differing voices can form an impressive social chorale. Certainly, thinking back on *Les Liaisons,* we are always conscious—beyond its people and their perfidies, or its other people and their plights—of a prevailing time and place, of something French; late eighteenth century; aristocratically worldly; preternaturally sex-minded.

In *Les Liaisons,* the letter-writing form seems inseparable from its subject matter, or from the approach to its subject matter. For, as Mme de Merteuil and the Vicomte dominate all that goes on, it is essential to their activities that they themselves remain apart and be forced to communicate by letter, confide by letter, praise and blame each other by letter, and finally quarrel and ruin each other by letter. Seeing eye to eye, working hand in glove, they yet operate separately. Moreover, though they are confederates in a cynical assault upon society, they are rivals even more through their personal vanity and egotism. Their letters to each other have a value that no conversations between them could convincingly have, for in their letters they not only confide their plans and progress, as they might in talk, but have also had time to reflect on what they have told each other; to condemn or deride, or make suggestions and counter-proposals. Laclos thus lets us see them in terms of themselves; in terms of their confederated attitude toward society; in terms of their competitive attitude toward each other. And if we add to this what we learn through other people's letters, we have psychological rewards quite as great as any dramatic ones.

I have begun with the framework because it so clearly *is* one, and because it is also something more. It dictates the tone, conditions the movement, and provides the peculiarly powerful effect of Laclos's novel. Though the chief characters are not numerous, and the secondary ones often scarcely take shape in our minds, we yet derive, from allusions to parties, balls, operas, and the like, and from a cluster of ostracized men and women and ruined reputations, the *sense* of a surrounding social world, of gossip always lurking and scandal ready to pounce, of social intrigue crisscrossing among the guests in a single drawing room. And we gain this impression of a rather extensive world at no cost to the intense relationships and detailed operations going on before our eyes. We are brought very close to what is happening by the letters—though much as we might be brought in mirrors.

The sense of a commodious background is important for our grasping the magnitude of what our two conspirators are up to. They are not just amusing themselves with particular people at a particular time: it is not merely Mme de Tourvel whom Valmont would conquer, or Cécile whom Mme de Merteuil would have him seduce (though the fact that the one is a chaste and moral woman and the other a young engaged girl makes them both very desirable targets). It is almost society at large that these two would systematically amuse themselves with, or revenge themselves upon, or assert their superiority against: as with a Volpone or a Horner, they crave such conquests as provide additional satisfactions—an end to fidelity, a loss of innocence, a surrender of principles, followed by guilty consciences, disrupted marriages, broken lives. For our conspirators, the art of coursthip, the art of seduction, the art of love are to coalesce into a kind of art of war; they won't simply grow bored with their lovers or mistresses, or callously cast them aside: they will betray them. They don't only seek, with a sort of moral nihilism, to corrupt people; with a sort of malign egotism they would deeply humiliate them as well.

Their confederacy is based on a shared pleasure in such

campaigning, on a shared attitude toward those they are
campaigning against, and on a certain appreciation of each
other. They themselves have enjoyed a successful love affair, in which two masters in the game of love have played
with a reciprocal adroitness. The termination of their affair
has had nothing finalizing about it, is less the end of a book
than the end of a chapter. Indeed, Valmont several times
suggests that they eventually crown their victories over
others by coming together again. Meanwhile, Mme de Merteuil is pleased to offer him an easy but piquant opportunity
in Cécile Volanges, whose mother has arranged for her to
marry, at fifteen, M. de Gercourt, a former lover of Mme de
Merteuil's. Gercourt is temporarily out of the country, and
Mme. de Merteuil bids Valmont add, to the joys of seducing
Cécile, the pleasure of having her betray her fiancé.

> She is really delicious! She has neither character nor
> principles . . . without wit and without finesse, she has yet
> a certain natural duplicity (if I may say so) which sometimes
> surprises even me and which will be all the more successful
> since her face is the image of candor and ingenuousness
> . . . I do not want Gercourt to escape; I spoke of him yester-
> day to the little girl and painted him in such colors that she
> could not hate him more if she had been married to him for
> ten years. I gave her a long lecture on conjugal fidelity;
> nothing could equal my severity on this point . . . I hope that
> by making her think that it is not permitted to yield to love
> except in the little time she has left before marriage, she
> will decide the quicker not to lose any of it.

Valmont, as it happens, is rather indifferent about Cécile,
from having, during a visit to his old aunt in the country,
met Mme de Tourvel, an attractive woman of firm conjugal
principles whose husband is also at a distance. This prude,
as Valmont first dubs her, becomes someone to besiege

equally for her physical charms and her moral virtue, for his sexual victory and her moral defeat. In spite of knowing his reputation with women, and of his own deliberate confessions about his past, she is drawn to him by the respect for her that accompanies his ardor. His love letters, a little pleading, a little recriminatory, are written with impressive hypocrisy. At virtually the same moment, he is writing to Mme de Merteuil of his actual plans from Mme de Tourvel's capitulation. Mingling feminine malice with a claim to superior generalship, Mme de Merteuil chides and mocks him for wrong tactics, for letting Mme de Tourvel lead him around by the nose. And indeed he is increasingly "led," not least by her opposition, an opposition in which virtue continues to repulse him, yet on such terms as to shut the door but not lock it.

Mme de Merteuil's amours being meanwhile rather on the flat side, she decides to be wooed by a too-self-assured fashionable rake, whose hour of conquest shall beget his moment of downfall; and with flawless planning, she contrives every move in the game until he is exposed and disgraced. His ostracism and exile reflect not just Mme de Merteuil's wicked glee, but a shallow society governed not by conduct but by a code of conduct, where exposure is the unforgivable crime. Valmont all this time is pursuing Mme de Tourvel pertinaciously enough to make her, as he did not foresee, flee his aunt's country house. This rouses him deeply: by running off, *she*—he insists—has deceived him. "Fool that I was! I dreaded her modesty, I ought to have feared her bad faith." It has, however, whipped him into a fury, half thwarted desire, half injured vanity, to possess her, and to be revenged upon her.

By now Valmont has also courted Cécile and seduced her, while Mme de Merteuil has in tow Dancey, the young man who wants to marry Cécile. And Mme de Merteuil has treacherously served as Cécile's confidante in one way and as Cécile's mother's in another, advising quite contrary plans of action and setting everything at sixes and sevens in a way to cause everyone harm. But a certain devilish cooperation over Cécile's destiny between the two confederates ceases when Valmont at last breaks down Mme de Tourvel's resistance. His account of his victory, of his own strong emotions and the lady's intense ones, so piques Mme de Merteuil with a kind of jealousy that she gets no pleasure from a virtuous lady's downfall, and no pleasure either from Valmont's protesting that he would fain return now to his confederate's arms. Valmont does actually copy out a letter that his confederate provides him with for brutally breaking off with his victim. But when he informs Mme de Merteuil of having done it, and for her sake, she answers him:

> You loved Mme de Tourvel very much and you still love her; you love her like a madman; but because I amused myself by making you ashamed of it, you have bravely sacrificed her. You would have sacrificed a thousand rather than endure one jest. Where will vanity not take us!

Meanwhile Mme de Merteuil, by way of Danceny, has in turn roused Valmont's jealousy. The two become enemies, each venting his malice on the other; and one and all, wicked and virtuous, innocent and guilty, are denied the happiness they looked for, and are doomed, most of them, to death or disfigurement or dishonor. The conclusion of the story has the harsh steel-on-steel sound of an avenging morality, but with virtue despoiled and not rewarded, and the stage left, as it were, in total darkness.

. . .

I have dealt at length with the enterprises and events of the book because it is by way of them that we are given Laclos's presentation, Laclos's exposure, Laclos's indictment of a society. There is little here of manners, little of the *spectacle* of society life or of its attendant ambitions. The ballroom is scarcely present in our thoughts, the bedroom seldom absent. Here, a hundred years after the Restoration in England, we encounter the same primacy of sex in a leisure-class society, the same obsession with it. There is something cruder and, all in all, healthier about Restoration gallantry: its lovemaking is not so finished an art, its rakes are much less enmeshed in rules; and the slapdash farcicality of the coarser Restoration comedies, where people hide in chests and cupboards or dress up in clothes of the opposite sex, is wholly alien to *Les Liaisons*. But in the Restoration, as in the France of Laclos, the fact that sex counts so signally makes it the master key to its society. From society's conduct in amour, and its code about amour, we can considerably infer its attitudes and morality concerning much else. Moreover, a world that raises love—not in the erotic but in the strategic sense—to the level of an exacting art is perforce involved in deception: in wiles as against fidelity, in something fought over rather than shared. In such circumstances, one forewent decencies while adhering to rules; and always one's vanity was at stake, because one's reputation in the matter was. Gallantry was an actual *career*—but, beyond that, was often a stepping stone to worldly advancement, for a lady's favors assisted her lover's fortune.

The central fact, however, is that a society so adroit at the arts of self-indulgence and self-seeking, and which encased a love of frivolity in a concern for form, must in time succumb to its shallowness, and decay beneath its veneer.

Where deception is an acknowledged art in amour, it must become one elsewhere. Where insincerity becomes second nature, one must assume it exists as much in others as in oneself. And when marriages are arranged with no thought of love or compatability, but only of rank and fortune, what personal or moral obligations can they encourage? Indeed, the suitability of marriage on the worldly plane quite outlaws the sanctity of marriage on any other. However wicked, Mme de Merteuil is no more cynical than her neighbor when she tells Cécile that even the most inconvenient husband is less inconvenient than a mother. As is well known, Laclos was inveighing in *Les Liaisons* against marriages of convenience; and their existing as an *institution* in French life has long tended to license infidelity and all its attendant deceptions. Certainly in any young bride—and all the more when girls were married off extremely young —the knowledge that her husband almost surely had mistresses, or had married her for money or position, must have had a chilling effect at just the age when she could have felt most ardent, and must have directed her ardor elsewhere. Yet the marriage of convenience need not so much have been a great evil in itself as the origin of what could grow into a great evil. It opened the way, in the upper levels of society, to the loss of devotion that goes with dalliance, to the suspicions that go with secrecy, to the need for victory that goes with sophisticated intrigue. Besides, where deceit could be assumed, espionage must quickly follow. Where irregularity invoked caution, go-betweens must soon exist. And where third parties shared lovers' secrets, blackmail could not but hover. Any treaty made between society people for mutual benefit could become one of mutual peril; trust involved mistrust; the slightest change in status led to treachery.

Certain people, to be sure, would resist their surroundings and even have generous feelings and impulses. But add to the sense of privilege the craving for pleasure, and the outer enamel of *politesse* covers nothing very warm or tender; outer enamel and inner hardness have become one. To succeed may well mean to make others fail; to have pleasure mean to give others pain; even survival may cause others to perish. Just living in such a world must reveal how predatory and unscrupulous men can be.

I have been characterizing the society of Laclos's France, a society much less exalted than Saint-Simon's several generations earlier, but not too different; a society which would soon hear the drum rolls of a revolution it hastened. I have doubtless painted it in colors a little too dark; even so, this makes the truth only a matter of degree, not one of kind. And if one paints it too dark, in the face of a Mme de Tourvel and one or two others, it is from wishing to emphasize that this world produced, helped mold, helped finally distort, our two villains. For unless we grasp all the vicious social elements that contribute to their beliefs and behavior, it is not easy to believe in *them*. Even so, it is not easy to believe in them. Villainy we can accept so long as there is a commensurate motive for it—enough understandable hate, or greed, or passion, or lust for power. We can also understand wickedness done on impulse, or in heat and hurry— particularly if we grasp what conditions it, and can see it fester within. But the operations, far less of the embittered heart or the unheeding flesh than, as here, of the corrupted mind; the mind plotting evil from frustration, or even ennui, its creativeness mere nihilism—we find such wickedness hard to swallow because hard to fathom. Such evil-for-evil's-sake wears no recognizable face, has no flesh-and-blood identity. Volpone, lying in bed pretending illness, suggests fable and allegory; even about Melville's Claggart and Billy Budd, in their sharply contrasted configurations, there is a poetic sense of allegory and abstraction; moreover, evil there stands opposed to good.

But in *Les Liaisons Dangereuses,* though Mme de Merteuil and Valmont are symptoms, we might in fact say malignancies, of a whole society, they are not dressed-up moral symbols; they are the creations of a moralist who is a psychologist even more. Few members of Laclos's society would go, certainly, to the lengths of Mme de Merteuil and Valmont, if only because few would possess their endowments. But, more to the point, conceivably *no one* not produced by that society would go to just such lengths at all. For what is depraved in our precious pair largely derives from a decadence involving their milieu; it need not make Merteuils and Valmonts, but it does make them possible. In a world that lives simply to gratify its appetites, appetites only roused by hothouse fruits and cunning sauces—a world, we might almost say, that creates a whole civilization for self-indulgent and corrupting ends—in such a world sensations supplant emotions, narcotics replace ordinary nourishment. In most overbred people who have also been overindulged, there exists a lurking ennui, a need for the new, the exotic, the *outré.* And if they have also been very much courted, they possess a sleepless vanity that must be stroked; and if they have never encountered opposition, they grow increasingly exacting about pleasure in the very process of being increasingly foiled of it. Some such people will doubtless turn savingly rueful, but most will have a fiercer craving for enjoyments, a less considerate feeling for others. Very few of them, however, will simply from boredom grow wicked toward others. They may harm those who get in their way, or make pawns of people as moves in the game, but they won't play the game just to make pawns of them. And they will not plot people's ruin for sport.

Indeed, to be so depraved they need almost be endowed with conspiratorial temperaments and malignly creative minds. They must also have great knowledge of their own world, and a certain resentment toward it. On just these terms, Valmont and Mme de Merteuil are concocting plots, are writing plays, using real people. But a superiority that *could* make them distinguished bears the seeds of what makes them depraved, for it makes them *feel* unboundedly superior; makes them despise a society that helped shape, or misshape them; and from having ill-used them, it makes them almost self-righteous about being revenged. Where a normal decadent craves new sensations but must wait or go looking for them, Valmont and Mme de Merteuil no sooner crave than they contrive them. And such dramatists must gain not just their own rewards, but other people's destruction.

More is involved in all this, however, than unprincipled contempt for others. There is a vast ego that must be gratified in itself, and accordingly, between Valmont and Mme de Merteuil, a vast struggle to dominate. As soon, indeed, as the two have set about "amusing" each other with their deviltries, they are committed to a competition in tactics, a battle of wits. Their by now inflamed vanities can in three important ways be gratified or hurt. There is the matter of the lovers and mistresses they are exerting their wiles upon —gaining their surrender, winning their adoration. There is, secondly, the matter of their skill, of how deftly they plan and carry out their campaigns: here the dramatist's, the artist's, vanity is involved. Finally, there is their competing against each other—with the vanity of *rival* dramatists, of rival sexes, at stake.

If there is something truly depraved about contriving such a game, perhaps it requires this conscious partnership to stimulate the depravity. In union there is incentive, there is that touch of mutual egging on that emboldens action; malice also loves company. What is important as well, there is the having a fellow playwright for one's audience. There is thus an inner and outer appropriateness to the form of *Les Liaisons:* in terms of storytelling, the two confederates *have* to write each other letters about what they are doing; but, in realistic psychological terms, they are partly *doing* it that they may have letters to write. Perhaps shared iniquity doubles the sense of pleasure while halving the sense of vice; more to the point, because it involves skill, it craves appreciation.

Their iniquity, one might almost say, consists in a systematic reversal of every moral value. And, as they are never stayed by compunction, so are they never pursued by guilt. Like the Devil, they most want to corrupt the virtuous and the innocent, and perhaps, like the Devil, they assail virtue and innocence from envying them. The great moral "drama" of the book is Valmont's assault upon Mme de Tourvel's virtue, in which, if you like, good and evil are contending in all their best black-and-whiteness. But there is nothing allegorical about their struggle—and it is a struggle; there is about it something real, personal, and more of both than Valmont had foreseen. In Mme de Tourvel's fierce and—as she at length must know—foredoomed resistance, in her love so intense that she dies of being rejected, we have the virtuous woman whose downfall is her vindication. To capitulate, for her, is to sin; to sin is to suffer—and to gain in stature, for her suffering creates a kind of moral tragedy. Valmont himself is not just irritated and jolted out of his complacency by the struggle to possess her; he is a little shaken and his ego is momentarily lamed. But ultimately, just as he could not own himself beaten by Mme de Tourvel's resistance of him, he cannot own himself beaten by Mme de Merteuil's gloating taunts; and rather than assent to her taunts, he capitulates to her letter. The taunts arose, of course, from her feeling beaten as a woman.

In both conspirators, an ice-cold cynicism was no match for an imperious ego. As partners, whoever was audience felt jealous of whoever was actor, or was roused to jealousy if the actor felt the lure of his prey. Theirs was simply an armed truce of egos, attempting confederacy but doomed to conflict. How could their partnership prosper when the one basis for its prospering—a perfect equality—was the last thing their competitiveness could endure? The classic situations of confederates-in-evil falling out and queering each other's game usually take on comic overtones; here the tragedy of their victims is fused with their own downfall. There is no comedy in their discomfiture unless we turn as cynical as they.

They are not precisely monsters, but there is something monstrous about them in the very sense that there is something overcivilized. Of the two, Mme de Merteuil, being much the more finished at the game, seems the more fiendish. Hers is the nimbler mind, the sharper insight, the more imperturbable treachery. If it is the mark of her fiendishness that with Cécile and Cécile's mother she is a double double-dealer, it is the mark of her finesse that she has managed to retain her reputation in society, where Valmont is known for a heartless rake. And, as the more hateful human being, she is the more vicious confederate—supercilious and abusive toward Valmont, given to slurs at his tactics, to sneers at his gullibility, to belittling and making a fool of him as a performer.

For him it is enough to be quite conscienceless and hence without compunctions. Mme de Merteuil, however, must go beyond exploiting possibilities—she must, wherever possible, double-edge them, and spoil any enjoyment for Valmont that is not of her making. Hers is not quite a motiveless malignity: it is rather a latent one always in search of a motive, something that sexual jealousy or feminine pique can provide, or that can be accounted a rightful revenge against society.

Valmont pretty much remains the self-indulgent worldling and inordinately vain "wicked rake." He is superficial, very much pleased with himself for being as clever *with* women as he is attractive *to* them; and he enjoys his alliance with Mme de Merteuil not least for the great sense of sophistication it provides. Her ambitions and designs are not so easily accounted for, on worldly terms, in the role she plays. We know how close to home this book hit with the actual society of its day, from how immediately and avidly they read it. Even if we stress its scandalous side, it could not have been such a scandal except as it did hit home; nor would it have been seized upon for erotic reasons, for though there is sex everywhere, there is indecency hardly at all. Still, though we know that society recognized itself in these pages, we, in all these pages, see scarcely anything of society. Here we run into a real limitation of the epistolary form, for though Mme de Merteuil is psychologically probed to the full, socially she is portrayed hardly at all. Thus I cannot help wondering—I don't know that others have brought up the matter—why this woman of such imperious will, with a *grande dame*'s poise, a *femme fatale*'s lure, and a diplomat's gift for dissembling, has yet no great *worldly* ambitions, no concern for politics, court life, princes, prime ministers. Had she had them, *Les Liaisons* must have been a quite different book, in purpose no less than plot. And had she had them—the issue here is genuinely psychological—she would have been a different woman. She would have been ruthless, but purposefully so; cold-blooded, but in pursuit of career. What we have instead is much more the cankering impulse to corrupt and defeat others than the wish to elevate oneself. Here we encounter a decadence wherein any relatively healthy craving of power gives way to a diseased connivance at displacement. But, as I have suggested, we must a little infer and deduce a world of politics and society in the book, for we are not shown very much of it. Still, one historical fact perhaps counts as the equivalent of pages of documentation: seven years after Laclos's novel appeared there came the storming of the Bastille.

Thus Laclos is not, here, the social historian of his own world, but rather the surgeon-general of its suppurating maladies; and, by dint of his probings and incisions, one of the great founding fathers of the psychological novel. Here, from our being gathered around a society on its deathbed, there is a magnificent sense of particular diagnosis, but a too-consuming atmosphere of disease; of such disease, moreover, as inspires no fellow feeling, or even identification, with the patient. But at times such patients exist, because certain social organisms have existed to produce them; organisms representing social dead ends and hence moral dark alleys. In Laclos we encounter all the fierce maneuvering and conspiring that we find in Saint-Simon. But with Saint-Simon—under a different monarchy and at a far higher social level—the maneuvers, the malice, are toward visible careerist objectives. Here the objective is not self-gain but self-gloating. An awful cynicism has made these people not weak-willed but stronger of will than ever, only without understandable aims. There is nothing here of the individual who flouts society, or defies morality, from being a law unto himself. There is only the nihilist's need to fool society and insult morality; and not a drunken ego but a poisoned one. The world Laclos pictures is so special that the effect can seem too extreme—the shoe fits, but as a kind of surgical boot. Yet time and again the single motive, the separate insight, the isolated act *is* truth; and our two conspirators are real, though perhaps not readily "human." The power of *Les Liaisons* is naked and intrinsic. It depends on no lurid or melodramatic flourishes, it stoops to no erotic or carnal episodes. Something clinically cold produces something ultimately terrifying.

JANE AUSTEN:
LADY SUSAN AND
PRIDE AND PREJUDICE

"THE WORLD IS TOO MUCH WITH US": WORDSWORTH'S sentiment is to be echoed by all of us at times in our reaction to the English novel. So immediate, so insistent is the sense of the world we encounter there in all its colored and concrete detail—of the village street, the London drawing room, the county ball; of trivial gossip or lustrous scandal, of matchmaking and moneymaking, of legacies and entails; so foremost and continuous is such subject matter that, need I say, England's contribution to the novel is overwhelmingly in the realm of manners. Grant though we may other distinctive strains—the novel of character, the novel of sensibility, or, much more rarely, the poetic novel evoking Wessex heaths and Yorkshire moors—yet clearly both the depth *and* the tumult of the soul belong to England's poetry. Its fiction is as generally wanting in profound inward visions as it is conspicuous for worldly sights and sounds; and for that matter, also a little wanting in psychological complexity and depth. The social scene in terms of manners, worldly interests, and class moralities is the main thoroughfare of the English novel from Fielding to Galsworthy.

In so dominating the English novel, these particular concerns perhaps also tend to make it dwindle—to make it too often a matter of surface, even when satiric, observation; to make too much of it exactly like too much else of it; to bulwark gentility while pretending to dislodge it; to prize snobbery in the very act of showing it up. (The sense of U and non-U is a hidden stream that subtly pollutes all but the best English social fiction; that, in all but the best, bulks larger than any question of true or false, passing or permanent, good or evil.) Snobbery plays the same lurking role in English fiction that adultery does in French, and in time becomes as unwelcome. County geography plays the same role in English fiction as a sort of cosmic lack of any does in Russian, and becomes no less hard to grasp. Perhaps the thing that in the end most unites English and Russian novels also most separates them, by symbolizing occasions so vastly unlike—I mean the endless drinking of tea.

But if, in English fiction, the world is too much with us, in the best of it the world is with us very revealingly and brilliantly. And if we grant the Restoration playwrights a place in the picture, as being the novelists of an age before the modern social novel was born, we have the world with us very historically too, from the days of Congreve—or for that matter, the days of Chaucer—straight on to our own day. If England has no single figure with the range of a Balzac, it has a succession of very substantial figures, each with his own niche, his own arm and stratum of society, each in his own generation.

Accepting the smallest niche, content with the most ho-

mogeneous stratum, and, by her early death, part of a very
short generation, Jane Austen yet seems, of all these novelists, the finest and purest. She is principally so by being in
the end the finest artist, which means that her materials
seem the least impure, that her course seems the least often
deflected. She knew only one kind of life—a rather aridly
provincial kind it would seem to many of us, and a trivially
worldly kind it would seem hardly less. Her experience of
the village street and the vicarage garden almost as much
lacks sheen as depth: it provided nothing in terms of ampli-
tude, it admitted nothing of high moral complexity, it
seemed unaware of impassioned individualist dilemmas, it
veered off from darkly guilty involvements, it was never for
long in London, nor ever really easy there, and it was never
in Paris at all. Jane Austen's is in itself a thoroughly unimag-
inative world—the basis of its interest is the view its
characters take of one another, the basis of its art is the
view Jane Austen takes of the characters themselves. We
are shown with how much genteel absorption, with how
much unbudging self-interest they play their roles; again,
we are shown with what incurious smugness they perform
their rites. Always, against their own small-scale worldly
values is opposed the detailed knowledge of their world, and
the unerring human values, of Jane Austen.

What, I think, makes Jane Austen oddly supreme of her
kind is that, together with a genius that enabled her to
distinguish every tone and accent of an enclosed provincial
world, she could in a certain day-by-day sense gladly identify with it. She led, and seems to have enjoyed leading—at
least she never seems to have resented leading—a decently
worldly, socially walled-in life. Whether, as Miss Mitford
was told by her mother, Jane as a young girl was "the
prettiest, silliest, most affected, husband-hunting butterfly

she could remember," Jane was part of the life around her, she picked up and passed on its gossip and small talk. In other words, Jane Austen was no more recluse than rebel, no more like Emily Dickinson than George Sand; like Emily Brontë than Mary Wollstonecraft. Fortunately, what we might remark on at times as a lack of temperament in her is triumphantly offset by her equilibrium, by her unclouded judgment as a writer of what she may seem to have acquiesced in as a woman. Perhaps no other woman of Jane Austen's capacities would have been content with her subject matter, which is to say, in the end, with her life. Every other such woman had, if not a fuller or more adventurous outer life, then a much more intense inner or secret one, whether of reverie to compensate for the outward flatness, or of emotions to belie the outward calm. About Jane Austen there is no more sense of renunciation than of rebelliousness; there is only, toward the end, in *Persuasion,* a certain wistful, regretful sense of loss.

All in all, it was of course a great advantage that Jane Austen was, in today's language, so well adjusted to the life about her; only so could she have been so richly immersed in it, so fully its mistress and hence so inexorably its judge. She had, on the one hand, sufficient personal limitations to be fully at home with it and to know its every inch and overtone; on the other, she had the artistic and critical endowments to be tough-minded and hawk-eyed about it, and hence to delineate, expose, and assess it for exactly what it was. The spinster of so often distasteful sharpness and by no means proven charm was, as a novelist, in equal parts discerning and detached. And that is the all-important point: obviously, it is not a writer's domestic virtues or faults that determine his stature; not whether he is personally a bully or an ingrate or a snob, but how he feels in the

depths of his nature about bullying or ingratitude or snobbery. Jane Austen would appear to have been a snob; what
only matters is that she gives us a hundred truthful and
incisive pictures of snobbery. What only matters is that she
rejected as a writer what she sometimes assented to as a
person; that her judgment condemns what her inclinations
succumb to; that she was willing and able—for that is the
real point—to condemn herself. And for this, the equilibrium I spoke of seems to me necessary: your cynic, your
determinist, your sentimentalist, your romantic, your rebel
all contrive some form of self-defense or self-justification,
of blaming destiny or society or heredity or acquired vi-
ciousness, something beyond one's power to change or control. Surely, too many even of those who write ethical
dramas of good and evil make themselves the self-exalting
or self-commiserating protagonists. Inside her own much
smaller and less passionate world, Jane Austen, as a master
of irony—and as that larger and greater thing which it is
less fashionable to investigate these days, a master of comedy—set down a quieter, more rueful, and rather amused
mea culpa. She would have confessed, I think, that her own
shortcomings and absurdities were no grander or more significant than anyone else's.

Now because Jane Austen lived in villages and country
places and wrote about the life of villages and country
places, we are not to suppose that her triumph lay in being
an expert miniaturist, or even an expert local psychologist
who knew everyone's mental quirks the way the family
doctor knew their bodily ones. She had far more than a
fund of shared experience for identifying with her characters, far more than an album of collected observations for
deducing their motives and desires. In treating her somewhat set cast of characters, she is as imaginatively aware as

any novelist who ranged humanity from cutthroats to cardinals. When we set her Mrs. Bennet and Mr. Woodhouse and Lady Russell against a Heathcliff or an Iago or a Raskolnikov, Jane Austen's sense of creation must tend to pale, and to seem more like re-creation. But beyond the fact that Shakespeare and Emily Brontë and Dostoevsky are confronting life on quite different terms, the creative impulse itself tends to operate in two different ways: on the one hand, which is Hardy's or Dickens' or Dostoevsky's or Emily Brontë's way, as a furnace; on the other hand, which is Jane Austen's or Turgenev's or Henry James' or Racine's way, as a filter. This, to be sure, is to attempt a useful contrast rather than a firm distinction, so that I may perhaps continue in the same undogmatic spirit to note that with the furnace it is something like genius that predominates, and with the filter, it is artistry; with the furnace something demonic, with the filter something disciplined. With the filter, the creative process may very well operate in reverse, as a rejecting agent which eliminates what is superfluous or excessive or uncongenial. But it will oftener operate as a kind of transforming agent, the filtered product being not just much purer but also much more concentrated—a distillation, as it were, or an essence. But the filter can have, in its way, as magical properties as the furnace does: it required something of a magician to create Miss Bates, to make a crashing bore irresistible; or, with Mr. Woodhouse, to make a cranky valetudinarian a delight.

Jane Austen chose in the end to stay with the Mr. Woodhouses and Mrs. Bennets, or at any rate with the Mary Crawfords and the Lady Catherine de Burghs. But that this was a matter of some thought to her, involving self-wisdom as well as temperament, is borne out by her relative success in a different style, in the style of *Lady Susan.*

Lady Susan was written no later than 1805, before Jane Austen was thirty. It is generally bracketed with her other fragments, *The Watsons* or *Sanditon,* though it is not, as they are, obviously a less than final draft; and it is not, as they are, obviously unfinished. To be sure, rather than fully rounded out it is merely wound up, and it would seem that this narrative in the form of letters was intended to be a good deal longer than it emerged; in other words, Jane Austen tacked on, to what letters there are, a few pages of orthodox narrative to make an end. But it *is* an end, just as *Lady Susan* is an entity: only as a novella instead of a novel. What it fails to have is the sort of development or, we might better say, the sort of density, that a full-length Jane Austen novel would possess. In a full-length Jane Austen novel, the fact that a number of characters are shadowy or sketchy would constitute a serious fault; at novella length, the fact that the title character is brilliantly realized greatly offsets what seems otherwise lacking.

So much for the technical side of *Lady Susan.* In any formal study of Jane Austen's art, there would be a good deal more to say; here we are principally concerned with Jane Austen as a novelist of worldliness, and on those terms we are given here something remarkably successful. We have, in *Lady Susan,* a study of a coldly self-seeking, self-indulging woman, unscrupulous about what she wants, but a woman who on the plane of outward behavior is always thoroughly well-bred. She is, again, an intrigante in a society that is hers by birth, rather than a mere adventuress invading it; and a woman who, in a certain sense, opposes her *own* values, however indefensible they may seem, to those of the world she preys upon. This opposition of values is one of class ethics, as against something larger or more humane: there is worldliness on both sides, two forms of behavior are in conflict rather than two views of life. To make a rough-and-ready analogy, Lady Susan is not the outsider who cannot get into the exclusive club, nor the rebel at odds with its standards; she is more like the club member who passes bad checks or cheats at cards.

Using—for almost the last time as a still received form of storytelling—an exchange of letters, Jane Austen gives us a woman of noble birth, nothing less than an earl's daughter; a woman without means who has a daughter of sixteen as well as herself to provide for. At thirty-five, Lady Susan is still beautiful; is intelligent, vivacious, educated, sophisticated; a mistress at controlling her emotions or anger; and able, in every drawing-room way, to get on with women as well as to infatuate men. Having more at stake, however, than drawing-room pleasantries, she is forced to show her hand. As the story opens, she is about to leave, under a cloud, a country house where she made a conquest of her host while professing friendship with his wife; and she has also snatched the suitor of her host's sister as a *parti* for her own daughter. She now invites herself to the country house of her dead husband's brother and his wife, while planning to put her shy sensitive daughter, whom she detests, in a fashionable London school. Lady Susan is suspect enough on coming to stay with her husband's relatives; they have among other things heard of her behavior during her visit elsewhere. But their informant, the sister-in-law's bachelor brother Reginald, now turns up to have a look at the notorious Lady Susan, is drawn into her web, swallows her story of having been wronged, and even comes to believe her against her daughter. Since she cannot marry her former host, who is married already, Lady Susan is prepared now to marry Reginald, only for him to come upon her with her true love and to break with her. She makes the best of it by marrying the nincompoop she had chosen for her daughter, while the daughter, we are encouraged to believe, marries Reginald.

Certainly such a story is nothing we associate with the Jane Austen of the six famous novels. And if it was to be a serious work, if it was to be more than the kind of high-society trash that the plot may tend to suggest, it would have had to be so along lines that never afterward tempted Jane Austen; it must indeed have possessed a tone that never again attracted her. The genesis of Lady Susan is of some interest: she was plainly suggested by the grandmother of one of Jane Austen's connections—a wicked, beautiful society woman named Craven and known as The Terrible Mrs. C., who, all tenderness to her children in public, in private beat and starved and locked them up. Thus Jane Austen did not begin with someone she knew personally, but only with someone she knew about; and she ended, I think we may say, with someone whose prototype she had in large measure forgotten about. The Terrible Mrs. C. had become somebody else, quite Jane Austen's own, and by virtue of Jane Austen's own imaginative insight. The character itself emerges so successfully that for anything like it we must look to other periods or literatures; must look back to the Restoration, or across the Channel to France, or forward, perhaps, to one or two of the intrigantes in Henry James.

For, though some of Lady Susan's prey are sketched so lightly, or so patly used as pawns, as to prove nothing of Jane Austen's skill and not quite enough even of Lady Susan's, Lady Susan herself seems thoroughly believable,

first from a real connection between her motives and her
maneuvers, and again from a real connection between her
personality and her view of life. Generally speaking, in easy
elegant worldly society, the intramural morals of its self-interested members are conditioned by either their incomes or
their sexual appetites. At times infidelity does involve
treachery to one's own friends, but oftener not. Most people
in good society will seldom flout its fundamental rules of
behavior. They will gossip and be malicious; if their era at
all permits, they will certainly drink and make illicit love,
and divorce and remarry among themselves; but if they are
in easy circumstances, they will not *for purely scheming
reasons* betray their friends, misuse their relatives, or callously lead on their admirers. In other words, were Lady
Susan well off, she might be just as unfeeling, but would
not need to be anything like so unscrupulous. She might
still be a homebreaker or adulteress; what, generally, she
would not be is a code breaker or adventuress. If her role
here derives from her character, it derives even more from
her circumstances. She is determined to succeed at the
social level that was hers by birth; marrying a crude parvenu would mean forfeiting as much as she would gain.
Though she never makes an upright move, she never makes
an unladylike one; and though she might violate all ten
parts of the Decalogue, she is never out of place in the
drawing room.

The sister-in-law, who is at all times on to Lady Susan,
provides, certainly, a kind of moral contrast, but on an
equally worldly basis. The sister-in-law is a good wife and
mother, is decent and honorable, is honestly outraged by
Lady Susan, is honestly concerned for Lady Susan's daughter and for her own brother Reginald. She is, in short, a
well-behaved member of good society. But she is just that:

there is a certain complacency about her, a real conventionality. If she is right in condemning and opposing Lady Susan, as much on disinterested moral grounds as on self-interested personal ones, she provides no very transcending contrast. On duller terms but no less material ones, the sister-in-law wants and is out to defend exactly what Lady Susan wants and is out to acquire; and the sister-in-law can in a sense enjoy the luxury of scruples from being nowhere menaced by a lack of income. She is the good woman who has no reason to be bad, the very personification of respectable worldliness. Lady Susan has none of her sister-in-law's taken-for-granted principles, the sister-in-law has none of Lady Susan's more sophisticated tastes; but at bottom theirs are exactly the same assumptions, born of the same social education.

Lady Susan is the victim of her education, of her world, not just because she is unprovided for in it, but because she is so unalterably its product. All her instinct as well as her intriguing is toward remaining in it; to remain in it, indeed, she will stoop to behavior that means being excluded from it. Aware of her gifts, she frankly feels—her letters to her friend Mrs. Johnson are always perfectly open about her true motives and feelings—so superior to those she would exploit as to justify her exploiting them. Out of an honest belief in her superiority, derived from sexual allure, social finesse, and intellectual vivacity, she finds full justification for an unscrupulousness dictated by financial embarrassments. As lacking in guilt as she is overflowing with guile, where she is not cold-bloodedly governed by the need to win she cold-heartedly takes pleasure in the sport. An adventuress only by circumstance, she is clearly an actress by nature.

But good actress though she is, she makes the fatal mistake of giving the same performance too often, so that no one can doubt that it *is* a performance. There is also a crack in her armor, a kind of carnal weakness rather than tragic flaw: she is too much attracted to her married lover, who, far from satisfying her worldly ambitions, can only hasten her social fall. As a character, or, one might better say, as a characterization, Lady Susan is very successful—which is all the more an achievement on Jane Austen's part in that she makes Lady Susan thoroughly selfish and heartless, nowhere displaying a decent or kindly impulse. Perhaps one reason why she yet comes off so believable is that there is what we might call no needless or pointless badness about her. She is always bad to a purpose, she is always intelligently selfish, by her own lights she always has a reason for being wicked; and though, as I have said, she relishes the pleasure of the sport, she has no motiveless malignity about her, she commits no infamous *acte gratuit*. As Elizabeth Jenkins says, she is an "extremely bad character but she is not a nightmare."

There is of course a good deal of irony about Lady Susan's campaigning and her decidedly pyrrhic victory at the end. As Marvin Mudrick, with his emphasis on irony, puts it: "She is the only person with passion and will in a milieu of circumscribed and will-less formality; and alone in such a milieu, the passionate and willful person must wither." Mr. Mudrick does not seem to me quite right in the matter; there is plenty of passion and will, or at any rate obstinacy and willfulness, in such a world. The obstacles to Lady Susan's success proceed, I think, quite naturally out of her aims: her ambition is too large because it is too small—she is like a subtle finished actress who would win acclaim on the London stage but is wasted on the provinces. She is partly, and here quite ironically, a victim of the class system from trying to exploit her own class; and partly a victim of her era. In a later age, she would conceivably have aspired on less narrow lines, she would have exerted her charms on a more spacious if more heterogeneous society. Though no less a lady, she would not have had to put all her eggs in the basket of ladylikeness; indeed, in a more cosmopolitan milieu, among more sophisticated people, where self-interest took less conventional forms, *hers* need not have been such devious ones. The way of that world would have been very much *her* way, the customs of that country much the same as her own.

But even in her own age, the more fundamental irony is not that a smugly respectable society defeats Lady Susan, but that she defeats herself by insisting on being so respectable. She loses by playing other people's rules and being caught cheating at them, where by establishing rules of her own she might very well win. The final, fatal irony seems to me almost the opposite of Mr. Mudrick's: it is that Lady Susan is so great a worldling she cannot do without respectability, just as her great blunder is in not realizing that respectability is the doughtiest of all adversaries. Lady Susan recalls to us certain characters in Restoration comedy, yet she has a special and subtler value in Jane Austen, by pointing up the very worldly basis not of a dissolute society but of a decorous one. However much we may speak in philosophic or metaphysical terms of appearance and reality, nowhere is the contrast between the two so decisive as in the realm of worldliness, where the surfaces, the set forms, in other words, the appearances, are everywhere and where, so long as the surface does not crack, reality fails to matter. Given the proper glove, it may conceal the most rapacious claw. Jane Austen's world, and hence its worldliness, is in the end more formidable than Congreve's by virtue of numbers and normality. Restoration society was in itself a Lady Susan, merely in luck for having in the King a kind of protector; and it too was finally done in by respectability, it too encountered Lady Susan's sister-in-law in Jeremy Collier. Lady Susan, in many ways, is an exceptional personality; her sister-in-law is an all-too-recurrent and quite central figure, with enough conventional virtue on her side to come out almost always ahead.

Despite its offering a fine single character rather than a wholly developed story, *Lady Susan* makes clear that Jane Austen might have won distinction in a different if adjacent vein to the one she finally chose. Her decision not to go on in the vein of *Lady Susan* was less one of self-knowledge about her talent than about her temperament. When Jane got the famous letter from the Prince Regent's librarian, suggesting that she write a historical romance founded on the House of Saxe-Coburg and she wrote back that she could no more write a romance than an epic poem, this was very fine in asserting her artistic independence, but no very extraordinary proof of self-knowledge. It wasn't because she refused to write like Walter Scott that Jane Austen showed great self-understanding—the disparity there was obviously immense; it was because she refused to write like Congreve. *Lady Susan* has not only a Congrevian enough heroine; at times its very tone and turn of phrase evoke Congreve:

> My dear Alicia [writes Lady Susan to her confidante]—of what a mistake were you guilty in marrying a man of his age; just old enough to be formal, ungovernable and to have the gout; too old to be agreeable; and too young to die.

Lady Susan makes us feel that Jane Austen could have mastered a brilliantly brittle manner, a certain enameled surface; just as after reading *Persuasion* we feel that she was moving toward greater mellowness and a more complex sensibility. But the manner—and the matter—of *Lady Susan* would have defeated, would have disabled, too much in Jane Austen if only because it would have meant leaving too much out. On one head, indeed, it would have meant bringing something foreign in: Jane Austen would have perforce been involved with the kind of situation she veered away from as a writer—that of illicit sex, something that lay outside her experience (whether largely or wholly is a matter of some dispute) and that clearly disturbed her equilibrium, and so must rather have paralyzed than stimulated her creative powers. But the vein of *Lady Susan* would have discommoded Jane Austen in another and much larger and more pervasive way; it would have hobbled the whole humorously comic side of her work.

> Follies and nonsense [says Elizabeth Bennet], whims and inconsistencies do divert me, I own, and I laugh at them whenever I can.

Elizabeth here is her creator's mouthpiece, and follies and whims and inconsistencies are her creator's meat and drink. Irony grew to be the vital force in Jane Austen's method, but comedy is the basis of her every glance. Just as the irony may deepen her world, so the comedy and humor enlarge it; yet enlarge it only to give it new limits, only to identify Jane Austen with the temperate zone of life and society. What *Lady Susan* lacks is the whole humorous side of its author, and it could never have had it. Any successors to *Lady Susan* in the same vein would have had to go deeper in that vein—where Jane Austen could hardly follow—or, through mere repetition, it would have at last run dry.

. . .

In turning to *Pride and Prejudice*, as Jane Austen herself probably turned to it after *Lady Susan*, it is less to speak of qualities often noted in a book so well known than to see in it a contrasted form of worldliness which became, with Jane Austen, the prevailing form. Here, as against the road not taken after *Lady Susan*, Jane Austen, reworking her youthful novel *First Impressions*, took for good and all the road that unites the worldly tradition with the comic one, that adjusts her temperamental approach to life to the kind of life she experienced at first hand. From *Pride and Prejudice* on, it is not the cold and brittle nature of her subject matter that will unite her with the tradition, but the essential worldliness of her attitude, an attitude so fundamental that in *Pride and Prejudice* it can permit itself romance and, with only a few spills, float a storybook plot and a species of storybook hero. The assumptions of *Pride and Prejudice* are so pervasively worldly—and here I mean Jane Austen's assumptions no less than her characters'—that the book at times can safely vault free of them. Take the heroine, take Elizabeth Bennet herself, with her sharp critical judgment, her independent thinking and superior values— take Elizabeth in relation to the book: so unquestioned are its *basic* assumptions that she can raise a question mark over everything else about it. Take equally the book's nonconforming figures—Mr. Bennet contemptuous of a dull circumscribed provincial society, Lydia wantonly defiant of it; at the same time, their relation *to* it is never for a moment ignored. The very center, and the very worldly center, of the society Jane Austen pictures—the business of marriage—never looms more formidably than with the three individualist members of it I have just named. Elizabeth's marriage is the very marrow of the plot; Mr. Bennet's wrong marriage is what has soured his disposition and probably disabled his capacities; Lydia's near-failure to marry after the elopement threatens the whole family with disgrace.

Surely it is the worldly assumptions, the worldly motivations of the book which enable Jane Austen to introduce, without serious damage, a Mr. Collins who hardly stops short of caricature, a Lady Catherine who smacks heavily of society melodrama, a Jane Bennet almost good and sweet enough for a sentimental heroine, and a Darcy haughty and aloof enough at the beginning, and noble and generous enough at the end, for romantic servant-girl fiction. And it is just these things that have pretty certainly endeared *Pride and Prejudice,* beyond all Jane Austen's other novels, to countless devotees of purely popular fiction. But because the worldly assumptions of *Pride and Prejudice* are so assured, the book is uncramped at a far more important level, a level of realistic portrayal, of comic overtones, of ironic commentary. The noteworthy thing about Jane Austen's comprehension and criticism of her world is that it is a comprehension and criticism from inside it, is that it *is* her world, and that its issues of status and money and marriage are real and large for her. She dissects it so clearly from having no resentful impulse to destroy it; were she more rebellious of it, she would in the end be less poised and hence less astute about it. In the same way, even the most skeptical of her characters gain in truthfulness from never challenging the rightness of their way of life, however much they may challenge what grows out of it. It is because Jane Austen sees what is unchanging and unchangeable in human nature and human relationships that she is so wonderfully a comic writer; and it is because she herself has no instinct to change what she finds, but seizes rather on its contradictions and ambiguities, that she is not satirist but ironist. This is how things are, says the comic realist in her; this is how things seem to be but aren't, says the ironist. But Jane Austen has neither the satirist's zeal nor the complete individualist's inner emancipation to believe that one needn't be governed by how things are, however much one may be affected. Nor does she quite grasp that accepting the facts of life is one thing, and acquiescing in other people's rules for living is another. She is a very great worldly writer because of her amazing perceptiveness about the ways of the world. But she is a little the *victim* of the worldly tradition also: in spite of setting her own values against its values, her own taste against its lapses of taste, her own corrective laughter against its constant laughableness, she never *quite* repudiates its point of view. Irony is in consequence more of a refuge for her than a release, more a way—to put it crudely—of settling scores with her world than of shaking herself free of it.

It is because Jane Austen never crosses the final frontier of social liberation, never quite discredits the assumptions of the world she writes about, that she achieves something valuable and irrefutable of a different sort. What I mean is that again and again the business of courtship is with her a process of education—but of human education, not social. Elizabeth Bennet is emancipated from prejudice, Emma Woodhouse from self-assurance, Catherine Morland, in *Northanger Abbey*, from misconception, even Marianne Dashwood, in *Sense and Sensibility*, from illusion. This education, in other words, is one (where the heart is concerned) in right feeling, and (where the mind is concerned) in good sense. False feelings and ideas are corrected and the human being learns much truth about himself, as the reader learns much truth about human nature. If this comes to pass because Jane Austen is extremely perceptive about the wellsprings of human nature, perhaps it also comes because she is not too critical of the foundations of human society. The basic worldly issues she never quite comes to grips with prevent her giving her heroines a complete *social* emancipation; they make her a higher kind of novelist than the purely social novelist can be, at the same time that they keep her from being the greatest kind of novelist, in whom social and human values easily unite, in whom social and human insights invaluably combine.

On the other hand, in few novelists are social and human materials so beautifully blended. So true is this that, far from merely carrying on the tradition of Fanny Burney, as the textbooks commonly put it, or used to put it, Jane Austen seems to me the meetingplace for the two great strains in eighteenth-century English fiction—she is Fielding's inheritor in portraying the social scene, but equally Richardson's in exploring the human heart. *Pride and Prejudice,* for example, gives us a detailed and superbly vivacious picture of village and country-house life in all its proud pettiness and monotonous gaiety; at the same time, it digs down into the feelings and reactions, the self-understanding and self-deception of a number of altogether human characters. And by doing both these things, it offers us, again and again, the inherent conflict between people's cravings and their conditionings, between humanity with all its desires and society with all its restraints.

The conflict is best seen *in* the characters themselves— most glaringly, if by no means most rewardingly, in Darcy. Here, at first, caste arrogance has so much the upper hand that even when Darcy cannot refrain from proposing to Elizabeth, the proposal includes an insulting list of her social disqualifications. Indeed, as his nobler nature comes gradually to the fore, it does so partly at a level of class embarrassment—of, beyond love for Elizabeth, shame for ungentlemanly actions and an unladylike aunt. The conflict has not so much been resolved as the bad angel in him has been routed. Darcy is not, of course, a real success: this only partly, I think, from his being rather wooden, for he might actually have been rather wooden. It is more that he is seen in a romantic light and grows somewhat too considerable and generous and noble; is that, where Elizabeth sees the truth and is educated, Darcy smacks just a little of seeing the light and being converted. Darcy, in a worldly sense the grandest suitor and the grandest catch in all Jane Austen, is the one person who is not followed through at a worldly level, but made into a storybook hero.

In his case the great theme of Jane Austen's, of humanity versus society, of true values in conflict with false ones, equally lacks sufficient realistic focus and ironic counterpoint. Where the theme pays off is in Elizabeth's gradual awareness of the conflict in Darcy—for, beyond her own particular involvement with him, her whole bent lies in sorting out true values from false ones, silly ideas from sound ones, truth from mere traditionalism. It is this indeed that makes her, in addition to her charming qualities, what we might call right-minded—which doesn't mean, on any specific occasion, in the right. Right-minded, I think, rather than in the best sense large-minded; and remarkably convincing and life-sized because she isn't. Like Jane Austen herself, for whom she so often acts as spokesman, Elizabeth dissects and often condemns the follies, manners, behavior, taste of her world, but seldom the basic assumptions. She can meet the situation, so to speak, of Lydia's elopement, but she no more questions the social disgrace involved than she condones the sexual misbehavior. It is part of Elizabeth's superiority that she would never marry the wrong man from purely worldly motives, but it is doubtful whether she would marry the right one, from a lower class or with a bohemian streak or a spotted past, and let the world go hang. Human right-mindedness, with her, would never constitute social wrong-mindedness; and this makes sense. She is anti-rebellious because she is unromantic—if also just a little because she is not, in the quite final sense, enlightened. And neither, perhaps, was Jane Austen.

In *Pride and Prejudice* worldliness is no key to the goodness or badness of people, ever. Thus Darcy's cousin Colonel Fitzwilliam must, as a younger son, marry with an eye to money, and this is from a common-sense and not greedy motive. He has no desire to marry rich, he simply cannot afford to marry poor. Charlotte Lucas is a pleasant, decent, intelligent girl, who shocks Elizabeth by accepting Mr. Collins; but as a girl who will have few suitors and for whom a respectable marriage is the central fact in life, it is better, in the world she inhabits, to marry an idiotic clergyman than to become a neglected old maid. If Charlotte lacks Elizabeth's standards, this is in part because she will never have Elizabeth's opportunities. Jane Bennet is kind, sweet, and tolerant, but we cannot say how much worldly thoughts color her decisions, for Mr. Bingley—who is her only decision—gives us no leave to. He is the perfect catch in a worldly sense. Yet as Jane is least tarnished by worldliness in her behavior, she is perhaps the least touched by unworldliness in her conformity: she never *questions* anything and is in equal degrees kindly and conventional.

Worldly pressure is surely a very strong reason for Mr. Bennet's accepting his matrimonial fate; for all his ironic, skeptical temperament and his constantly assaulted sensibilities, it would never occur to him to leave his wife or live apart from her; and if the father here has decided influence on the husband, the strictures of gentility, the sense of fitness even in this connoisseur of misfits, have equal influence. The world is too much with even Mr. Bennet for him to flout it; he can only make fun of it. We get this whole side of him at the very outset, when he teases his wife about not going to call on the new rich young tenant of Netherfield Park; but "Mr. Bennet was among the earliest of those who waited on Mr. Bingley."

Oddly, or logically, enough, the one unworldly character in *Pride and Prejudice* is Lydia, who is unworldly in the exact sense that she is imprudent. In her, self-interest bows to self-gratification; reckless about her own reputation, thoughtless of her family's, shameless in her behavior as a true and convincing wanton, she alone in the book would settle for Love in a Cottage or, for that matter, for Sex in an Inn-Chamber. By our standards, no less than by those of Jane Austen's day, Lydia is hopelessly selfish and shallow; but today she would hardly so disgrace her family as to deny her sisters husbands or her parents an altogether assured place in society. Today, in other words, she would scarcely constitute the point on which everything material in *Pride and Prejudice* pivots, round which everything moral in *Pride and Prejudice* turns—the thing that calls forth not only what is noble in Darcy's love but what is a little incommensurate in Jane Austen's own judgment. It is sound realism, here, to elevate a provincial small scandal to the level of possible family tragedy; but Jane Austen, by bringing too little ironic awareness of her own to bear, is herself fairly guilty of moral provincialism.

The behavior of her characters over Lydia's behavior is beautifully believable, a mirror of the social morality of the world it involves. What gives us pause is that the reactions of the more enlightened characters seem to have the author's stamp of approval. We know that in matters of sexual misconduct, Jane Austen was ill at ease, so much so that her sense of comedy might desert her and her sense of values begin to fall away. I say ill at ease, not shocked, not dismayed: in the *Letters* and indeed in the general attitude of *Lady Susan* she faces facts readily enough. Yet, in the books she saw through the press, it would seem that she acquiesced in the prevailing county or genteel attitudes toward sex, and so displayed a quite literal moral provincialism—for in Regency days, London society was not very straitlaced while being often enough scandalous, and could offer, indeed, a pair of shrugging shoulders for every pair of pursed lips. Jane Austen was never hypocrite or prig and never pursed her lips; nor did she, really, ever avert her eyes. But, having looked, she sometimes turned away.

She spoke rightly of working on two inches of ivory—her perceptions, sensibilities, sense of balance, her blend of the comic and the ironic, make her unsurpassed in her own sphere. Her perspectives, however, can be limited and even inadequate; she is a little myopic in the degree that she is sharp-eyed. So far as she is a social novelist, she rightly looks at things in terms of accepted right and wrong. So far as she explores the human heart, she rightly looks at things in terms of subjectively arrived at ideas of right and wrong. Between the two there is often personal conflict, social conflict, moral conflict; out of these conflicts come personal education, social criticism, moral emancipation, and sometimes human growth. What is missing—and perhaps quite wisely—is a sense of what goes beyond right and wrong into regions of good and evil, which means the presence in her novels of baser but also larger natures, of people with greater scope and imagination wrestling with greater cravings and crises. Jane Austen's wrongdoers may have a weakling's charm or a scoundrelly dash, but they quite lack stature. With a more complex morality, as with a more complex worldliness, which means with a Lydgate in *Middlemarch* as well as a Kate Croy in *The Wings of the Dove*, Jane Austen was not to be concerned. Part of Elizabeth Bennet's right-mindedness rests on how superior it is to the world it is part of, just as Mr. Bennet's cynical view and ironic comment are constantly watered by the dullness of the world they jest at. But on just such grounds, the people about Elizabeth and her father do not bring into play the great worldly complications to be met with in Stendhal or Henry James or Proust. To judge, however, by Jane Austen's last novel, in *Persuasion* she was beginning to move from a world of ironic assent into one of individual assertion, so that in time she might have shifted the center of her books, and the stress of their worldliness, from courtship to selfhood. The choices before her heroines would have become more difficult, the temptations in her more complex characters might have turned darker. Jane Austen was right to abandon the manner of *Lady Susan* for that of *Pride and Prejudice,* if only from being a great mistress of comedy. But after *Persuasion*, perhaps long after *Persuasion,* she might have returned to some of the possibilities in a *Lady Susan* and, among characters less vague or less villainous, involving crises in an ampler sphere, she might have achieved a great mastery of high comedy, with its among other things tragic intimations.

IX

BYRON'S *DON JUAN*

Sooner or later Byron will enjoy a decided vogue again. He will never, of course, be so famous as he once was—he once, after all, intoxicated all England and half of Europe. He carried a sable and self-conscious melancholy to its farthest height; he turned pose into poetry. A dashing hero with some of the glossiest attributes of a villain, he was first swooned over and then hissed, the greatest social success and the greatest social scandal of his age. The whole thing has something excessive about it; there are writers whose careers are an affront to realism, an offense against art. Disraeli's, for example, is too flashy; Beckford's too opulent; Byron's too lurid. Anyone with blood so blue ought not to have blood so black—not kings' and madmen's both. If one is a lord and romantically handsome, need one also walk with a limp? Byron inherited a dank, half-ruined abbey where it was only decent to drink wine from a skull; he could ride like a streak; he swam the

Hellespont. He hated and cursed and sobbed over his mother; committed incest with his sister; snarled on his wedding day at his wife. For love of him, titled ladies stabbed themselves with scissors; for love turned hate-wise, had him burned in effigy. After a life of pleasure and excess, he died in squalor fighting for the independence of Greece. And amid all this fame and obloquy, this dandyism and violence, the Lady Carolines and Lady Oxfords and Countess Guicciolis, Byron, before dying at thirty-six, constantly wrote letters, insatiably wrote verse.

It is all too purple for any self-respecting storyteller, let alone real life. That it happens to be true may be the most fantastic part of all, but is not much my reason for recapitulating it here. My chief reason is that for any even brief discussion of *Don Juan* it happens to be immensely relevant. I don't mean in any strictly factual sense; I mean that only someone with the endowments for living so privileged and tempestuous and superbly exuberant a life could have written so worldly and torrential and superbly exuberant a poem. *Don Juan* is not an example of literature compensating for life, of the romantic imagination fleeing mean streets for fairyland. *Don Juan*, to be sure, gallops with imagination; shoots the very rapids of romance. But on that side it hardly bounds more swiftly than Byron's own life did: while, from another side, it is crammed with knowledge of highborn sin and folly, with intimate understanding of the great world. To create Haidée and hymn the isles of Greece it was doubtless enough for Byron to be a poet. But to portray a Donna Julia or Lady Adeline, to move through ballrooms and glide up staircases with so much assurance, Byron needed also to be a peer.

Don Juan is not autobiographical: Byron set down here

something better than autobiography, he set down himself. Here at last, after so many studied twitchings of his mantle, here amid a hundred extravagances and excrescences, in a rush of words, a pell-mell of impressions, here where the operatic tumbles sheerly into the farcical, where the beetles of mockery kill the flowers of romance, stands revealed the whole unruly man. *Childe Harold* is in large part Byronism, but *Don Juan* is Byron.

Don Juan is also one of the most staggering performances in literature. So far as I know, there is nothing truly like it—for one thing because no one more of an artist would have dreamed of doing it as Byron did, while no one less of a genius could have contrived to do it at all. In its obstreperous magic, its aristocratic vulgarity, in the eloquence of its praise and far greater eloquence of its abuse, there is such swagger as even Byron never elsewhere attempted; but also such power as he never elsewhere achieved. What he did in *Don Juan* was, fortunately, not portray but express himself.

Than Byron there is in general no stagier actor in our literary history; but the immensely rewarding thing in *Don Juan* is that Byron altogether eschews the leading role, the center of the stage. In return, it is true, he insists on being almost everything else connected with the production: now dramatist and now drama critic; now heckler, now prompter, now minor actor muttering brash asides; frequently stealing a scene, unblushingly interrupting the show. Hence what we get is as much production as play, as much rehearsal as performance, as much brilliant confusion as clear sense of design. And for Byron it is all wonderfully in keeping and wonderfully liberating: he has found his happiest calling—not actor but showman.

This exchange—of posturing for showmanship—works tremendous good: instead of a personal desire to attract attention, there is the professional ability to command it. And, indeed, filled as it is with such antics and interruptions as no formal work of art could endure, *Don Juan* is most accurately called a show. Nor are we merely hanging on to a metaphor; nothing else—not satire, not epic—so truthfully describes *Don Juan* (which is as often comic as satiric, and less epic than picaresque). Nothing except a show dare be so explosive in its energy, so filled with fireworks and gaudy trimmings, so played in the very lap of the audience; can contain such tossed-off insults, such haphazard profundities. And one of its most showmanlike qualities is that, though episode after episode may be treated tongue in cheek, the episodes themselves are never thrown away, never whittled down to a mere satiric point. Juan's intrigue with Donna Julia is almost as good Boccaccio as it is Byron; the storm and the shipwreck have their quota of excitement, the harem scenes their quota of indecency. Byron deals in meaningless wars but not sham battles; in too lush Mediterranean scenes, perhaps, but never painted backdrops. And writing of Juan and Haidée he can, of course, be genuinely romantic, and chronicle a romance that is genuinely tender and moving:

> *Alas! they were so young, so beautiful*
> *So lonely, loving, helpless . . .*

It is the one haunting episode in the poem, its innocence and ecstasy staining our memories more deeply than all the cynicism and worldliness. Nor do the digressions and asides in *Don Juan* come through as mere random frivolities: they not only lend variety, comic vigor, and change of pace, but often help to create suspense: the retardation of Haidée's father's entrance, for example, is managed to excellent effect. For all its waywardness, the storytelling in *Don Juan* is seldom flabby.

But it is for its satire, in the end, or at any rate its elements of laughter, that *Don Juan* must really be praised: for the spectacle it makes of high life, the farce it makes of pretension. Its wars bring nothing about; its lovers (save only Haidée) are all untrue. Juan—an acceptable *jeune premier*, but the least interesting thing in the poem, a merely acquiescent rake, an insipid grandee—is exposed, now in chains, now in triumph, to all the best barbaric society, the most sumptuous misrule, in Europe. But since there's no place, for the satirist, like home, Juan is brought at last—and just when the story needs a complete change of air—to England. In England, Byron's vision narrows but intensifies, his coloring is soberer but his brushwork more expert; we pass out of a world of swashbuckling and opéra bouffe into that of Congreve and Pope. There is no longer any stalking strange beasts through exotic forests with barbaric weapons, but a stiff ride with the hounds after hypocrites and snobs; a long day on the moors bagging philistines and pharisees; a large coaching-party clattering at the heels of politics. The subject being the most nearly "civilized" one in the book, the treatment is, with justice, the most nearly savage: yet the slashing at morals is maintained at the level of manners, with a wonderful accumulation of detail; it is Byron seeking heavy damages for exile, perhaps, but not cheap revenge; and it concludes, in midair, on a wild high note of farce.

A powerfully charged, helter-skelter production, indeed: exhibiting that ebullient gaiety so often twin-brothered by

loneliness; that peculiarly magnanimous love of liberty of
one who takes inordinate pride in rank; that overemphasis
on sex of one never quite at ease with women: the production of a poet in whom two centuries meet with a great
clang but no very deep hostility; the performance of someone versed in English and European and Eastern ways who,
if he was in Shelley's words the Pilgrim of Eternity, was
also, in Mr. Wilson Knight's, our only cosmopolitan poet.

As with anything so recklessly creative, *Don Juan* has its
share of unconscious confession, curious oscillation, odd
twistings and turnings. Yet I do not think it superficial to
suggest that what the poem is enormously outdistances
anything it may mean. The critical malady of our age is an
indifference to sheer creativeness as a thing—of power and
of pleasure—in itself. In its itch to correlate and laminate
and explain, current criticism has half lost the instinct to
respond and enjoy. Worse, in its obsession over what makes
the clock tick, it all too often fails to notice whether it tells
the right time. Most great books, it is true, are complex and
not lightly mastered; they need to be unraveled and ex-
plained. But with something like *Don Juan*, the overwhelming thing is to pitch in, to participate. For you cannot
explain inexhaustible energy and high spirits; you can only
explain them away. And you lose out if you so concentrate
on the targets in *Don Juan* that you only half appreciate the
hits; if you care more for Byron's motives than his manner;
if you persist in making a laboratory of an amusement
park. The motives, to be sure, aren't to be brushed aside;
the targets, after 150 years, are still there to shoot at. But
what is most exhilarating in *Don Juan* is not so much the
satire as what might be called the satiricalness. Obviously
what makes any great satirist is much less the occasion for

scoffing than the disposition to scoff; for the true satirist, opportunity, so far from knocking only once, knocks all day long. In themselves, ruling classes may or may not be always rotten; but for satire, obviously, they are always ripe. Furthermore, there is about *Don Juan* too great a love of battle for its own sake for us to identify each sideswipe as a blow against tyranny or time-serving, against this vice or that. All the same, the man who wrote *Don Juan* was very far, at bottom, from being either a cynic or a trifler: its cascading poetry, its tumultuous energy cannot consort with the merely cynical and small; and amid the impudences and extravagances, there sounds again and again the war cry of the intransigent rebel. Though Byron himself, as Mr. Quennell has remarked, abandoned Juan for Greece out of a "haunting death-wish," *Don Juan* is a very dazzling exhibition of the life force.

It is difficult, again, to find anything resembling a level of achievement in *Don Juan,* for it dashes up and down the whole ladder of comedy like a monkey. It shows none of the instinct for tone of a satirist like Pope. Pope, for the most part, confines himself to the rapier and the poisoned dart; but Byron (though he worshipped and at times resembles Pope) grasps hold of any weapon, sharp or blunt, subtle or crude; and not guns, swords, arrows only, but stones thrown at windows, firecrackers tossed under chairs, and occasionally a massive field piece, as in the onslaughts against Southey and Wellington. *Don Juan* mingles the wit of the salon with the horseplay of the schoolroom, sensational rhymes with impossible ones, all varieties of facetious nonsense, insult, abuse, pleasantry, unpleasantry. Now it is the buxom widows at the battle of Ismail who wonder despondently why the ravishing hasn't begun; now

Guests hot and dishes cold . . .

or

He was the mildest-mannered man
That ever scuttled ship or cut a throat . . .

or

And whispering "I will ne'er consent," consented . . .

or

So for a good old-gentlemanly vice
I think I must take up with avarice . . .

But it is the profusion, succession, accumulation of jibes, jokes, comments, epithets, apostrophes, the rhymes and running fire throughout sixteen cantos and some sixteen thousand lines that make *Don Juan* the most tumbling and impromptu of epics.

A portrait of a civilization, *Don Juan* is also a kind of pastiche of one. It is immensely "literary"—crammed with poetic tags, critical and biographical tidbits, historical and mythological allusions. In his turning—to sharpen his satire or brighten his narrative—to history, literature, all the compass points of culture, Byron is like Pope, and achieves a like glitter. For satiric purposes, *Don Juan* is even more a parade and parody of quotations than *The Waste Land;* while it is a virtual anthology of worldly wit and wisdom— Pope and Horace, Chesterfield and Montaigne, Johnson and Swift.

In her first passion woman loves her lover:
In all the others, all she loves is love.

And if I laugh at any mortal thing,
'Tis that I may not weep.

Byron has made both these sentiments his endlessly quoted own; but the first of them, of course, is pure La Rochefoucauld; the second, pure Beaumarchais. And of what is entirely Byron's own in *Don Juan*, how startlingly much has passed even beyond common speech into rank cliché: *"Man's love is of man's life . . ."; "But words are things . . ."* and so on; even *"Stranger than fiction,"* even—though I fear fortuitously—*"Sweet Adeline."*

We come last to the fact that *Don Juan* is a poem, which is perhaps the most crucial fact of all. Three things, it seems to me, save *Don Juan*, with its prodigious breakneck energy, from coming to grief, from skidding or careening off the road. Byron's great comic sense, which checks his impulse to rant, proves a stout wall on one side; his feeling for tradition, his sensibility for the highbred, the historic, the classical, walls him in on the other. But it is the requirements of verse itself, of rhyme and meter and stanzaic form, that keep a smooth road under him. By virtue of these things indeed, Byron—for all his antics and vulgarities—is an aristocratic poet. As to how decisive such qualities can be, we need only turn to the most democratic of poets, Whitman, who lacked the first quality, never fully acquired the second, and almost wholly rejected the third; and may see how much more impurely and wastefully his genius operated. Byron's sense of the past, of the poetry of history, is much more evident in *Childe Harold*, yet certainly not missing here:

> *I've stood upon Achilles' tomb*
> *And heard Troy doubted: Time will doubt of Rome.*

But it is the actual versification, the use of rhyme, meter, touches of poetic diction, stanzaic form, that lifts and liquefies *Don Juan*, that helps give it the "beauty" that Shelley noted. Of immense value is the heightening power of the verse, the regularity that goes with the rush, giving it not an eccentric but a dramatic speed. Or consider the splendid exordiums to so many of the cantos, with their sense not of breaking new ground but of instantly getting *off* the ground: for this, too, we have the élan of the verse to thank.

To perceive the difference—and distance—from prose, we have only to compare *Don Juan* to the long work in English that, all in all, it perhaps most resembles—*Tom Jones*. Certainly both works are in their way first-rate. Both, again, are epical: the one a panoramic entertainment with all England for its stage; the other a kaleidoscopic spectacle, with all Europe. In both the well-placed hero is a youthful rake who comes to know one pure love and countless varieties of lust. In both, the pre-eminent aim is an elaborate satiric survey of manners: in both the author's strongest hate and most frequent target is hypocrisy. In both, conventional morality is regarded with scorn: Fielding and Byron alike forgive many "sins" and castigate many "virtues." Fielding and Byron alike, moreover, deliberately and unceasingly obtrude themselves, interlarding their story with personal comments and confessions, curtain speeches and familiar essays, parodies, denunciations, every variety of obiter dictum. And yet . . . well, I have actually, and understandably, never seen the two compared. For it is somehow like comparing a solid with a liquid, a side of beef with a great bowlful of rum punch, a stagecoach with an Indian canoe—prose, in short, with poetry. As poetry, *Don Juan* is disfigured by some slipshod verses and some ghastly rhymes; it is blunted by Byron's sometimes being too busy with satiric weapons to care enough about artistic tools. But as poetry, Byron's masterpiece remains curiously true to itself: it sails off into highfalutin now and then, or nosedives toward bathos, but it never merely dodders into prose.

X

EUGENE ONEGIN

NEXT TO A FEW OF THE GREATEST WORKS OF POETRY and drama, what I could most wish to read and fully appreciate in the original is Pushkin's—I abandon at once the Russian spelling—*Eugene Onegin*. And of these things Pushkin's is the most completely frustrating, for though my Greek is much worse than spotty and my Italian covered with rust, at least I know a little how Homer and Aeschylus and Dante tend to sound in the original, I have a faint sense of the greatness of the Greeks in their own language and a fair sense of Dante in his. But with Pushkin, with *Onegin,* one is encountering something so special that to know no Russian is a double loss: one is not just deprived in translation of much of what makes him uniquely great, one is equally deprived of what makes him constantly delightful. In a translation such as Babette Deutsch's, which at its best has real virtues, we are made to feel the *fact* of Pushkin's greatness, but are never quite given what constitute great effects; again, for a number of lines or a stanza or two, we savor what makes him delightful, but then what we get is spruce, or jingly, or a little verbose. The translator of Pushkin is to be sympathized with *: that special amalgam of gifts which, to be approximated in English, seems to involve comparing Pushkin successively with Horace, Byron, Keats, Stendhal, André Chénier, Praed, and Tolstoy; an amalgam, moreover, that has made Pushkin both the prime figure of Russian poetry and the forefather of the Russian novel, not to speak of his being the inspiration of Russian opera—*Ruslan and Ludmila, Pique Dame, Onegin, Boris Godunov,* and *Coq d'Or.* This amalgam is of course what baffles the translator and hence robs the English reader of Pushkin's very essence. However much we may lose of Dostoevsky or Tolstoy, we have a full sense of what makes them great and individual; even with Chekhov there is not the equal loss of verbal magic or unparaphrasable effect, and in a first-rate production, something of what is lost can be regained.

Pushkin's very special qualities, and special effects, in *Onegin* seem to have baffled even the Russian imitators who sought to capture them. *Onegin,* says Prince Mirsky, demanded "two qualities that are extremely rare in conjunction—a boundless spontaneous vitality and an unerring sense of artistic measure." This is to say that he was as natural a genius as he was instinctive an artist, as creative as self-critical, as free-flowing as channeled. Such a combination of genius and artistry brings, above all others, Mozart to mind. But though this is to indicate the marvelous rareness of Pushkin's gifts, it is not quite to define the special nature of his poem—or, as it might better be called,

* Nabokov's close rendering, however notable for accuracy, is hopeless for transmitting Pushkin's art.

his novel in verse; and here Edmund Wilson is more immediately helpful, when in the matter of *Onegin* he speaks of
Pushkin's "peculiar combination of intensity, compression
and perfect ease." Intensity and ease are not often happily
married; yet they pretty plainly seem so here: the intensity
we must at times infer, the perfect ease we can, I think
even in translation, feel. Which suggests another combination, and one no less remarkable—the happy marriage here
of poet and novelist, of something more than poet and
storyteller; of someone who achieves magical effects with
language, atmosphere, the visible world, while simultaneously telling a story, developing a theme, creating and counterpoising characters, projecting in the most vivid fashion
social and personal scenes. *Eugene Onegin* is not only a
novel of manners in all that it pictures of high life, of
domestic life, of country life, of bachelor life; it is a novel of
contrasted attitudes and temperaments, and thus of contrasted values: Eugene and Tatyana and, to a lesser degree,
Lensky are as representative figures and as differing natures as we can ask for in good fiction. But we get them
with all the vivid force that we ask for in good poetry; and
again with all the brilliance that we can ask for in gay and
witty writing, and in a polished and worldly writer.

Onegin opens briskly, indeed at a kind of gallop; for
Eugene, a gay young dog and dandy, is bounding along to
the bedside of a dying uncle, whose heir he is to be, and
reflecting as he rides:

> *My uncle's shown his good intentions*
> *By falling desperately ill;*
> *His worth is proved; of all inventions*
> *Where will you find one better still?*
> *He's an example, I'm averring;*
> *But God, what boredom—there, unstirring*

> *By day, by night, thus to be bid*
> *To sit beside an invalid:*
> *Low cunning must assist devotion*
> *To one who is but half alive:*
> *You puff his pillow and contrive*
> *Amusement while you mix his potion:*
> *You sigh and think with furrowed brow*
> *"Why can't the Devil take you now?"*

Thus in a single stanza we are given one of the most worldly of situations and easy and sophisticated of tones, together with something of the character of Eugene himself. That a rich uncle one is inheriting from should be dying in the country is a great bore for a dashing young man about town, who, we are told,

> *keen as brandy*
> *Went forth in dress—a London dandy,*
> *His hair cut in the latest mode;*
> *He dined, he danced, he fenced, he rode.*
> *In French he could converse politely,*
> *As well as write; and how he bowed!*
> *In the mazurka, 'twas allowed,*
> *No partner ever was so sprightly.*

He was not without accomplishments:

> *with the spark of a bon mot*
> *He set the ladies' eyes aglow;*

He could

> *Quote Virgil, not a long selection,*
> *And always needing some correction*
>
> .   .   .
>
> *Theocritus and Homer bored him*
> *If true delight you would afford him*
> *You'd give him Adam Smith to read.*

A deep economist, indeed,
He talked about the wealth of nations;
The state relied, his friends were told,
Upon its staples, not on gold . . .
His father listened, frowned and groaned
And mortgaged all the land he owned.

But his principal accomplishment was l'amour—

He early played the fond deceiver
And feigned the pang of jealousy,
Rejoiced the fair one but to grieve her,
Seemed sunk in gloom, or bold and free.

Which made for an active life:

After an evening's dissipation
He will lie late, and on his tray
Find notes piled high. What—invitations?
Three ladies mention a soiree,
Here is a ball, and there a party,
His appetite for pleasure's hearty—
Where will my naughty lad repair?
For he is welcome everywhere.

And we follow him as he promenades, and sets forth in the
snow at dusk in a sleigh, to where "Glass after glass is
drained"; and goes on to the theater and the ballet,

               to taste the blisses
And breathe the free air of the stage,
To praise the dancer now the rage
Or greet a luckless Phèdre with hisses:

The theatre's full, the boxes glitter,
The stalls are seething, the pit roars,
The gallery claps and stamps, atwitter,
The curtain rustles as it soars;

and afterward,

> The house rocks with applause; undaunted,
> And treading toes, between the chairs
> Onegin presses; with his vaunted
> Aplomb, he lifts his eye-glass, stares
> Askance at fair, unwonted faces,
> Remarks the jewels and the laces,
> And notes complexions, with a sneer
> Briefly surveying every tier.

And to complete the scene:

> While in the lobby sleepy flunkeys
> Are guarding fur-coats faithfully;
> Within you hear the feet still pounding,
> The coughs, the shouts and hisses sounding,
> The noses blown and without pause,
> Above it all, the wild applause.
> The carriage horses, chilled with waiting,
> Impatient, twitch beneath the lamp,
> The coachmen round the bonfires tramp,
> Their masters wearily berating.
> But our Onegin's out of range
> Of curses: he's gone home to change.

All this eventually begins to pall. Seduction, says Pushkin, ceased to be amusing, and

>   he could make no bon mot
> Or wash things down with Veuve Clicquot
> When his poor head began to ache;
> And though he was an ardent rake,
> The time came when he quite abhorred
> Even the pistol and the sword.

It was an age of Byronism and English fashions; and as against that female ailment, the vapors, he had that male malaise, the spleen. True, says Pushkin,

He spared us one piece of folly:
Although he grew more melancholy
He did stop short of suicide.

He scorned women, and locked himself in to read and write.
But after a short time,

He's done with women, and it looks
As though he's also done with books.

Society and solitude, gaiety and gloom, had about equally,
now, left this intelligent, but dilettantish, this appreciative
but Byronically posturing young man at loose ends. At just
this point, our dissatisfied worldling and equally dissatisfied
flee-the-worldling is summoned to his uncle's bedside; but
this time the new form of boredom he seems faced with is
spared him. When he reaches his uncle's country house, his
uncle is already dead.

He takes possession of his uncle's estate and attempts the
business of managing it:

His early years were all a waste,
And this routine was to his taste.

adding:

For two days he found it quite diverting . . .
The third day interest abated
And he was not the least elated
By grove and stream and field and steep—
They only sent him off to sleep.

Fortunately, in his new boredom, he meets a young neighbor, a poet named Lensky, fresh from a German university
and filled with German idealism. Lensky, who in his romantically exalted fashion has long loved and been faithful
to a "nice" uninteresting girl, seems to Eugene incredibly
naïve, but he is likable and a new type and they see a good

deal of each other. And when Onegin goes visiting Lensky's girl with Lensky, he meets her sister Tatyana, a strange shy wildly romantic girl—

> *She is the novelist's creation:*
> *Julie, Clarissa or Delphine;*
> *She wanders with imagined lovers*
> *Thru silent woods, and she discovers*
> *Her dreams in every circumstance*
> *Of some imported wild romance.*

Tanya, at first sight of him, falls passionately in love with Eugene: Werther, Grandison, St. Preux, all the romantic heroes,

> *All these our tender dreamer fused*
> *Into one image . . .*
> *Onegin's form, Onegin's face.*

But though Onegin had noticed her as a hundred times more interesting than Lensky's choice, he had not been personally aroused; and the poor girl goes about for days, in a fever and torment, waiting for him to come visiting again. When he does not come, she pours out her love in a movingly honest and impassioned letter to him. Two or three days later he does come to see her, with a sense of the beauty of her letter, with decent feelings and honest words —*if* he wanted to marry, it is she he would choose:

> *If for a moment I found pleasure*
> *In cosy scenes of fireside life,*
> *You, you alone would be my wife.*

But, he goes on,

> *I must confess, though loth to hurt you,*
> *I was not born for happiness;*

I am unworthy of your virtue;
I'd bring you nothing but distress.
My conscience speaks—pray let me finish;
My love, first warm, would soon diminish:
Our marriage would mean misery,
Then you will weep, but who supposes
Your grief will bring me to remorse?
I shall lose patience, then, of course:

What is there more to be lamented
Than this: a household where the wife
Whose spouse has left her, discontented,
Grieves for the wretch throughout her life?
While the dull husband . . . jealous in a frigid way
Can only curse his wedding day.
And I am such.

And in taking his leave he preaches self-control to the half-out-of-her-senses, tear-blinded girl.

He sees her again at a big party that her family gives, and she is again all hot and cold in his presence. And, finding the party—which Lensky had dragged him to—boring, he revenges himself by idling flirting with Lensky's girl. He has dance after dance with her, he makes up to her with all his dash and charm: so that Lensky in a heartsick rage leaves the party and straightway challenges Eugene to a duel. Realizing how wrong his behavior has been, Eugene is ready to make things up, but then begins to worry that by not going through with the duel he will make a fool of himself, be subject to whispered jokes and to that worldly scorn that is bred of worldly quarrels. And so he meets Lensky and indeed, by rather dishonorably raising his pistol while the distance is still being paced off, shoots him dead before Lensky can even aim. And it becomes apparent that

subconsciously Onegin has resented Lensky even while liking him—has resented his feeling an unselfish love, as he
could not do; his being a poet, as he could not be.

Onegin now goes away from his place in the country, and
Tatyana in time goes to it in all its desertedness, goes day
after day, reading the books in Onegin's fashionable library.
She refuses other suitors, and at length her mother takes
her to Moscow, where she goes out into society and is
eventually married to a general. When in due time Onegin
himself appears in Moscow, he discovers that she has become a poised, splendid, much-admired great lady. Eugene
would now make up to her but she ignores him; he writes
letters to her but she does not answer them; and after a
period of self-immolation he goes one day to her house,
finds no one at the door, walks in, encounters her reading
the letters he has been writing to her, and falls at her feet.
She is momentarily touched, but then she makes him get up
and recalls to him the reversed scene when she, in spirit,
was on her knees before *him* and he read her a sermon.
That she can forgive him, for he was honest:

> *Far from Moscow's noise and glitter*
> *You did not like me . . . That was bitter*
> *But worse what now you choose to do!*
> *Why do you pay me these attentions?*
> *Because society's conventions,*
> *Deferring to my wealth and rank,*
> *Have given me prestige? Be frank!*
> *Because my husband's decoration,*
> *A soldier's, wins us friends at Court,*
> *And all would relish the report*
> *That I had stained my reputation—*
> *'Twould give you in society*
> *A pleasant notoriety?*

Even the old harshness of speech, she adds, is preferable to "this insulting passion." And she goes on to say that all her present splendor means nothing to her, that she would give everything to be back in the country where she first met him. But now it is too late:

> *Now my fate is quite decided,*
> *I was in too much haste, I fear;*
> *My mother coaxed and wept; the sequel*
> *You know: besides, all lots are equal*
> *To hapless Tanya . . . Well, and so*
> *I married. Now, I beg you, go.*
> *I know your heart; I need not tremble*
> *Because your honor and your pride*
> *Must in this matter be your guide.*
> *I love you (why should I dissemble?)*
> *But I became another's wife:*
> *I shall be true to him through life.*

> *She went. Onegin stood forsaken,*
> *Stood thunderstruck. He could not stir.*
> *By what a storm his heart was shaken:*
> *What pride, what grief, what thoughts of her!*
> *But are those stirrups he is hearing?*
> *Tatyana's husband is appearing.*
> *At this unlucky moment, we*
> *Must leave my hero, ruefully,*
> *For a long time . . . indeed, forever.*

This seems to me, in its suddenness and theatricality, and at the same time its artistic completeness, one of the great leavetakings in literature. Pushkin need say no more; he in a sense dismisses his hero at the same moment that Tatyana does. "Onegin's portrait," as Pushkin says, "has been finished." It has been done with quick, light, creative strokes that are at the same time incisive ones. Onegin is the young worldling par excellence of a certain class and

period, temperament and taste. He is no mere society playboy or rake, leading a life of wholly frivolous pleasure;
himself intelligent and perhaps not ungifted, a man capable
of sensitive perceptions who has come under the spell of
Byronism, Onegin is perhaps best described as a dandy-dilettante. It is not simply the activities of a dashing young
man of the world that engross him, but rather the attitudes.
It is not the vulgar fashions that he cares about, but the
picturesque and recherché ones. His is the essential dandyism that regards dress as not just decorative or becoming or
beautiful, but as expressing a mood or portraying a role;
everything, indeed, is to be significantly stylish, symbolically expressive. His in the same way is a dilettantism that
turns to art most readily when he is out of sorts or at loose
ends; you cannot imagine him normally staying away from
a ball to read a book, except as a pose, except that it may
make for publicity. Yet he gets pleasure, a right and educated pleasure, from books, indeed from the arts generally;
he does not just ogle ballet girls, he appreciates the ballet.
He enjoys the advantage of having one foot in the social
world and one in the artistic; but more than this in the end
is an advantage, it is a misfortune. For he is never quite
happy, or entirely at home, in either world: the social world
that suffices for the ordinary playboy must all too often bore
him, while the world of seclusion, of thought and expression and feeling, must all too often leave him restless. For
such a dandy-dilettante, his greatest advantage is really his
youth and his personal dash and charm: they shelter his
shallowness, they embellish his poses, they even make him
cut a figure of sorts. But the truth is that for all his desire to
be expressive, there is little to express; he can only adopt
attitudes, enact roles, stage-light situations. For achieving
his effects, he is dependent upon the very society that he

pointedly eschews or showily turns his back on; just as, in his dilettante moods, he models himself on the fashionable writers he has read or met. Tatyana, examining the books in his country house,

> *found the margins most appealing:*
> *The pencil marks he made with care*
> *Upon the pages everywhere*
> *Were all unconsciously revealing:*
> *A cross, a question mark, a word—*
> *From these the man might be inferred.*

For an Onegin, the world is too much with him even when he has taken leave of the world. It is not only that whenever he goes in for the simple life he is deeply aware that he has gone in for it, but also that as soon as it becomes a way of life—as soon as there are no new fields or paths or brooks to discover, no new romantic views or picturesque customs to be found—he turns bored. He does not like solitude, he likes the idea of liking it. He cannot be simple, he can only be *simpliste*. In the same way, he perhaps cannot be truly unhappy, he can only be Byronically melancholy, self-dramatizingly sad. At his best, he has a real air; very often he has only affectations. At his best, he has sensitive feelings about life, sensitive reactions to situations; but he is oftener sensitive about the kind of figure he will cut, the kind of impression he will leave behind. He is thus not only a man of the world, but the world's man, its ultimate slave, its eventual faintly tragic victim. If such a dandy-dilettante is a good deal of an eternal type, in another way he is a pure period type; but Pushkin, with his brilliant vivacity and superb detail, has given Onegin, if no full face, at least a profile of his own.

And Pushkin, best of all, has dramatized—and simultaneously criticized—Onegin's make-up by bringing it into crucial relations with others, by setting it against first Lensky and then Tatyana. At the first, and even the second, glimpse Onegin shines by contrast; he has what the other two lack, all the social graces; he has dash and poise, an air of wit, of cultivation, of connoisseurship; he is the kind of man who, in a pinch, can convey a critical judgment simply by looking bored. Obviously, too, Lensky admires him, and Tatyana loves him at first sight. Yet we have but to note just once his behavior toward Lensky, and just once his behavior toward Tanya, to get to the root of him. He knows how wrong he was with Lensky's fiancée at the ball, he knows too how shamefully absurd it would be to go through with the duel, yet the thought that by not doing so may invite a few sniffs and sneers from society is enough to make him change his mind. In the same way, as Tanya points out, his feverish pursuit of her as a Moscow great lady is predominantly a desire to publish his conquest of her and add to his reputation as a society rake. These two things are the key to his character and the measure of his limitations; they epitomize him, they type him. In that sense they are a more decisive criticism of the essential Onegin than something as shocking as his not giving Lensky quite an even chance in the duel, for in this he unconsciously seeks revenge that is a form of tribute, in this he is actuated, without knowing it, by envy. In the same way, by refusing Tanya's love, by refusing to marry her, though the consequences were to be grave, he was being honest about himself, and was only dishonest when pursuing her as a great lady.

When I say the consequences of Onegin's refusing Tatyana's love were to be grave, I mean chiefly in terms of Tatyana. Hers, as between the two, is both the moral and the personal victory; hers, by Onegin's standards, is indeed a dazzling success story; but it is she who is the truly tragic figure of the story, from being pushed into so unwanted a role and coming to live so wasted a life. In the shy girl we first meet, who is incapable of pretense or concealment, and whose untutored heart bursts with the most passionate love for Onegin, we have also a type, and also a period type. But in her passionateness, and in the poetic accuracy and delicacy of her creator's perceptions, we have suddenly a human being—one of those figures who stay with us not from how thoroughly we know them but from how intensely we feel them; not in detail, but in essence. The Tanya whom Eugene suddenly encounters as a great lady is someone whom *we* suddenly encounter in the same way: we have not watched her working into a new role, and when in the great scene she speaks to Onegin for the first time since he has again become aware of her—and for the last time, it is to be assumed, in their lives—every word is crucial, a false sentence, even a few wrong syllables, can be fatal. For she is grown into the kind of woman she should never have been, playing a part she seemed in no way ever able to play; and with a calm glacial dignity she refuses for good and all the man she still loves. The scene not only has a great moral force: *that* it might possess from the nature of the situation and the poet's power of words; it has also a convincing trenchancy, an exalting stature, as between man and woman no less than between differing natures and ways of life. The poet triumphs here by his boldness, his succinctness, his speed, by compressing the whole psychological analysis into a few salient facts, a few freighted speeches, a recollection of what was, a recognition of what is: a novelist would not have been so daring, nor trusted to so little; nor, without the heightening power of verse, have been capable of so much.

It has been well said that Pushkin's greatness in creating Tatyana lay in his almost miraculous ability to make of her at the end a virtuous wife and yet neither a prig nor a puritan; nor, we might add, a conscious martyr. Perhaps, best of all, he does not let the spirit of the final scene sound the final note of the story: he resumes the light, informal manner of so much of the book, the briskness and gaiety acquiring now a wistfulness, the modest ending having its own kind of human magnificence. In Pushkin's diminuendos, we sense something of Turgenev and, with a lesser kinship, of Chekhov. And it is a commonplace that the Tanya-Onegin relationship—the weakling and the woman of strength, the worldling and the woman of character—has been a recurrent one in Russian literature. But, as Prince Mirsky has said, "the classical attitude of Pushkin, of sympathy without pity for the man, and of respect without reward for the woman, has never been revived."

I have summarized this story at considerable length, I have quoted from it in considerable detail, because it seems to me that Pushkin managed to enfold his criticism in his chronicle. For all the personal, or seemingly personal, comments that he introduces, for all his quick sallies and short sermons, his asides and digressions, it is in this tale of Onegin and his way of life, as set lightly against Lensky, and graphically against Tanya, that we find our whole sense of comparative values. To be sure, the more than eight years that Pushkin spent in writing his poem also chronicle the moral and artistic growth of the poet himself. The young man who, inspired by Byron's *Don Juan*, set light-heartedly to work on *Onegin*—with his own kind of dazzling youthful gifts—was far removed from the mature artist who wrote the final scenes; and in that sense, we may doubt whether the young man would have had the moral insight, let alone the creative power, to tell the story quite as it came to be told, or to be concluded. We might say that, in a sense, the account of Onegin's deterioration is the mark of Pushkin's development; that the protagonist and his creator started off in a strong autobiographical alliance, as both of them dashing, privileged young men of the world, and increasingly diverged as Pushkin learned from life and from his endowments as a student of life and a writer, while, with no such endowments, Onegin acquired no such knowledge either. In Pushkin's own life there was enormously much, of course, of Onegin's—in his youth Pushkin drank and gambled, danced and fought duels, had a succession of love affairs, attacked autocracy and epigramatically thumbed his nose at the Czar, and was more or less exiled with an army appointment in southern Russia. As the politically agitated years passed, he became much less of a firebrand; he returned to Moscow, a gayer blade than ever, and more than ever a social success, and finally met and married a beautiful young girl, who with the passing years proved flagrantly unfaithful, which provoked the duel that caused Pushkin's death. This is the Onegin side of Pushkin's story; but the whole other side of Pushkin's life, the political troubles and financial debts, the vagabond streak and clutter of adventures and experiences, and above all his position in the literary world and his considerable productivity, contributed equally if less directly to the writing of *Onegin* and the insight with which it was written; while beyond that there was the ever more deft and accomplished artist.

There is, indeed, almost every species of good writing— dark and bright, mocking and tender, gay and serious, brilliant and passionate—in this remarkable novel in verse; writing that proclaims Pushkin's knowledge of human nature, his acute observation of the physical world, his thorough familiarity with sophisticated life and the social scene; writing that at the same time, in a rather taxing fourteen-line stanza, can be wonderfully lyrical, immensely poetic, or have the crackle of epigram, the ballroom gloss of *vers de société*. No other criticism of worldliness, no other taking the measure of a worldling can so draw blood from the worldling's own weapons, his insouciance, his suavity, his dash. No one, more than Pushkin, has so brilliantly described the social scene or so ably appraised it, but it is the measure of the poem's high excellence that it describes and appraises so much else, and can elsewhere be as intense and poetic as here it is glittering and sharp.

Let me quote a few of the ways in which, even at brief length and in translation, Pushkin excels. Here is pure society verse, pure portrayal of manners:

> They take her to the Club for dances,
> The rooms are thronged and hot and gay.
> The blare, the lights, the shining glances,
> The couples as they whirl away,
> The lovely ladies' filmy dresses,
> The balconies where such a press is,
> The young and hopeful brides-to-be,
> Confound the senses suddenly.
> Here dandies now in the ascendant
> Show off their impudence, their vests,
> Their monocles that rake the guests.
> And here hussars on leave, resplendent
> And thunderous, flock eagerly:
> They come, they conquer and they flee.

Again, there is a speculation on what Lensky's future might have been, had he lived:

> He might have altered and deserted
> The Muse—to marriage been converted,

And worn in comfort, far from town,
Horns and a quilted dressing-gown;
He might have learned that life was shabby
At bottom and, too bored to think,
Have been content to eat and drink,
Had gout at forty, fat and flabby;
He might have gone to bed and died
While doctors hemmed and women cried.

Here is Onegin during one of his reading bouts:

Again a book was his sole crony—
He read at will: Gibbon, Rousseau,
Chamfort and Herder and Manzoni,
Madame de Stael, Bichat, Tissot;
Devoured Stendhal, the arrant skeptic,
And Fontenelle, acute, eupeptic;
He read miscéllany and journal,
The magazines that like to scold
Us all, and where I now am told
That my performance is infernal,
Though once they praised my magic pen:
E Sempre bene, gentlemen.

And here is Pushkin, not high and Keatslike in poetic description, but homely and domestic, rather after the fashion of the Dutch genre painters:

Here's winter! . . . The triumphant peasant
Upon his sledge tries out the road;
His mare scents snow upon the pleasant
Keen air, and trots without a goad;
The bold kibitka swiftly traces
Two fluffy furrows as it races;
The driver on his box we note
With his red belt and sheepskin coat.
A serf-boy takes his dog out sleighing,
Himself transformed into a horse;

One finger's frostbitten, of course,
But nothing hurts when you are playing;
And at the window, not too grim,
His mother stands and threatens him.

From these translated quotations alone, one might deduce no more than Pushkin's great adroitness in small
ways, and fine eye for detail. But in the original I would
suppose that from just such passages there emerged a marvelous expressiveness, a delicate play of mind, a large gift
of observation, things that exceed the most accomplished
lightweight, that indeed stamp Pushkin as not a lightweight. And how little he was one stands forth when we
recall that these quotations are hardly more than garnish-
ing for a poem that exhibits great mastery of narrative, of
characterization, of theme; and that, for all it may pause or
digress, has beyond its shapeliness an organic form. We
can only praise and value Pushkin the more for his gaiety
and elegance and his dandyism since they did not prevent
his achieving in the same work what would not only father
much important fiction but was in itself important fiction.
Certainly the great scenes in the story of Eugene and Tanya
—the first meeting; Tanya and her nurse; the scene in the
garden; Tanya's journey to Moscow; and the final scene in
Moscow—certainly these scenes, to re-dignify a much-
abused word, are unforgettable.

THE CHARTERHOUSE
OF PARMA

FOR MOST DISCERNING READERS—THERE ARE THOSE, to be sure, who find Stendhal uncongenial—*The Charterhouse of Parma* ranks among the greatest of novels; but scarcely anyone, I think, would deny it a place with the very greatest novels of worldliness. It is this for two substantial reasons: because of its tone—its attitude of an urbane, unillusioned, enormously perceptive *homme du monde;* and again because of the level at which the worldliness operates. Our very scene is the court of a small early nine-teenth-century principality. We are concerned with, so to speak, *professional* worldlings, with courtiers and politicos, great ladies and ministers of state. One's every move, be it never so trivial, tends to be a calculated one—because any move, in an audience chamber or merely on a dance floor, may have consequences. One's every word, even the merest banter, needs to be weighed, for every word will be commu-nicated to others. The favor of the prince is no sooner won than it may be lost again; the favorite of the prince is no sooner established than he may be dismissed. Every social occasion is endowed with political significance; every comic contretemps may have tragic repercussions; every forgotten indiscretion may be strategically brought to light. At any given moment, the ruler's policy may derive from the ruler's vanity, just as his personal fears may occasion his whole court's fright. Moreover, the worldliness is all the greater here, all the more concentrated, because the scene is so limited, the stage so small. At this miniature court of this toylike principality, everyone is the warier for being involved in the same wiles, for giving ear to the same gossip, for coveting the same places, for clinging to the same ropes, for being equally a contestant, a competitor, a conspirator. The whole thing has, in its blend of rather sinister worldly disguises and ticklish worldly missteps, now the sound of melodrama and now the tone of farce. But there are deeper sounds too, and profounder intimations—all that high comedy has to tell us, in its own way, of what is tragic in life.

For *The Charterhouse* goes beyond the usual worldling writer catching his worldling characters out; goes beyond a tearing off of masks and a mockery of pretenses, beyond even the most extensive representation of social stances and sophisticated gambits. One reason why it is so great a novel of worldliness is that, without relaxing its worldliness, it transcends it—not by introducing copybook figures of greater nobility or idealism, not by counterpoising booted-and-spurred abstractions of ethics or philosophy, but by creating three particular magnificent characters, one of whom—Count Mosca—sums up what can be said both for and against the enlightened worldling, two others of whom —the hero Fabrizio, and the incomparable Duchess of Sanseverina—stand less outside the worldly scene than above it. It is not so much that they are incapable of mastering its ways as unwilling to submit to its laws; as that they are moved, in the great crises of their lives, by grander personal desires, by more urgent personal visions. They do not evade, they do not in the didactic sense renounce the worldly life; they enlarge upon it.

But behind them is their creator; *in* them, indeed, is their creator, in each of the three there is one side or another of Stendhal. And Stendhal is more brilliantly endowed than even they are. E. M. Forster speaks somewhere of a not too happy encounter with Howard Sturgis, who conveyed the impression—Forster noted with amused malice—that Forster's books contained him and not he his books. Certainly Stendhal's books do not contain him, he contains them. We are particularly aware of this in *The Charterhouse*, aware not only of someone who can command a whole orchestra of human musical instruments, fiddles and flutes, trombones and tubas; who, again, can create an entire small state rich in history and geography alike, but someone who most of all can imbue the whole with something complex and multicolored, a kind of compass with all its varying points; a contradictory whole that subtly rejects what it seems to accept, makes comedy of what it seems to hold sacred, blithely stands on its head what it seems to have stood on a pedestal. It is a method that uses every kind of contrast as a form of criticism yet seems to find all forms of contrast inadequate as a guide—so that the final irony is the inadequacy of irony.

If we begin at the simple level of story, how superbly engrossing a story—or, rather, an opera or cinema—we have. Here, as would seem at first, we have in Fabrizio an ideal *jeune premier*—a young man almost as innocent as Candide, but with some of the qualities, too, of a romantic hero. Actually the son of a French officer with whom his nobly born mother had had an affair, Fabrizio is legally the son of a reactionary Italian marchese, a man between whom and Fabrizio there is bad blood. The Marchese del Dongo's sister, however, is infatuated with Fabrizio from his childhood; between these two is to develop an extraordinary relationship. At seventeen, Fabrizio, fired by an admiration for the Bonaparte who occupies his country, runs off to France and manages to be blurredly present at the battle of Waterloo. This is the first of the book's peculiar triumphs —the wholly unromantic, antiheroic account it offers of Fabrizio's confused and aimless wanderings on the day and very site of Waterloo.

Fabrizio eventually gets back to Italy; there are some piquant and revealing episodes of home life, but with Mosca's infatuation for Fabrizio's now widowed young aunt, the story begins shifting to its main theater of action, to Parma —where Mosca is Prime Minister—and the court of Parma. The Parma of Stendhal's novel is a wholly imaginary small autocratic state, existing in a period suspended outside time —a world that in some ways suggests the Machiavellian Renaissance and in other ways shows touches of post-Napoleonic Europe. If it is Ruritanian in its compactness, if it can be Graustarkian in its events, it is very much, in its motivations, of the real world of society, and of the real world of politics in its maneuvers. It is a kind of chessboard: a chessboard in the subtlety and stealthiness—and often the irrevocability—of its moves; a chessboard, again in the danger of ably defending one part of the board while leaving others open to mortal attack; a chessboard, too, in the differing rank of the pieces, in the consistent sacrifice of pawns, and even knights and bishops, to win the game; and even in the arbitrariness of the colors—for the two political parties in Parma, though one purports to be liberal and the other reactionary, are in their tactics indistinguishable, just as in their relations with the prince and his police they are almost equally impotent. The Prince, Ernesto IV, is a near-despot with much intelligence of a kind, with sardonic guile and malicious worldly understanding. His model is Louis XIV, his manner rather less effective; he is vain, deceitful, touchy, given now to mature insights, now to childish tyrannical impulses, and often simply frightened and unnerved.

Mosca, Ernesto's Minister of State, Minister of Police, Prime Minister, is—as success in serving so devious and whimsical an autocrat would imply—a finished man of the world, adept at maneuver, adroit at all the arts of management, persuasion, diplomacy; unillusioned, unsentimental. He is not, however, the baser sort of finished worldling, bred to cynicism and callousness, but someone capable of humane judgments, tending toward humane policies, acting harshly where he must but benevolently when he can. His passion for Fabrizio's aunt is the turning point of his career: indeed, for love of her he is ready to abandon his career, to leave the Prince's service and live in modest retirement. He lacks the means to offer a good marriage, as he lacks the freedom: he is married already, though separated from his wife. Fabrizio's aunt, though Fabrizio is her real love, is yet much attracted to Mosca, and very much impressed by him. To join him at Parma as his obvious mistress would be hopelessly ill-advised; he therefore arranges for her to marry an aging duke who will settle money and estates on her and, in return for being created an ambassador, never see her again. She therefore comes as a duke's wife to Parma so as to be, under impeccable circumstances, a prime minister's mistress. She—whom we can

now call the Duchess of Sanseverina—is surely among the
most delightful women in all fiction; but she is not simply a
romantic heroine or charmer, she is a great woman with
whom personal feeling and personal relationships are para-
mount. She is willing to play for big stakes over real issues.
Beautiful, highborn, enchanting, she becomes the focal
point of Parmesan social life. Living in the world, she
knows all its ways, and on occasion employs its methods,
wears its masks, stoops to its duplicities; but the Duchess is
not essentially a woman who seeks power or would dominate the powerful. Quite the other way; it is personal fulfillment in the amplest sense that she wants—the attainment
of an enlightened rather than emulous way of life, and of a
world of happiness that lies beyond outward victories and
sophisticated temptations. To say that this fearless woman
of generous instincts is a force for good in the world suggests liberalistic virtue and ethical exertion; with her what
counts is not so much goodness as largeness, a kind of
affirming courage, a contempt for the prudential hesitations
so instinctive with the people about her. To get what she
wants or destroy what she hates, she can be ruthless; but
what she seeks in life is essentially ample and noble.

The third of our chief figures might seem to be the
simplest. But Fabrizio is not simple at all, he is much less of
a type and much more of an original than he at first seems
to be. He goes through the motions of a certain kind of life,
but he is untouched by much of it because it leaves him
unattracted and unfulfilled. What is simple about him is his
fundamental self, his wish for a life half born of 'romantic
dreams and chivalrous idealism, and half imposed on him
by his never being really at home with courts and society.
Again and again, as he lives the customary life of gallantry
and sex, he is pervaded by the feeling that he is incapable of

love: which, as Martin Turnell remarks, may reveal a secret fear (and one that Stendhal shared) of impotence. But it may also be, I think, that he cannot find love in court surroundings, because *there* he can never find its face— since love, for him, must have an air of difficulty, inaccessibility, high romance. Love, at any rate, only comes to him when, imprisoned in the great tower of Parma, he encounters Clélia under the most high-romantic—indeed wildly cinematic—circumstances. And indeed he is happiest as a prisoner in the tower, not just because he has fallen passionately and exaltedly in love, but because he has come upon a life that, despite its difficulties, *is* richly private, fundamentally hidden and dreamlike. The aristocratic young courtier in him that he has inwardly always rejected is now replaced by the knight errant gazing daily at his *princesse lointaine,* whom he has inwardly always envisaged.

At the same time, it is important to grasp that Fabrizio is no simple romantic innocent, is not even of the never-fully-mature type of a Tom Jones—the sort of hero who has countless experiences but very few adult reactions. Fabrizio can play the young man-about-court, and even the distinguished cleric, not only adroitly, with considerable ironic enjoyment; he can also, on occasion, be very much the haughty patrician. It is his *nature* that is unsophisticated, not his conduct; as, again, his misfortune is much less an inability to speak other people's language than a failure to find others who speak his. He is one of those people, it seems to me, who go through life most happily talking to themselves. This in some sense, of course, is the artist's nature—and this side of Fabrizio reflects a side in Stendhal: that side of the artist which, for all its mingling with the world, remains aloof and alien, secret and uncorrupted, just as in Mosca, Stendhal gives us what was guileful, ironic, mature, and worldly-wise in himself.

These three characters occupy the foreground of a novel whose background is a mesh of social and political intrigue, a maze of social and political maneuver, and all the paraphernalia of worldly calculation. Never elsewhere, in this sense, has anyone so fully as Stendhal held the mirror up to the very opposite of Nature, so fully held it up to masquerade. The commonest approach of current criticism toward *The Charterhouse* is as a political novel, and certainly it is notable as just that: indeed, the very framework—of a small autocratic state where every one is jockeying for power—implies political action inside it. All the same, I think that a distinction needs to be made about *The Charterhouse* that so far as I know has not been: which is that it is essentially a novel of political *intrigue* rather than of political ideas, a kind of handbook on political tactics rather than a textbook of political thought. And in this sense it seems to me a political novel folded into something broader and more commodious: in other words, it is ultimately concerned with intrigue itself, with methods, with stratagems, whether political or social or sexual; whether inside ministries or throne rooms or boudoirs; whether in pursuit of power or position; whether a matter of false friendships or false vows. It is because *The Charterhouse* is concerned with worldly motives and ambitions on the political *and* the social *and* the personal side, having as much about it of Castiglione's *The Courtier* as of Machiavelli's *The Prince*, that it is a supreme novel of worldliness first, and a remarkable political novel secondarily.

Very much of the secondary, and sometimes primary, pleasure that the book provides has to do with political machinery no less than political machinations. One of the most delightful of creative enterprises for an author is setting up a history, a geography, a cosmology of his own; inventing a state, a capital, a dynasty such as Stendhal has done here, a miniature world which shall be made to seem real and in time take on more than factuality—take on depth and significance. Stendhal's world has, in small compass, everything needed for Stendhal's purpose. Martin Turnell refers to it as a police state, and to the Prince as a dictator; but that, I think, gives it too purely modern a slant. Parma is rather a remnant of autocracy, of something despotic by inheritance, than a foretaste of totalitarianism, with its pretense of a welfare state and a usurper-despot. Indeed, what is so peculiarly operatic about the manner and even the events of *The Charterhouse* springs from how old-fashioned and ornate an autocracy it is; any police-state conception, even as opera, lies far in the future and the world of *verismo*. More important, a police state cannot easily ascend to high comedy, cannot explode at will into extravagance, or plummet into farce. What gives *The Charterhouse* both its Renaissance cunning and its rococo court life is its air of the ancien régime—and at a moment in the consciousness of Europe when the ancien régime has crystallized as precisely that: when a new order is challenging it and triumphing over it.

In this world of Parma, which a little recalls the old description of Russia under the Czars—"autocracy tempered by assassination"—the ultras and liberals intrigue against one another with the utmost unscrupulousness, the great difficulty being that they tend to function with the utmost impotence and that their political aims are mangled by their personal ambitions. The official chief Liberal is the governor of the Citadel, which is to say the head of the jail, and most of his prisoners are fellow Liberals whom he

treats with all possible harshness. The farcically ironic use
to which Stendhal puts the whole party system, the space
he happily lavishes on all the stratagems of party function-
aries, as against how little he does with beliefs and ideas,
further stresses how much more this is a novel of political
intrigue than of political thought. Mosca, who, though
Prime Minister of the reactionary party, is Parma's best
proponent of liberal tolerance—to *practice*, indeed, any
kind of liberalism he must preach its opposite—even Mosca
is concerned not with how best to persuade or convince
Ernesto IV, but with how best to manage him: whether
with coarse flattery or veiled threats, but in any case with
the arts of the diplomat rather than the arguments of the
statesman. And as the plot thickens, it becomes Mosca's
problem to manage the Prince as much in terms of the
Duchess and Fabrizio as of Parma's internal and foreign
affairs. Moreover, at one of the great crises of the story,
Mosca's horrible ministerial blunder constitutes one of
Stendhal's most brilliant satiric triumphs. When the Duchess, as the price of her remaining in Parma, forces the
Prince to remove the prison sentence he has imposed on
Fabrizio, and astutely stipulates that "these unjust proceed-
ings shall have no consequences in the future"—in other
words, that Fabrizio shall go permanently free—Mosca,
drawing up the document for the Prince to sign, from a
form of diplomatic caution that has become second nature
with him, omits the safeguarding phrase, and so gives the
Prince the chance to throw Fabrizio into the Citadel. This
way in which he instinctively serves the Prince's interest
rather than that of the woman he passionately loves is a
just insight into human conditioning. Certainly it would be
possible, but I think unsound, to bring Freud into it and

suggest that, by omitting the crucial phrase, Mosca is unconsciously conspiring the downfall of his rival with the Duchess.

The whole scene that culminates in Mosca's drawing up the document is full of the most adroit and delicious high comedy, one of the scenes that contribute generally to *The Charterhouse's* high distinction, but more particularly to its definitive portrayal of worldliness and its comic verve and wit. The scene itself is too long to quote, but we would be slighting the whole polished surface of the novel if we did not suggest by quotation Stendhal's manner, now of commenting on his people and now of characterizing them.

The wit at times is pleasant and dry, but hardly vintage, as in the description of the Princess of Parma as imagining herself "to be the most unhappy person in the universe, a belief which made her perhaps the most trying." Again, the book exhibits what might best be called high playfulness, something not easily removed from its context, it springs so fully out of the moment; but perhaps this small soliloquy of Fabrizio's, when he is in prison and falling in love with Clélia, will do:

"But . . .," Fabrizio said to himself in astonishment, "I am forgetting to be angry. Can I be one of those stout hearts of which antiquity has furnished the world with several examples? How is this—I who was so much afraid of prison, I am in prison and I do not even remember to be sad! It is certainly a case where the fear was a hundred times worse than the evil. . . . Can it be the surprise of all these novel surroundings that is distracting me from the grief that I ought to feel? . . . In any case, it is indeed surprising to . . . have to reason with oneself in order to be unhappy. Upon my soul, I come back to my theory, perhaps I have a noble character."

In a different vein, there are bits of maxim making: "The lover thinks more often of reaching his mistress than the husband of guarding his wife; the prisoner thinks more often of escaping than the jailer of shutting the door." With such bright pleasantries the book is dotted, but they are merely the salted almonds or the *sauce piquante* of Stendhal's brilliant feast. We must go beyond salon sarcasms, we must go to the worldly devices whereby people manage to function or advance themselves or survive. The Prince, talking to the Archbishop about Fabrizio's killing the actor who got in the way of one of his amours, remarks:

> In the Devil's name, one gets things of that sort done for one by somebody else . . . *besides,* one doesn't kill a comedian like Giletti, one buys him.

That represents someone very exalted speaking; here is the worldly reaction of a petty police official to whom Fabrizio has handed Giletti's passport, pretending that it is his own:

> Our hero was sufficiently alarmed, as we have seen; he would have been a great deal more so could he have read the thoughts that were disturbing the official's mind. This man was a friend of Giletti: one may judge of his surprise when he saw his friend's passport in the hands of a stranger; his first impulse was to have the stranger arrested, then it occurred to him that Giletti might easily have sold his passport to this fine young man, who presumably had been doing something disgraceful in Parma. "If I arrest him," he said to himself, "Giletti will get into trouble, they'll see at once that he has sold his passport; on the other hand, what will my superiors say if it's proved that I, a friend of Giletti, put a visa on his passport while it was carried by someone else?" The official got up with a yawn and said to Fabrizio: "Just a minute, sir"; then, availing himself of a professional formula, added: "A difficulty has arisen!"

—which is to say, he goes into another room and finds a pretext for having the passport stamped by someone else.

Here is the Sanseverina giving Fabrizio worldly advice, on his way to becoming an archbishop:

> Believe or not, as you choose, what they teach you, but *never raise any objection.* Imagine they are teaching you the rules of the game of whist; would you raise any objection to the rules of whist? I have told Count Mosca that you are a believer, and he is delighted to hear it; it is useful in this world and the next. But, if you believe, do not fall into the vulgar habit of speaking with horror of Voltaire, Diderot, Raynal and all those harebrained Frenchmen who paved the way to the Dual Chamber. Their names should not be allowed to pass your lips, but if you must mention them, speak of these gentlemen with a calm irony: they are people who have long since been refuted, and whose attacks are no longer of any consequence. Believe blindly everything they tell you at the Academy. Bear in mind that there are people who will make a careful note of your slightest objections; they will forgive you a little amorous intrigue if it is done in the proper way, but not a doubt: age stifles intrigue but encourages doubt. . . . The second idea which Count Mosca sends you is this: if there should occur to you a brilliant argument, a triumphant retort that will change the course of the conversation, don't give in to the temptation to shine; remain silent; people of any discernment will see your cleverness in your eyes. It will be time enough to be witty when you are a Bishop.

All this is the polished floor, and the often dangerously slippery one, over which our characters dance and our story moves. The story itself, however, is in no sense merely of the ballroom. Much of it, as we observed earlier, is operatic; almost all of it, which intensifies what is operatic, is Italian. Behind the uniforms and medals there are passionate bodies, and behind the masks, devious minds. In the course of the book Fabrizio kills a man; the Duchess has the ruler of Parma killed; the ruler himself kills whoever seems to menace him; the Duchess has the strongest amorous feelings for Fabrizio, as has Mosca for her, and Fabrizio for Clélia. Fabrizio escapes by a silken rope from a high tower; opportunists everywhere conspire, ruffians everywhere lie in wait, politicians everywhere bide their time. The effect of so much melodrama laced with so much urbanity is sometimes merely storybook, and at other times rather dreamlike and surrealist. At still other times, it becomes a particular type of opera—one in which the libretto runs to crude action but the music to refined commentary. Accompanying the flash of a stiletto will be an aria full of exquisite perception or ironic mockery. As the plot plunges into some new thicket of intrigue, the orchestra sounds chords of civilized ennui or despair. In a work like *The Charterhouse,* story and theme, action and reaction, surface and subsurface, present and past, often play antiphonal roles. And so, most of all, do the romantic and the realistic in Stendhal's cosmos—or perhaps we might better say the romancer and the psychologist in Stendhal. The story lets us revel in the merely witty, entertaining, thrilling, almost frivolous, only for us to suddenly find ourselves—with all the torches extinguished—in the dank vault of self-interest, hearing strange animal screeches of treachery and malignity. And this most operatic of stories is of course recounted in Stendhal's bare Code Napoleon style; amid all the sword flourishes and rapier thrusts of his characters, he himself uses a plain pen.

Having eaten our cake and enjoyed every rich crumb of the story, just what have we besides? I'm not sure just what: as no one can be more explicit than Stendhal, so no one at times seems more enigmatic. The sense of enigma derives, to some degree, from a total absence of dogma: the essence of Stendhal's urbane worldly-wiseness is that one can pose no lasting answers or solutions. It is as easy to blueprint an imaginary principality as it is hard to chart the course of man's emotional or moral destiny. And so, when most serious or engaged, Stendhal may turn most whimsical and flippant: balked of reality, he will permit himself to play the conjurer. Doors sometimes magically fly open in *The Charterhouse*, with no realistic concern about any hand or key to open them with. Stendhal in one way is immensely creative in *The Charterhouse*, and by different standards hardly creative at all. Thus there is no immediacy about his people, no sense of what we might call the next door neighbor; nor do characters or events come upon us as things known or seen. Stendhal, in other words, does not create in the sense that he seems to re-create, as Jane Austen does, or Fielding, or Tolstoy. Perhaps one reason why Stendhal does not do this is that from his inventing *everything*—even his own detailed history and geography —very little seems familiar or near at hand. Despite what a Mosca may owe to a Metternich, and even a fictitious Parma to a historical Modena, the book is a perfect tissue of the artificial and imaginary. In going so far outside ordinary nature, Stendhal is equally going inside his private self. And that, thought at first it might not seem so, makes for less unity of effect than would the usual vision of the outside world. For where, by one's interpretation of things and view of life, one can harmonize the diversities of the outside world, when it is the contradictions of one's own complex inner self that provide the substance of one's book, the result may well be clouded and enigmatic. What in other words we have in *The Charterhouse* is neither any

sort of subjective or autobiographical novel on the one
hand, nor any sort of objective and photographic novel on
the other. We have instead a Stendhal who, however detached he may seem, is not so much detached as diffused.
He has changed the banknote of his whole self into a number of coins, he has distributed himself among various
characters—Mosca, Fabrizio, Palla, the Prince, the Duchess. Or say that there is a general flavor to the book in
which we discern a variety of flavorings—this herb and
that condiment, a certain strange syrup and some very old
brandy—removing any of which would be to mar the taste.
The enigma of Stendhal is not, I think, so much any failure
to communicate his feelings or thoughts as the impossibility of consolidating them; the impossibility for the contradictions to be neatly resolved, for the coins to turn back into
the banknote. *The Charterhouse* is perhaps the greatest of
worldly novels because it comprehends all worldliness
within itself, but itself emerges as more than a critique of
worldliness. Indeed, simply by its projection of Stendhal's
own intellect and nature, it points up the inadequacy of all
general critiques; it stresses how much all answers can
leave unanswered. Hence the final taste of the book has
incongruous and disconcerting and unruly flavors. Irony
and comedy join hands, tragedy and farce embrace, passion
sits cheek by jowl with mockery, charm with brutality,
idealism with crime. The showman links arms with the
philosopher, the fool with the sage; and along with torches
that penetrate the darkness, fireworks glitter idly in the
night. All this is perhaps not too far from Paul Valéry when
he says that for him Stendhal is "a type of intelligence
much more than he is a man of letters"—the wonderful
play of Stendhal's mind and the way it becomes concrete
through his characters and his cosmology; the way too, I

myself would add, that it becomes a system of values by refusing, in any final sense, to formulate one.

The book's whole storybook setting is really an embodiment of Stendhal's mental universe; and it perhaps makes less for something enigmatic than for something too diversified to be defined. Most books that seem to us very "personal" seem so, no doubt, because of the unmistakable signature they bear—whether of style, as in Sterne or Sir Thomas Browne; or in attitude, as in Jane Austen or Pope; or in a kind of unique vision, as in Melville or Dostoevsky; or sometimes in mere faultiness or excess, as in Thomas Wolfe or Tennessee Williams. *The Charterhouse* is much less personal than immensely individual, bearing the stamp of a complex temperament and intelligence, being not a mirror but a hall of mirrors. We get the whole diversified Stendhal because he is projected by way of his substance, not his manner; of his story, not his storytelling; of his distributing, not his dramatizing, himself. Henri-Beylism, to revert to Stendhal's real name, is in this sense the complete reverse of Byronism.

Thus, in the book, where there is personal harmony there is no philosophical unity. The contrast in attitudes between, say, the Duchess and Mosca, between her purposefulness shaped by passion—what Stendhal calls *espagnolisme*—and his cautious sense of the world—what is half ironically called *logique*—creates a private conflict that is one of the eternal collisions of civilized morality: whether, one might say, to go at life on the other man's terms or on one's own; to go at it discreetly or defiantly; to keep as much as one can, or play for all or nothing. It is the opposition, no doubt, of the lion and the fox. We tend naturally to exalt the lion, and we do well to, except—and here the fox begins to speak —that if those who lack a lion's strength would themselves survive and serve others, they must needs take on some of the fox's cunning; for there are also wolves in the world, and vultures, and hyenas. In Stendhal, as in so many superior natures, the idealist and the enlightened worldling strive to complement each other, though at times their strife merely cripples both. In *The Charterhouse* it is Mosca, not the Duchess, who wins—Mosca who indeed wins the Duchess, without winning her heart or for that matter winning her for long; for she but a short while survives Fabrizio, who has had her heart always. Still, as we are told in that very last sentence of the book, in that mockery of a fairy-tale ending, Mosca was "immensely rich." And indeed he lived on, immensely powerful and useful and rich, when all the others were dead. And there is a kind of purely practical justice about his triumph. That the civilized man of sense, the benevolent compromiser who can use the world's weapons against the world, shall succeed is perhaps all we can realistically hope for in the world of politics. For if power corrupts, perhaps it is then best held by those who know it does, and are just a little corrupted—vaccinated, as it were, against corruption. And it is Mosca too, in the end, who alone of the great trio *understands* politics: the Duchess is impatient of its rules, Fabrizio is indifferent to its ends. The Duchess and Fabrizio represent at bottom the private life and what reflects Stendhal's inner world: the Duchess is an aspect of what is single-minded in the artist's aim, Fabrizio of what is inviolable in the artist's nature. The two of them are inseparably mingled in Stendhal's approach to things, as they are incestuously joined in Stendhal's story. Except that, as I'm not sure has ever been stressed, the whole problem of incest is oddly ironic for being actually illusory—Fabrizio is no blood nephew of the Duchess, and we have here one more chance to speculate on appearance and reality, on what might be called the morality of mirage.

Here, then, is a novel of many and opposed attitudes; a hall of mirrors full of brilliant but conflicting lights. What gives it formal unity and workable proportions is the setting —the creation of a wonderfully compact small state that acts as a stout cord around a rather unwieldy bundle: for along with all the enchantments of make-believe go all the hardheaded involvements of politics and society. But beyond what is fantastic and what is all too realistic, there is something particular and grand, appertaining to Stendhal's "happy few," to his sense of an elite. That is what is so splendid about the book, that it deals convincingly with immensely superior people. Their superiority is not altogether a moral one—we know how ruthless on occasion they can be; even less a spiritual one—there is nothing exalted about them, no more a religious sense of sin than a mystical sense of sainthood. Their superiority is not humanitarian either; they are no more concerned with self-sacrifice than with sainthood. Their superiority is a matter of personal texture and stature, of something large, distinguished, aristocratic: they are, in the real right sense of the word, the best people, and their satisfaction lies in living for and with one another.

It is part of Stendhal's own nature, but also of the age he lived in, that these people impose themselves on us with a quick, assured sharpness; they do not go swathed in a latter-day, a Henry Jamesian or Virginia Woolfian, sensibility. As there is nothing gross or piglike about them, there is nothing bird-pecking; they are unafraid of being vulgar, and so they *are* not vulgar. They are superior too, without being literary: they have not their author's manner, but the grand manner.

Not sensibility of the modern kind is what so enriches this book, but that gaiety which Stendhal considered a mark of healthy art, and that great eighteenth-century endowment which Valéry noted, "the priceless gift of vivacity." And Stendhal would have been amused, Valéry goes on to say, "had he been given a glimpse in a crystal globe of all his doctoral future—of how his witticisms were twisted into theories, his manias into precepts, of how his brief maxims were the basis for interminable commentaries, his few favorite motives the source of volumes of exegesis." Well, some exegesis is always indicated with a great writer, and much of it can be useful; but with Stendhal, I would venture to say, it has proved particularly tiresome and costly, by giving modest nourishment to others at the cost of dehydrating Stendhal himself—Stendhal, who of all writers perhaps loses most by dehydration, because his verve, his mockery, his mellowness, his impudence, his quick dancing impulses, his quick flashing insights, his ability to shadow the tragic in the sunlight of comedy, to glimpse the profound in the caperings of farce, are the very essence of his art. The element of quicksilver in him is the chiefest part of his artistic gold. *The Charterhouse of Parma* is not least operatic, in that it has something of the unparaphrase-ableness, the untranslatability, of music.

XII

VANITY FAIR

VANITY FAIR, I THINK, IS THE ENGLISH NOVEL THAT
would come first to mind as the prime instance, the
perfect example, of worldliness in the long and, on the
whole, constantly worldly English tradition. The very title is
a kind of proclamation. Here, it trumpets forth, is a world of
people concerned with, agitated by, emulous of the shows
and vanities, the puppetry and pageantry of life; the gratifi-
cations of personal and social position and success. The
heroine—for if this is subtitled "A Novel Without a Hero,"
no novel ever had a more memorable heroine—represents
everything that constitutes getting on in the world, on
whatever terms, by whatever means; in temperament as in
ambition, Becky Sharp is worldliness incarnate. The ever-
changing scene of this very long, very broad, ultimately
rather panoramic novel is always concerned with the *fortunes* of its characters. In addition, Thackeray time and
again intrudes himself upon the scene as an overt moralist,

to comment in one way or another on the character, the manners, the motives of those he is writing about—and even, at times, of those he is writing for.

We thus have one of the great and central examples of a tradition. We have, no less, one of the great and central examples of an age—the Victorian age; and, I think, of a reading public—the large middle- and upper-middle-class reading public. The Victorian coloration of the book is all the more striking from the subject matter itself being laid in pre-Victorian times: between what Thackeray is writing about and how he is writing it there is a curious but palpable contrast; as there is, once again, between what he is writing and whom he is writing it for. Conceivably no age was ever more worldly than the Victorian—though here of course one must define and distinguish. We have seen how in matters of worldliness the eighteenth century is a notable hunting ground. The eighteenth century has a certain intellectual and cultural temper, a certain cultivated, formalized way of life—well-bred, high-bred, overbred, and glossily ill-bred; full of class feeling, which often means a great lack of feeling for any other class; in one sense extremely enlightened, in another shockingly prejudiced; in one sense patrician and aesthetic, in another peculiarly philistine; wary, worldly-wise, skeptical, believing that the gentlemen or lady, the *grande dame* or man of the world, should no more raise his moral voice than his social one, should be no more edifying in one way than argumentative in another; should prate no more than he should brawl.

Thus, among the worldly, matters were most properly ordered in eighteenth-century England. Yet, as I have said, perhaps no age was more worldly than the Victorian. No age, you may retort, was ever so committed to things hostile to worldliness—to humanitarianism, to good works, to moral uplift, to destroying social abuses and reforming wrong conduct; no age had such a sense of Sunday about it, and of Sunday psalm singing and soul saving. Even if we confine ourselves to literature, it was an age when great numbers of middle-class people read and listened earnestly and attentively to the Carlyles, the Ruskins, the Dickenses, the Arnolds; when middle-class reading societies, like middle-class choral societies, abounded, as did equally middle-class societies for the enlightenment and emancipation and reformation and conversion of every sort of backward or unprincipled or debauched or heathen group.

Good works of a kind abounded indeed; the good life, in Victorian England, was very much of a duty and an ideal. But the good life was, wherever possible, combined with good living, and the golden ladder to Heaven provided splendid mundane stopping-off places en route. In the course of the ascent, the final destination might even be forgotten, the very light of Heaven be dimmed by the resplendent gas chandeliers of Bayswater. And good living at home meant driving hard bargains abroad; meant adhering to a strict sense of getting ahead, of keeping afloat, of watching one's chances and counting one's shillings and counting one's spoons: there was to be no foolishness about the pursuit of the main chance; it was a solemn pursuit, it was a lifetime occupation.

Victorian worldliness particularly stands out in the sense of being so much more truly extensive: it embraced not just the wellborn, but the great and growing middle class; and it took the form of an unblushing materialism. If there was much more worship of God than, say, a century earlier, there was also much more worship of Mammon; indeed, with the Victorian middle class, God and Mammon became interfused, almost interchangeable, deities. Clearly one reason why the dismal Victorian Sunday was so set apart for serving God was almost blatantly to differentiate it from six days of serving His rival. Not the least ostentation of an ostentatious age was Victorian piety: the dismal glum Sunday afternoon was as showy a production as any garish weekday party or ball.

All this is unfair to the many people who were truly religious and by nature humble; but it is scarcely unfair to the age itself. It was an age of seemliness, of lip service, of hypocrisy, an age whose worldliness lay ultimately in its otherworldliness, in how many were to be *refused* admittance to the Good Life, in how much one might with an easy conscience amass, compared with how little one would, with great show of conscience, give away; in a horrifying social snobbery, a lip-smacking sexual prudery, a massive material vulgarity—never, it seems to me, were so many people cut dead right at the very doors of the church, and not only for being seen with the wrong man, but for being born in the wrong street. Never, again, were there greater compensations for leading so-called *un*worldly lives. It could almost be said that the amount of pleasure many "good" Victorian women got from sexual scandal exceeded what they might have got from sex itself; and surely the modesty that impelled them to clothe themselves from throat to ankles only doubled their opportunities to drape themselves in velvets and festoon themselves with jewels. Victorian clothes, Victorian meals, Victorian houses, the Victorian female figure were all of them testimonials to a constant flow of blessings, howsoever derived; in Victorian times English morality might in one sense lead the way, but it went hand in hand with hypocrisy, and hand in glove with materialism.

We are thus brought smack up against the Victorian

reading public, that mass of readers large enough to make a novelist's fortune, yet—for the novelist—a stumbling block to freedom of expression and, eventually on his own part, to freedom of thought or belief. The novelist's own mind went swathed in proper garments. Nothing, taking *Vanity Fair* as a story—it must also be taken as a theme—approaches in interest and power its account of Becky Sharp's career. And yet, at stage after stage of her career, we are left to infer and even guess at her precise sexual involvements: far from entering any unsanctified bedrooms with her and George Osborne, or with her and Lord Steyne, we have no knowledge of where the bedrooms may be. Even in the great climactic, unforgettable scene of discovery, when Rawdon comes home from the sponginghouse and finds Becky with Steyne, however much she may be condemned for heartlessness toward her husband, she cannot on the evidence quite be for infidelity. And though I think the reader's feeling—an author-guided feeling—that Becky is essentially a rather cold woman is right, it is surely a little intensified by Thackeray's never revealing her where she might be aroused, in any scene or even moment of passion.

Thackeray also went with his age in portraying contrasts between vice and virtue—though, of course, long before Thackeray was born, this was less any proof of the good life than a commonplace of bad fiction. Here, however, and I shall have more to say of this later, Thackeray did not ultimately subsist in clichés. Also, the more he was prevented from a frank treatment of sex and from a personal vision, as against a conventional view, of virtue and vice, the more he was encouraged to be unequivocal and indeed relentless about the self-interested motives of human nature and the essential make-up of the social scene; in return for drawing a curtain over Venusberg, he provides, as fully

in depth as in detail, an unequaled panorama of Vanity
Fair. Here, rather than suppress, he almost gloatingly exposed.

In spite of its having in Becky Sharp as vivid a single
character as perhaps exists in English fiction, *Vanity Fair* is
as incontrovertible a social novel as any that fiction can
offer. It is not for nothing that it originated with Thackeray's "Pen and Pencil Sketches of English Society"—that it
had, so to speak, a theme before it had a plot, and a
background before it had characters. And the theme, in the
end, counts more than the plot, and the background carries
as much weight, for what Thackeray wanted to say, as the
characters. For in all Becky's efforts to get on, she herself is
no more exposed or condemned than is the social world she
is challenging, wooing, hoodwinking, defying; her own values are not more castigated than are those of the world she
aspires to. The book is a large and full-blooded novel by
virtue of its author's ability to create living characters and
memorable scenes; but however preeminent for its creation
of character, it remains of permanent serious interest for
its criticism of society. Partly from having got started with
his "Sketches," partly from borrowing Fielding's method of
interpolating little essays and intruding himself into the
story, Thackeray explicitly announces, at one point or another, the themes that he orchestrates and integrates in the
novel itself. Moreover, in such passages he sets not the
themes alone, but a tone—it is almost a tone of voice—that
would identify him anywhere. Consider him on the subject
of matrimony:

> What causes young people to "come out" but the noble am-
> bition of matrimony? What sends them trooping to watering
> places? What keeps them dancing till five o'clock in the
> morning through a whole mortal season? What causes them

to labor at pianoforte sonatas . . . and to play the harp if
they have handsome arms and neat elbows, but that they may
bring down some "desirable" young man? What causes
respectable parents to take up their carpets, set their houses
topsy-turvy, and spend a fifth of their year's income in ball
suppers and iced champagne? Is it sheer love of their species
and an unadulterated wish to see young people happy and
dancing? Psha! they want to marry their daughters.

Hear Thackeray again on the subject of rich relatives—
expectations, bequests, inheritances, disinheritances are of
the first importance in *Vanity Fair:*

> She is my aunt, say you, in an easy careless way, when
> your friends ask if Miss MacWhirter is any relative. Your
> wife is perpetually sending her little testimonies of affection;
> your little girls work endless worsted baskets, cushions and
> footstools for her. What a good fire there is in her room when
> she comes to pay you a visit, although your wife laces her
> stays without one. The house during her stay assumes a
> festive, neat, warm, jovial, snug appearance not visible at
> other seasons. You yourself, dear sir, forget to go to sleep
> after dinner and find yourself all of a sudden (though you
> invariably lose) very fond of a rubber. What good dinners
> you have—game every day, Malmsey-Madeira, and no end
> of fish from London.

And in giving us the way of the world in its materialistic
motivations, Thackeray gives us the lesser ways of the
world in the matter of class rituals and social habits; *Vanity
Fair*, preeminently a society morality play, is only a little
less a novel of manners. This, if we make allowances for
differences of decor, might come straight out of J. P. Marquand:

> The faithful chambers seem, as it were, to mourn the ab-
> sence of their masters. The turkey carpet has rolled itself up,
> and retired sulkily under the sideboard; the pictures have

hidden their faces behind old sheets of brown paper; the ceiling lamp is muffled up in a dismal sack of brown holland . . . the cellaret has lurked away behind the carpet; the chairs are turned up heads and tails along the walls; and in a dark corner opposite the statue is an old-fashioned crabbed knife-box, locked and sitting on a dumb waiter.

On the other hand, Thackeray's account of how the Rawdon Crawleys managed to live well "on nothing a year" has very much of a period air:

It was wonderful to see the pertinacity with which the washerwoman from Tooting brought the cart every Saturday, and her bills week after week. . . . Nobody, in fact, was paid, not the blacksmith who opened the lock, nor the glazier that mended the pane, nor the jobber who let the carriage, nor the groom who drove it, nor the butcher who provided the leg of mutton, nor the coals which roasted it, nor the cook who basted it, nor the servants who ate it; and this, I am given to understand, is not unfrequently the way in which people live elegantly on nothing a year.

Even in England, with its many caste survivals, few lower-class landlords today would long let themselves be exploited by upper-class tenants; or tradesmen in general extend unlimited credit. Today's hard-up person in society lives well on nothing, if he does at all, not in the privacy of his home but by giving publicity, by lending his name to what he wears or what hotel he favors or restaurant he frequents or champagne he drinks or airline or steamship line he uses: by making a walking advertisement of himself, or a high-styled sandwich board.

Thackeray, furthermore, is the great depicter, is, I think we may say designedly, the great English novelist of snobbery. It is not by accident that he gave the word its modern, as opposed to its earlier, signification. Until his day the snob stood opposed to the nob; the nob was the man with position, the snob the man seeking it; the nob sat high, the snob was the climber. The distinction comes out in Lord Steyne's speech to Becky on the subject of her own climbing, of her wanting a place at Steyne's wife's dinner table:

> You've got no money and you want to compete with those who have . . . All women are alike. You will go to Gaunt House . . . It's not half so nice as here. You'll be bored there. I am. My wife is as gay as Lady Macbeth, and my daughters as cheerful as Regan and Goneril. . . . Ho ho! You'll be asked to dinner next week. And *gare aux femmes*, look out and hold your own. How the women will bully you!

So much for what is actually derived, or might be, from the "Pen and Pencil Sketches of English Society" and for what gives *Vanity Fair* its thematic whalebone. All this, along with the constant incursion of puppet-show symbolism, has its bad side as well as its good: it makes for diffuseness in the way of narrative and didacticism in the matter of tone. It is not for nothing that Thackeray was descended from a family containing at least nineteen clergymen. But all this side of *Vanity Fair* makes for what is good and bad in the Victorian novel as a whole, one might almost say in the Victorian scheme of things. Yet *Vanity Fair* gives us, even where it is didactic, a feeling of largeness, equally in criticizing something as in creating. Partly by intruding himself, partly by using the pen and pencil sketches, Thackeray seems to amplify his theme, to magnify his picture, to multiply his people. The main characters are actually rather few, even if we include all the Crawleys; yet there is somehow an almost whirling sense of movement, of activity. If the plot were neater, the action less broken in upon, the driving force more purely creative, we should have, certainly, a finer novel, but perhaps a less genuinely spacious picture. And it may be that half the effectiveness of Becky Sharp lies in Thackeray's keeping her offstage for long stretches of time; consciously or not, we are always waiting for her to reappear.

Becky, besides being one of the great characters in English fiction, also seems to me an extremely useful *type* of character: her aims and ambitions, that is to say, enable the author to move in many directions and to traverse vast social distances. Such types doubtless tend to dominate the social novel: Tom Jones is, very notably, another of them. He is the warm-blooded young man who won't stay put and who, as he peers and pokes about, as he consorts with high and low, has picaresque adventures enough to achieve a kind of panoramic experience. Becky, the climber-adventuress, as she moves all over the social terrain, as she passes from one level of English society to another, opens all doors, if not always for herself, at least for the reader. And as she advances, she makes all the set moves whereby one conquest is but the prelude to another, one foothold but the stance for climbing higher. Thackeray does an exhaustive job with Becky, he thoroughly reveals so sleepless an opportunist through tremendously varying her opportunities; and he thoroughly reveals the nature of her role by exhibiting her equally among men and women; and by stressing how, with a Becky, it is the good women, the well-off married women, who at once discern the worst in her and encourage it, who at once see her for what she is and make her what she would not be. Here Lady Susan comes to mind. In the kingdom of worldliness those who are both rich and respectable have a power scarcely to be combatted. The spectacle, a thousand times repeated in Victorian fiction and drama, of the woman in good society gathering her daughters about her to create a tableau made of ice, as the adventuress, the bad woman, comes upon the scene, represents, more than all the haughty duchesses and high country-house walls, the real enemy in the social game of Victorian life.

For Becky, however, it was a perfectly legitimate enemy, since hers were from first to last illegitimate tactics. Save only Amelia for a long while, Becky fools none of the women she comes up against, and is by many of them instantly recognized for what she is. As a maneuverer, Becky hardly ranks amont the great *intrigantes*, though hers, most of the time, is a very difficult role, for she hasn't a shred of position, or the semblance of a protectress, or sixpence of capital, to help her along. Even among the men, George Osborne is in the early days against her, and Dobbin always. But if no consummate deceiver, she is remarkably convincing in her ability to please, in being in all kinds of ways useful or entertaining or sympathetic; in being, indeed, the perfect companion or nurse or hostess or *maîtresse-femme*. She is right in thinking—and it is a key remark—that "I could be a good woman if I had five thousand pounds a year." Had she position and security, she might be a very good woman indeed; for though unprincipled and heartless, she is good-humored, unmalicious, and unprejudiced in her views. She is a bad woman but not a petty one, just as she is a bad woman made worse by an uncoguid and class-ridden society. Though not a faithful wife, she made Rawdon till near the end a wonderfully good one; all in all, she had about equally the gift of brightening lives and blighting them, of making herself indispensable and making trouble for others.

It is easy to see Becky as bad and Amelia as good, the one as villainess and the other as heroine; and Thackeray himself lapses into homily and sentimentality about their roles, and such roles in general; but it seems to me naïve to accept any such distinctions inside the larger moral framework of the book itself. The book is often deplorably Victorian but it has at bottom a quite un-Victorian disillusionment and dryness of mouth; it sees life—or at least the varied, even the commodious life of the comfortable classes —as sunk in materialism and calculation and hypocrisy.

Thus Amelia, though so often sentimentalized, does not get off scot-free; it remains for the one person who is genuinely her moral superior, for Dobbin, not merely to diagram her behavior but also to denounce it, to upbraid her for her own kind of selfishness, as we might upbraid her for her own brand of Victorianism. There are moments when the virtues of the Victorians seem as unalluring as do the vices of a different era, and perhaps for a sound reason: the virtues of the Victorians can be inseparable from their vices. The Victorians fear God, but fear public opinion even more; to the degree that they are upright they tend to be intolerant; and in the name of morality and decorum, they close now their eyes and now their minds. More even than, in virtue's name, the Victorians were hypocritical, they were cruel—cruelly smug, cruelly snobbish, cruelly self-righteous. They had—so Becky might have reasoned—*their* tricks, their wiles, their defenses; and how much worse in the end were hers? Thackeray himself, unhappy at his public school, struggling in his early manhood not just to make a living but against actual want, and coming flush up against a system and a set of values that, for all he deplored and disparaged them, he all his life acquiesced in—Thackery himself must sometimes have shared Becky's psychology, if not her personal traits, and might at such times have said, like Flaubert of his Emma, "Becky Sharp is me." Thackeray too lived off his wits; he too—sharing Becky's gift for mimicry—parodied but also pandered; he too must have felt a colossal contempt for those he deferred to, if only for his being, like Becky, so much gayer, so much more gifted. But he was victimized by the very social canons that he held up to view and even to scorn. Hating snobbery, he yet led a kind of snob life, bowing at any rate to the code of the old school tie and the London club.

A hater of hypocrisy, like Fielding and Byron before him, he yet went halfway toward condoning it in the name of social decency, speaking indeed of "the decency of secrecy." And in prudishness and propriety he can be very Victorian wherever the printed word is concerned—"There are things," he writes, "we know . . . perfectly well in Vanity Fair, though we never speak of them." He is often—there seems no better word—genteel. He is very often—there is no better phrase than Frank Swinnerton's—a clubman of genius.

And yet, though his genteel timidities, his gift for cutting dead whatever seemed beyond the pale greatly limit him as a novelist in the finest sense, they also help him as the kind of novelist we here appraise him for. They make him at once the critic of worldliness and the spokesman; at once an analyst of Victorian manners and morals and their precise delineator. Many of the things that may detract from *Vanity Fair* as a novel add to its value and vividness as a document; moreover, in the matter of chronicling the social scene, Thackeray is as valuable where he accepts the faults of his period and his public as where he denounces them. *Vanity Fair* is an inside job, with the peculiar overtones of the ever-so-slight outsider. Since it was written, we have at various levels had repetitions in modern dress of it, or variations on it; even in America, its tradition continues in Scott Fitzgerald and J. P. Marquand and John O'Hara. It is interesting to recall that when Fitzgerald was asked about French influences on his work, he stressed that Thackeray had greatly influenced him since a boy.

Thus, in not telling the truth about the sexual lives of the Victorians, Thackeray *is* telling the truth about the Victorians themselves. The taboos of a society can be as revealing as its predominating traits; and from what is never allowed to appear on the surface we may often infer a sense of the depths. The sex life—in some cases, the lack of sex life—of the Victorians remains a subject of peculiar interest: consider, among writers alone, the case of Carlyle, Ruskin, Dickens, Mrs. Browning, Lewis Carroll, Rossetti, Swinburne, and how many others. It is worth remembering too that in Victorian times emotion as well as sex was suppressed; that there arose, side by side with the sentimentalism, a new English conception of "manliness," of the stiff upper lip and so on, which has left a strange backwash of sentimentality, infantilism, and essential *un*manliness.

From Thackeray we do not get, in the end, anything like the whole truth about universal human nature, but we do get, memorably, the truth about middle-class and very class-conscious Victorian England. We get a kind of gentleman's-eye-view of things, a view that is somewhat narrow, with the viewer somewhat blinkered; but what he sees, he sees with marvelous distinctness; and what he shows, he shows in superb detail. The detail, indeed, is superior to the design. Thackeray is not a great architect of fiction, partly because he seems an indifferent planner, because he moves rather from one situation to another than, by a charted route, to a predetermined end. Like Dickens and many Victorians, he was artistically penalized by the way he was professionally rewarded—his novels appearing first in serial form. The old writer's gag, "Had I had more time, this would have been shorter" is perhaps one key to the length of so much Victorian fiction. What we rather facilely speak of as the amazing energy of Victorians may often rest on the constant deadlines that serialization made necessary; as, again, it may have to do with the whole Victorian love of size, and taste for excess—three-decker novels went with triple window curtains and seven-course dinners. The result, in any case, compelled the writer to rely all too often on mass rather than form, on accumulation rather than intensity.

Whether by severe standards *Vanity Fair* is an altogether great novel may be open to question—though one might also question the questioning. But surely of very few other works of fiction would one say with such promptitude and certainty, "This is a novel," for at every level *Vanity Fair* provides much that each class of novel reader looks for. In the popular sense, which is never a despicable one, and which indeed has often kept valuable work alive when more critical audiences had buried it—consider all the years that Dickens was out of fashion—*Vanity Fair* has a narrative power, a vividness of characterization and a succession of imposing scenes that are hard, of their kind, to surpass. At a higher level, it offers much truth about human nature, a superb portrayal of manners, along with enough wit and sophistication of tone to give the book virtues far beyond its story or its storytelling. Applying the highest standards, one can easily, and properly, insist on how much more satisfying and distinguished *Vanity Fair* might have been had Thackeray's outlook been less genteel and his method more disciplined. Rather much of the book is told a little flabbily, rather much is left untold, rather much of a different sort *might* have been left untold. An ounce of moral vision would have been far better than the pound of moral sentiment Thackeray so often provided. But for all the little homilies and essays and personal intrusions, there is surely a vital point of view in *Vanity Fair,* as there is a unifying theme—indeed, the fullest development of that theme, and constant exploration of it. And there is a quick gift of characterizing, of bringing alive, someone in a sentence. Take George Osborne: he says of his wife, "I'm very fond of Amelia—I adore her, and that sort of thing." George is one of the successful characters, one of those about whom (except in his relations with women) Thackeray tells us the whole truth. Becky we have spoken of, and with her certainly we are given the whole truth, except in *her* relations with men. Only a novelist of great power and constant perceptiveness could create either one; but Thackeray creates someone else who is indeed, in sheer unforced undiminished realness, a triumph—I mean Rawdon Crawley. As for small touches, they are as telltale as the famous one of the little shirt for her son that Becky was carefully hemming for all to see, and that, says Thackeray, "had got to be too small for Rawdon long before it was finished." I bring in such touches, less in the way of merit than of appropriateness, for how they belong in a novel that shall portray and assess a whole social organism. Within its limits, *Vanity Fair* is a comprehensive picture of worldly living; within its limits, it is an incisive criticism of worldly life. It remains, in both the depreciatory and the admiring sense of the phrase, a monument of Victorian fiction.

XIII

BARCHESTER TOWERS

IN THE LITERATURE—AND THE LEGENDRY AND ICO-nography and anecdotage—of worldliness, no one comes in for more vivid notice than the clergyman. The notice may be particularly vivid for seeming so oddly out of place, the worldliness particularly striking from our expectation of spirituality. But, whether as realistic figures or satiric ones, as mitered priests or mendicant friars, as merely all-too-human figures or as hypocrites or aspirants to social position or ecclesiastical power—whether as one or another of these, or as more than just one, we encounter them again and again, in Shakespeare's Wolsey, in the great satires, and even the plays, of Dryden; nor can we forget Hogarth's fat, well-fed priest hugging his side of beef while a few yards off stands a gaunt, starving soldier. We remember from real life English bishops like Burnet, or French and Italian cardinals, who rose to high places, pulled strings, and sometimes governed thrones. Nor can we forget that

Swift was a dean who longed to become a bishop. As against these were the far smaller figures with ambitions much less formidable, who yet led lives of leisured piety in country vicarages and provincial towns, and fribbled and fox-hunted and won a place, and sometimes a life's partner, among the gentry. And nowhere are we so often reminded of the clergy enjoying this world's good things as in the English novel. The English novel being, above all, a novel of manners, it can hardly include a picnic or party without a clergyman; it cannot be set in a village and not give due place to the vicarage; it cannot portray an established family without its clerical younger son; it cannot raise a clamor over a local scandal or an issue like divorce without bringing in the voice of the Church. From the fashionable clergyman who draws great crowds for his magnetic preaching, the handsome clerical bachelor who is the prey of every matron with a marriageable daughter, the clergyman who went into orders to be given a bountiful living, to the ambitious time server and—witness Jane Austen's Mr. Collins—the silly snob, the English novel has a long procession of men of God who are hardly to be denominated men of godliness.

English literature offers us, for very good reasons, a clerical worldliness that is lived out in the world. That reason is England's prevailing Protestantism and the nature of its Church. Its clergyman, to begin with, may marry—which means live like other men, and like other men have families, and like other men wish their children to prosper and themselves to win a place in society. In the very forefront of this, moreover, stands that crucial figure, the clergyman's wife. Of her, more later; but the mere mention of her calls up a host of worldly situations and perplexities and plans. The Church of England is not, however, simply Protestant;

alongside its faith we must set its fortune. It is the established Church, and very much part of the English Establishment. It is the wealthy Church, the correct Church, the
fashionable Church—its bishops, and its bishops alone, sit
in the House of Lords; its cathedrals and its cathedrals
alone are the ecclesiastical monuments and the architec-
tural glories of England—that the greatest of them were
originally Roman Catholic is half-forgotten. But the Church
of England has almost always offered a certain comfort to
the mortal self as well as the immortal soul, has rather
looked askance at what in the eighteenth century was dero-
gated as "enthusiasm," has preferred the decorous to the too
devout, and modulated tones to fervent hallelujahs. With
the Church of England an immediate concern with the
higher life, an inflexible judgment against worldly temptation, has been a little frowned upon, has been associated
with Chapel rather than Church, with Dissenters and
cranks; and preaching in the wilderness has seemed going a
little too far, quite beyond the necessities of the grouse
moor and the hunting field. There have been no end of
genuinely devout and spiritual Anglican priests, some of
them great poets—John Donne in one way, George Herbert
in another; but during the long golden day that extended
from Augustan times to Edwardian ones, the Church of
England had a distinct social character, just as the House
of Commons and the two universities had a distinct social
character—which may help account for how decidedly the
English novel has had a distinct social character.

There has been a very decided social basis, moreover, for
wellborn young men becoming clergymen of the Church of
England. It was, as a matter of fact, one of the few fitting
things they *could* become. During a great many generations, the wellborn were debarred from what was called

"trade": even medicine and the law were not thought really suitable, though the law might perhaps be linked to a career in politics. But, except for the army and navy, or a seat in Parliament, the Church was the only pursuit open to a young man of standing. I say "pursuit," since in terms of his own inner feelings it could scarcely be called a vocation; and in terms of his not making concerted efforts to distinguish himself, it could scarcely be called a profession. A well-connected young man was assured of a living, something that could be bestowed on him by a relation or friend or neighbor who had it to give; and the young man's incumbency at St. Kilda's-in-the-Thicket did not prevent his gaining another living or two elsewhere. Thus a younger son went into the Church as another younger son, who was possibly more muscular or gregarious, went into the army; and with what his living brought in, and he might have from his father, he lived very well. If he had little from his father, he might still live well off the dowry that came with his wife. In some cases, where he had only his living to depend on, the incentive toward a career would be decisive. In some cases, he would have as little to rise with as to live off, and get nowhere.

Just as the Church was one of few suitable pursuits for a wellborn young man, it was one of the most desirable for young men of a different sort. It would naturally be so for those with truly religious feelings or spiritual ideals. These, and there were many such, really felt a vocation and, just so, are outside our purview. With a great many others, we may allow that a sense of vocation entered in, but that other considerations did also. A young man who was rather more scholarly than spiritual might take orders but live at the university, becoming a Fellow of an Oxford or Cambridge college as Dr. Arabin, in *Barchester Towers,* is. The combination of a clerical and an academic life was for a long time a tradition in England; as indeed there was a tradition of men of letters who had taken orders with or without occupying pulpits—the right to put Reverend in front of their names belonged to Donne, Herbert, Herrick, Swift, Sterne, Cowper, Coleridge, Kingsley, Lewis Carroll, and a number of others. As there has been a kind of clerical worldliness in English life which we shall examine in *Barchester Towers*, so—and it is worth a digression, since we shall not examine it elsewhere—there has been a particular kind of academic worldliness. The dons and Fellows at Oxford and Cambridge lived, in their own way, very snug; and in their own way looked about them very sharply. Their life was peculiarly circumscribed and, in tone and appearances, strangely celibate. But in the midst of their studies or their devotions they had a keen eye for their well-being and advancement; they played the insistent parochial politics native to institutions of learning; they gossiped, they insinuated, they conspired; they joined forces or horse-traded; they raised a decisive eyebrow or let drop a succulent remark; and all such plots and feuds and conspiracies could concern something more than their careers, could be half the business of their richly ascetic lives. They dined and drank well, and might rub shoulders with the great and the high-placed; they won recognition for their scholarship, they gained reputation for their wit; they had, some of them, their vices, and others their eccentricities; and one way or another, they made of their withdrawn way of life almost a kind of miniature great world, with just enough of material comfort and social elegance and political maneuver to endow the common room with the amenity of the drawing room, and the academic grove with the fierceness of the arena. It is partly what they stood for and jealously guarded during many generations that has made Oxford and Cambridge stand so haughtily apart from all other English universities, stand so haughtily above them in social prestige and the whole conception of the Establishment. For what has set them apart is rather something worldly than scholarly, is rather a lustrous appearance of learning than a profound love of it. Academic worldliness is of course ironic by its very nature, and so can be wonderfully comic in its manifestations. Almost all the novels written today about professors and campuses are too overtly satirical, often too obviously spiteful, for this; in general, American university life lacks the amenity, the aplomb, the practiced use of the saber, the superlative backhand strokes achieved during many generations at Oxford and Cambridge. Worldly motives abound in American colleges, but the methods are not very worldly; it is not the velvet glove that they feature, but the boxing glove.

To return from our digression—which is not altogether one, since in *Barchester Towers* not only is Mr. Arabin of the university as well as of the Church, but also the Master of Lazarus at Oxford plays a real part in getting Mr. Arabin made archdeacon—*Barchester Towers* is a novel wholly concerned with clerical politics and ambitions and pulling of strings, and with the life of the clergy in the community and in society. The clergy dominate the story, to begin with, from its being laid in a cathedral town; but as a cathedral town, Barchester is as distinctly a provincial capital as another town might be a provincial political capital or a banking or manufactuirng center. That is to say, the gradations of rank, the customs of society, the sources of gossip, the center of thought pivot as much on the Church as elsewhere they might on the Parliament House or the stock exchange. An ecclesiastical crisis is Barchester's biggest news. A clerical feud is Barchester's biggest social predicament. A clerical faux pas is Barchester's choicest gossip. An invitation to dine at the Bishop's can be Barchester's social event of the month; being left out of his garden party can be the social disaster of the year. Moreover, there are all the internal politics among the Barchester clergy themselves, who are as distinctly hierarchy men as there are organization men today.

Being a cathedral town, Barchester breathes a certain air of decorum that may seem to set it apart, though it is not easy for us, after a hundred years and more, and in America rather than England, to know in what degree this is clerical rather than provincial decorum, or, more than either, mid-Victorian. But it would not seem that the decorum has undue clerical roots. In a non-cathedral community, there might, to be sure, be more card playing and going to race meets; there would certainly be a greater sense of people in other professions, and of men in business and trade; but otherwise the atmosphere would seem to reflect a period provincialism. A young vicar might have to mind his morals very particularly; but in a mid-Victorian provincial town almost everyone had to mind his morals rather particularly. In any case, though a Barchester might be immensely concerned with church going, nothing in *Barchester Towers* suggests overwhelming feelings of piety; and though the Barchester clergy might be greatly occupied with religious observance and matters of doctrine and ritual, there is no sense of great religious dedication. If most of the clergy have a sincere sort of belief, on the ecclesiastical side they have also a sharp eye to business, and an eye turned outward, to living in the world. As members of the cloth, they wear the Church's uniform, and to a degree it conditions their behavior, not least toward their superiors;

but we cannot say, as we might of an army uniform, that it fully dominates their lives.

Barchester Towers, whatever shortcomings we may tax it with elsewhere, is a first-rate chronicle of clerical worldliness. It has the interest and, indeed, leaves the impression of a *social* novel. It reflects, to be sure, ecclesiastical issues that very much agitated the England of its time, or of just before that. We are not far distant from the Oxford Movement; and we breathe, right in Barchester, the air of High and Low Church factionalism; indeed, Trollope's novel, with Archdeacon Grantly on one side and Bishop Proudie on the other, divides into High and Low Church parties. The gauge of warfare is thrown down at the outset by Mrs. Proudie and Mr. Slope in the matter of Sabbath Schools and wanting to do away with Sabbath traveling on the railways. And the general High-Low issue—sometimes High enough to arouse cries of Romanism, sometimes Low enough to provoke mutterings of Chapel—was a very real and persistent one which over a long period bored into the lives of parishoners and communities. In the light of that, however, we can the better judge its relatively minor role in Trollope's novel. Principles exist, and for all the more reputable members of Trollope's clergy, principles enter in; but the preeminent struggles are for personal victories—for place, for domination, for power.

Barchester Towers is, to begin with, chiefly a social novel because of the ticklishly varying social positions of its clerical participants. Bishop Proudie, Mrs. Proudie, and Dr. Stanhope have connections with the peerage; Archdeacon Grantly is rich and locally wellborn; his father-in-law, Mr. Harding, is well enough born but not rich; Bishop Proudie's chaplain, Mr. Slope, is a fiercely ambitious parvenu; Dr. Arabin has sound roots and the prestige of Oxford behind him. The lesser clergy of the novel are, except for the Quiverfuls, significantly lesser *characters*, but the Quiverfuls are significantly so much at the bottom as to belong to another race—their hideous struggle to exist centers on feeding their half-starved bodies, not on holding up their heads in the world. They and their fourteen children stand for many clergymen's families, with no private income, no pastoral sinecures, no hope of preferment. There was a sharp dividing line between those in the Church who had incomes and connections and often several livings, and those for whom it was economically a struggle and socially an ordeal. Moreover, we cannot fail to note how the ill-fed Quiverfuls, as part of the plotting and politics of *Barchester Towers*, come hair's-breadth close to being tragically ill-used as well: they are more than pawns in a game of bishops and rooks; they are at moments outright catspaws.

Church politics here, if of final importance for personal ambitions and ecclesiastical policy, merge with drawing-room contretemps. *Barchester Towers* is in the great English tradition of the social novel by being often a comedy of manners, very particularly of bad manners. This means that, however prominent the clerical collar, the Victorian bustle will very likely be more so. Mary Bold is the heroine of the book, with all the hub-like position of a heroine. She is the daughter of Mr. Harding, round whom rages the matter of the wardenship he has resigned; she is the sister-in-law of Dr. Grantly, the wealthy, doughty, opinionated archdeacon in command of the established High Church forces; she is, as an attractive widow of means, the object of Mr. Slope's matrimonial attempts and of Bertie Stanhope's matrimonial scheming; and she is the object, finally, of Dr. Arabin's love and desire. But though she is the heroine of the book, she is no vital part of its social comedy or

political drama; it is Madeline Neroni and Mrs. Proudie
who are memorable on these accounts, the first as a kind of
disabled *femme fatale,* the other as a kind of overbearing
grande dame. Mrs. Proudie is by all odds the book's most
vivid character, and for long periods is its dramatic center,
for she is not only the Bishop's wife, with all that signifies
of social prestige, the Bishop is distinctly Mrs. Proudie's
husband, with all that implies, for her, of political power. It
is Mrs. Proudie who during most of the action cracks the
whip, or seizes it from whoever in defiance of her would
crack it; it is she who first sponsors Mr. Slope, who makes
up the Bishop's mind for him, or changes the Bishop's mind
for him, or at worst confuses or addles it. It is her Low
Church policies that both start the plot boiling and then let
it thicken. It is she, too, whom we have to thank for some of
the best comedy of bad manners, and even the drama. Mrs.
Proudie is an excellent kind of stage figure, whom Trollope
has tailored to a particular role: she has real convictions
about the Church and an interest in its concerns; she is not
at all frivolous and has no wish to be fashionable, nor to have
tea-table or dinner-party triumphs. Trollope tailors her,
however, for a particular role without depriving her of a
general one: of the dictatorial, interfering *grande dame,*
cousin if not sister to Jane Austen's Lady Catherine and
Wilde's Lady Bracknell.

Barchester Towers is a social novel, again, for portraying
clerical life in terms of community life, the two things in a
sense running parallel. A different kind of novelist, more
concerned with the emotions of contending churchmen,
with bigotry and tolerance, spiritual growth or decline, community life as a moral problem, poverty and suffering as a
moral responsibility, a clergyman's doubts as to his fitness
or his worries concerning his faith—a different kind of

novelist might make use of the community life to portray the clerical problems, or the clerical conscience, or the fight *against* worldliness and its temptations. And *it* would be very little a social novel. If *Barchester Towers* is very much one, the reason, very simply, is that Anthony Trollope is a social novelist. But that in no way denies the relevancy or truthfulness of his picture, or the fact that one whole side of the Church of England was a social organism and that in varying degrees a clergyman of that Church was a social animal. Dr. Stanhope is a prebendary of Barchester possessing two rectories and the cure of three parishes. Yet, says Trollope, "Years had now passed since he had done a day's duty"; and a moment later Trollope adds that "he had resided in Italy for twelve years." Indeed, he only reappears in Barchester from being summoned home by the crisis over the new Proudie scheme of things. This is an extreme example, but without its being in Victorian life a rare occurrence. What it points up first of all—whether they spend twelve years in Italy or in their own rectory gardens—is the more than worldly, the truly material nature of many clergymen's "livings." They were a genteel form of income, and often pure sinecures. They left one free to lead pretty much a life like everyone else, and pretty much a life of leisure. But even the clergyman of the Church of England who took his duties more seriously, or thought rather of career than of comfort, might by virtue of his birth, or the efforts of his wife, or the tenor of community living, be a full participant in social life, and as much influenced by rank or wealth or prestige as anyone else. That there is much more talk of parties in *Barchester Towers* than of prayer is one evidence of how true to life the book is. That Miss Thorne's fête champêtre occupies eighty pages of the book is, I grant, partly to be accounted for because it lets Trollope do a number of things, by way of story and background, that he wants to do. All the same, it truthfully illustrates the importance to the community of a party given by the most exalted member of it.

The hierarchical nature of clerical life in a cathedral town, with its own forms of rank and prestige, also brings into play the class structure of English life generally; it is not accidental that those in the upper strata of the hierarchy are in the upper strata of society as well, with most of the lesser clergy given just such walk-on roles as they would have occupied in Trollope's day. The great exception is Mr. Slope, and in Mr. Slope we get a good many of our thematic traits. We get first, in the best traditions of the social novel, the man on the make. But Mr. Slope is not simply a social climber who wants to make a good marriage and to sit at the right dinner tables; he is a clerical careerist who would sit very high in the Church and have not just position, but power. Mr. Slope is nothing more than Bishop Proudie's chaplain, and is that as Mrs. Proudie's protégé. Accordingly he needs to be a courtier as well as a politician; to insinuate himself to the point where he can manipulate others, then manipulate others to the point where he can install himself.

Climber and politician, he is also a hypocrite. I don't know that there is anything insincere in his Low Church views themselves; they may be his by inheritance or early conviction, and as a politician he must necessarily have joined a Church party. Or he may have veered toward Mrs. Proudie's tenets as part of her taking him up. But, however sincere, his clerical views must always ride pillion to his personal ambitions, and his views become blurred from looking in so many careerist directions at once. In any case, his doctrinal views are never reinforced by religious or ethical feelings, are not even tinged with honest bigotry. In the moral sense he seems, for being a churchman, all the more offensively ambitious and scheming. To be sure, his sliminess and utter lack of principle make him out at times almost too bad to be true, and almost too bad to be successful. Yet, overdrawn though he is, and tending though he may be to overreach himself, a good deal of him might be true, and the man as a whole is not untypical. But the psychological side of Mr. Slope, whatever its importance to Trollope's story, is not of great importance to our theme: what Mr. Slope tends to illustrate is a persisting ambitiousness in the Church of England's clergy. We have noted that side of it which supplied gracious livings to the better-born, enabling them to be, as it were, gentlemen of God. But like most established religious institutions, the Church of England has always had its great opportunities for career, has always been a ladder to power and a stairway to place, a mitered battleground and a cloistral arena. The Englishman is a political animal, often a very adroit and astute one, and at Cambridge or Canterbury no less than at Westminster. Mr. Slope is no Trollopian Tartuffe; he is a representative figure. Moreover, his own crudities and unprincipledness, recalling to us his difficulties as a flagrant outsider, remind us of the smoother worldliness, the more sanctified plotting of the Dr. Grantlys. The Church of England very particularly offers careers to gentlemen because it is the Church of gentlemen, the lower-born qualifying for more dissentient and nonconformist theologies. But, as the Church of gentlemen, it attracts those who, like Mr. Slope, want secular rewards as well as ecclesiastical power. For, as the Church of gentlemen, it is also the Church of wealth.

Of *Barchester Towers* as a novel I shall not speak at length. For one thing we must see and judge it as part of the whole run of Trollope's Barsetshire novels, beginning with *The Warden* and ending with *The Last Chronicles of Barsetshire*. Thus, unless we have read *The Warden,* which concerns the fight over Mr. Harding's wardenship, we do not know certain people in *Barchester Towers* so well as we might. This does not affect the virtues of *Barchester Towers* as a single work, but it does limit our sense of Trollope's talent as the creator of a very extensive world of his own. Like Balzac, or like Faulkner in our own day, Trollope uses people and places over and over again. Unlike Balzac and Faulkner, however, he is little concerned with what once was known as the passions, with the harsh dramas or darker visions of men. A Mr. Slope, with his tincture of the villain; a Mrs. Proudie, with her resemblance to a virago; a Mme Neroni, playing the temptress on her invalid's sofa— these are as dark figures as Trollope can offer us. If they do not create mere tempests in teapots, the fact remains that we are very little conscious in the novel of genuine tempests, and very much conscious of tea tables. In his many books, which vary more than we might suppose, Trollope does delineate, does in some degree explore, does very much preserve a world, does portray, beyond manners and customs, the prejudices and thoughts and opinions of a many-sided English social life. His storytelling, his borrowing from Fielding and Thackeray their habit of first-person interpolations, gives his fiction something rather noticeably fictional. Set him against Jane Austen, and there is much less subtlety and sensibility; against Thackeray, and there are fewer telling strokes; but there is about him, taking all his novels into consideration, something much more generally spacious, and there can be, as here, something more *specialized.* Jane Austen abounds in clergymen: one aspires to Elizabeth Bennet's hand, another to Emma Woodhouse's, a third marries Fanny Price, a fourth, Catherine Morland.

But Jane Austen never pictured a whole clerical world or ran quite the whole gamut of clerical worldliness.

Trollope's portrayal of it is often best suggested in his own words, whether the tone be comic or satiric, moral or factual. For example, when in Bishop Proudie's youth, more liberal ideas were permeating the country and "it appeared clear that high-church principles were no longer to be the surest claims to promotion," he acquired a Whiggish view of theology. "He bore," says Trollope, "with the idolatry of Rome, tolerated even the infidelity of Socinianism, and was hand in glove with the Presbyterian Synods of Scotland and Ulster." In much the same way we are introduced to the absentee Dr. Stanhope, summoned back from Italy: "As Dr. Stanhope was a clergyman, it may be supposed that his religious convictions made up a considerable part of his character; but this was not so. That he had religious convictions must be believed; but he rarely obtruded them, even on his children." And so for the others, until we have in Stanhope a clergyman with no feeling for his role, and in Slope one whose feeling is far too fanatical; in Bishop Proudie someone worldly-minded too soon, and in Arabin someone worldly-wise too late. As for our other two clerics of importance, one brief colloquy will do. Our not-at-all worldly Mr. Harding says to his importuning son-in-law: "I doubt if there is any true courage in squabbling for money." And Dr. Grantly answers: "If honest men did not squabble for money, in this wicked world of ours the dishonest men would get it all; and I do not see that the cause of virtue would be much improved."

Trollope's own attitude is the realist's, not the reformer's. He is conversant with the world he treats of, which he portrays in the form of comedy. He is in a fair degree critical of the world he treats of, which he impugns in the form of satire. He is not a master psychologist; he has no revolutionizing insights into man's inner nature. But he has much knowledge of general human nature and of how it is modified by particular environments and social climates. He knows our strongest desires and ambitions, our recurrent feelings and reactions, our likeliest masks and pretenses. He knows, above all, the Englishness of his people, which can mean all that is smug, ambitious, mealy-mouthed in Barchester, and in how many questionable ways these people can regard one another, judge one another, play-act for one another's benefit, conspire for one another's good or ill. His portrayal often constitutes an exposure but is almost never a protest. The impression he leaves is of social realism, social comedy, and satire—the way of the world in cathedrals as well as in clubs or country houses. And at times it offers, too, the way of the world among writers of fiction. "The end of a novel," Trollope begins the last chapter of *Barchester Towers*, "must be made up of sweetmeats and sugar-plums." This is but to echo the deliberately shameless happy ending of *The Beggar's Opera* and to make us feel, just a little, that the author has joined hands with his own main-chance characters. But the fault with Trollope is perhaps less moral than artistic; there is something of the mere storyteller about him as well as a much larger element of the novelist. Certainly *Barchester Towers* is a true novel. Some of its cathedral-town atmosphere and detail has been questioned; but to an outsider, and after the lapse of a century, it has, I think, documentary as well as dramatic truth about it—which is to say that while particular characters and scenes palpably smack of fiction, the general scene seems rooted in fact, as the comedy of it seems ringed with criticism.

XIV

WASHINGTON SQUARE

CERTAINLY NO NOVELIST IS MORE CELEBRATED THAN Henry James for delicate probing, subtle analysis, subterranean movement. We are often not just taken behind the scenes, but below the surface, moving among muted voices in dim-lighted rooms, among murmured obliquities, almost soundlessly ruffled undercurrents. It is the merest cliché that no novelist has in a certain sense more the quality of the subterranean, more the accent of the merely whispered; but none either, in a certain sense, possesses a quality more concrete; possesses a greater feeling for, or interest in, or mastery over the capturing and illuminating of *scene*. We know James, of course, as a greatly gifted travel writer, observing England, France, Italy, America; but the English, French, Italian, American scene also figures brilliantly and even decisively in his fiction—equally in terms of varied categories of culture and of the activities and attitudes of society. Scene figures in the most concrete way of all, in the way of material possessions, of things, of money, these in turn bespeaking status and rank. If there is something inward and downward, and often subtle and tenebrous, about the psychology of many James stories, there is something equally outward and richly visible and immensely concrete about their settings. One has a sense of piazzas and front parlors, of watering places and hotels, of country houses and palazzos, of dinner parties and balls; one has the vividest possible sense of London and Paris, of Venice and Rome, of New York and Boston. One has, in all its forms and observances, a sense of the world. James, indeed, ranks with the most informed and investigative portrayers of worldly life, and ranks no less as one of the great commentators on the *morality* of worldliness.

The morality of worldliness in James is not something that makes his treatment more overt or didactic than it exists in earlier writers; if anything, it is more ambivalent and complex. Fielding, the first important English novelist to treat thematically of leisure-class worldiness rather than of the dog-eat-dog kind—Fielding and his descendant Thackeray are far more explicitly didactic; and if James seems far more a moralist than, say, Jane Austen, this in the end is less a matter of didacticism than of dimension. Jane Austen, in her judgment of specific character or behavior or belief, is implacable; but this derives from her comic perceptiveness, her ironic reflectiveness, her satiric relish. Every patch of Jane Austen's little world has been carefully and very richly plowed; but the world is small, the soil pretty predictable and familiar, and in her sense of right and wrong there is little awareness of what we might call good and evil. These doubtless were part of a wider and duskier, a more violent and tormented world; a world, much of it, invoking a troubled chiaroscuro, a Gothic vision, a romantic guilt that Jane Austen, far from creating, might doubt or deride. But the duskier regions, the deeper intimations do, as we know, exist and, for all his specific worldliness in a Henry James, as in a Melville for all his symbolic whales. Again and again we find real villainy in James: sensitively cold characters, exquisitely cruel ones, and people whose deep betrayals are proportionate with their large temptations. The great world in James is brought into spectacular collision with the moral world; and James's subterranean quality has at its best some of the rumble and power of an earthquake. This vision of worldliness is what is sometimes so splendidly enlarging about James's fiction, as there is equally in him a melodrama of worldliness which can be grandiosely lurid. But in book after book involving worldly motives, desires, ambitions—whether early, as in *The Portrait of a Lady*, or very late, as in *The Wings of the Dove*, right and wrong become intertwined with good and evil, and along with moral impact we find moral perturbation.

There is one of James's novels, however, which without lacking a peculiarly Jamesian ground bass, is of worldliness all compact, is indeed in the artistic sense superbly compact, superbly organized—something which carries on from the manner of Jane Austen without repeating it; something with social aura enough to evoke a society, an age, a milieu, to be of its kind a beautiful period piece— which yet narrows down into an intensive story and study of a very few people. This is, of course, *Washington Square*.

Washington Square sufficiently carries on from Jane Austen for the three characters who assault its heroine's life to have very rough counterparts, if you will, in *Pride and Prejudice*. Very superficially Dr. Sloper is not too unlike Mr. Bennet, the mainspring of his ironic and cynical attitude being love for a wife who has died, as in Mr. Bennet it is loathing for one who has failed to. Mrs. Penniman, again, is as silly and romantically meddlesome as Mrs. Bennet is in more purely prosaic ways, and is as subject to contempt from her brother as Mrs. Bennet is from her husband; while Morris Townsend is as much a fortunehunter as Wickham, with much the same surface plausibility and charm. And though the setting is mid-nineteenth-century New York rather than an English county fifty years earlier, it offers much the same social characteristics—a compact and stable society; family and clan relationships of a set, old-fashioned sort; and a world in which well brought-up young girls are involved in innocent pursuits and subject to parental injunctions.

Where *Washington Square* quite differs from Jane Austen is first of all in its concentrated treatment, its severe unity of plot and theme. We deal, really, with Catherine Sloper in relationship to three people, and with nothing else. The social background is so beautifully implied that all we have need of is a very few minor characters and social occasions. In the same way, there are no subplots or secondary actions; breadth, range, populousness have everywhere been sacrificed to concentration. Hence what distinguishes *Washington Square* from Jane Austen in terms of structure comes to distinguish it equally in terms of tone. This story of a girl squeezed from three sides by three people, this story of a quietly passionate nature, of an "undiverted heart" splintered by three self-regarding minds—one given to romantic nonsense, one to realistic maneuver, one to chilling superiority—acquires a certain charge, a certain increase of feeling from the lack of feeling, or the false feeling, in the characters affecting Catherine. Social and material elements are outwardly as central here as in Jane

Austen, but they come to be James's framework rather than his texture, rather his source than his text; and where in Jane Austen the personal and the social life are blended, here we come to be held by a sense of individual destiny. The four people who make up James's story are, by their fewness no less than their force, vivid and distinct; they constitute—even Mrs. Penniman in her way—not social types but dramatic roles.

No outright stage directions could introduce them more pointedly. Catherine's father was "some fifty years of age; his popularity was at its height; he was very witty and he passed in the best society of New York for a man of the world—which indeed he was in a very sufficient degree." And James hastens to add: "He was not the least of a charlatan." Dr. Sloper's sister Mrs. Penniman had "a high standard of gentility . . . and a certain foolish indirectness and obliquity of character. She was romantic, she was senti-mental, she had a passion for little secrets and mysteries" and "she was not absolutely veracious." Knowing how ro-mantic his sister was, Dr. Sloper told himself that when his daughter was seventeen, his sister would "try and persuade her that some young man with a mustache is in love with her." And he added about Catherine herself: "It will be quite untrue; no young man, with a mustache or without, will ever be in love with Catherine."

Which brings us to Catherine, who, says James, was "not ugly—she had simply a plain, dull, gentle countenance"; she was "imperturbably good, affectionate, docile, obedient . . . extremely fond of her father and very much afraid of him . . . her deepest desire was to please him, her concep-tion of happiness was to know that she had succeeded." "Dr. Sloper," we are told, "would have liked to be proud of his daughter, but there was nothing to be proud of." From shyness Catherine seemed stolid, but in reality "she was the softest creature in the world."

She had from her mother some $10,000 a year—perhaps $30,000 in our money—and the prospect from her father of a great deal more. And being without a mother, having a father who sniffed at her and an aunt far less foster mother than matchmaker, Catherine was soon in the matchmaker's toils; for, meeting a handsome, attractive, attentive, virtually penniless young man at a party, Catherine was at once in love with him and seemingly much courted. Matters soon quicken, with Dr. Sloper inspecting young Townsend at dinner and deciding against him. By Dr. Sloper's standards, Morris is no gentleman, is too insinuating and familiar. Morris grasps the doctor's dislike of him at once—a dislike so great, her father soon tells Catherine, that should she marry Morris she will end their own relationship and be disinherited.

In this crisis in her life, this necessity to choose, Catherine's choice of Townsend is naturally approved of by her theater-minded aunt, who also suggests to Townsend that by marrying Catherine without her father's money he may win round her father as not having married for money at all. Townsend wonders, and is not reassured by Catherine when he lets the face of his venality peep from behind his mask of devotion. He thereafter postpones and procrastinates, enabling the doctor to take Catherine abroad on a trip that, intended to make her get over Townsend, only intensifies her feelings; but when she comes back, Morris is ready to break with her—$10,000 a year isn't a good enough match for him—and he does break with her in a scene that half breaks her heart. She grows older, she grows into an old maid, inherits a fifth of her father's fortune and lives on with her aunt in the Washington Square house, until when she is forty-five and Townsend has roamed and married and become unmarried and come back to New York, the aunt brings him back into Catherine's life, ready now—with his fortune still unmade—to make it with her. But she will have none of it; she has forgiven him but cannot forget how badly he treated her. "I felt it very much," she says, "I felt it for years"; and she dismisses him, and seats herself again with her fancy work—"for life, as it were."

Though Henry James excluded *Washington Square* from his great New York edition, it may conceivably be his best novel—which is not for a moment to say his greatest. That place I would assign to *The Wings of the Dove;* and there are other James novels much greater than *Washington Square,* or at any rate much richer. But *Washington Square* is that rare thing, an almost perfect piece of sustained writing, and one that makes no sacrifice of substance for the sake of form. Rather, along with the shapeliness and formal balance we associate with the minor classic, it has qualities found in more assured and robust works: a controlled intensity of forces and feelings, a way of moving the heart by striking quietly at the heart, and a moral pulse and current that bestow a certain stature on what might otherwise stop at shapeliness.

Thematically it is equally classic as cliché, that oldest of worldly melodramas about the heiress, the fortunehunter, and the disinheriting father. The plot and character relationships being as borrowed as anything in Greek tragedy, there is nothing unfamiliar we need learn or need adjust to: we even know, among other things, all the usual ways of developing such materials, and hence can the better approve or assail what James adds or subtracts, emphasizes or ignores. And if this is true with the conduct of the plot, how much truer will it be with the behavior of the characters and with the pattern of their relationships.

James's pattern beautifully concentrates the action among a very few characters and into vividly expressive scenes; better still, it quickly indicates what James is peculiarly about, which, despite how modest the book can be and how comic, is a kind of moral drama. For here, very simply, is Catherine, a girl with hidden depths of feeling, simple and shy, whom no one really sees or thinks of in terms of *herself*—which is crucial. Her aunt sees her as a vicarious romantic opportunity; Townsend sees her as a very unromantic opportunity; her father sees her without interest as a person and so uses her as almost a plaything, to be looked at with careless contemptuous intermittent curiosity, with more amusement than affection, with more disappointment than dislike—someone who, having no appeal to his feelings or his mind, becomes a mere object of his wit and creature of his will.

The reader will have noted that I ticked off Townsend's and Mrs. Penniman's attitudes toward Catherine in a few words, while needing a good many more just to start characterizing her father's. And he indeed is much the most complex character of the three, his much the most crucial role. Where Catherine's aunt is simply given to self-dramatization and Townsend altogether actuated by self-interest, Dr. Sloper is a figure of *selfishness*—a delicately chilled, sensitively brutal selfishness; above all, a kind of gratuitous selfishness. His judgments and motives about Catherine's romance are up to a point unexceptionable. He is correct about Townsend as a man, and doubtless equally so about what he would be as a husband. On a practical basis, he is a sound worldling and a proper father. On a human basis, a witty urbane man of the world who had a charming wife must be disappointed in a colorless daughter, must find her boring, must find himself very little involved. Where he is less right is in thinking he can understand her because she is nowhere complex, or can coerce her because she is nowhere rebellious; and where, of course, he is wholly wrong is in wanting to coerce her. It would be one thing to use all his influence and power of entreaty to keep Catherine from marrying Townsend; it is another to pass from pleadings and advice to ultimatums and penalties. Yet even here a certain kind of dense "heavy" father, however misguided, might be guided by affection, or feel he must make his daughter unhappy to spare her greater unhappiness. Dr. Sloper, however, is not deeply concerned with saving Catherine from unhappiness; and knows also that, if she gives up the marriage, he will bother very little *about* her unhappiness. At first sensible, his opposition becomes willful and altogether unfeeling. Even Townsend comes to see that the thought of being disinherited horrifies Catherine, not for being cut out of her father's will but for being cast out of her father's life. As for her father, he is almost for the first time interested in his daughter, but now only in the way of manipulation and management. He is not cruel from concern or selfish from love; he is all but pointlessly cruel, and turns disingenuous and unscrupulous into the bargain. When he tells Catherine that she should have spoken to him before getting engaged and she answers "It was because I was afraid you wouldn't like it," he pounces immediately with "Ah, there it is—you had a bad conscience"; and her "No, I have not a bad conscience, father!" is the key to his own motive; her being afraid is altogether the truth.

And because Dr. Sloper could not help knowing in what awe and dread Catherine held him, he must have known, for her to oppose him, how deep were her feelings for Townsend.

The opposition between the two is not a usual one, is indeed one reason why *Washington Square* is so successful; for the two are unyielding in terms of character, not just in point of view, are figures of drama and not of drawing-room allegory. James takes a relationship that could easily be sentimentalized or moralized over—the brilliant man of the world with everything except a heart, the unprepossessing daughter with almost nothing but one—and brings into play very subtle elements of sentiment and morality. Clifton Fadiman has remarked that the moral of the book is "To be right is not enough." And on Dr. Sloper's part, to be sure, an ounce of love for Catherine would be worth a pound of rightness about her. But there is more here than that, so much more that *that* can hardly be the moral. Dr. Sloper's peculiar selfishness lies in his displaying, in the absence of love, no fatherly wish to be right for *her* sake; it is almost as though he made use of being technically in the right to cause her pain; as though, in the knowledge that he was right, he was entitled to be cruel; as though, in his awareness that Townsend might break Catherine's heart, he himself was entitled to break it.

Though both Jane Austen's Mr. Bennet and James's Dr. Sloper are disappointed worldlings who find an outlet in cynical wit and a refuge in irony, they could hardly be more different. As a family man, Mr. Bennet is guilty of sins of omission, but in a pinch he always does from a sense of duty what he cannot from affection; he is not the first man so situated as to turn caustic in order not to be cruel. But where life has put vinegar in Mr. Bennet's blood, it has turned Dr. Sloper's to ice. There is a sin of commission in him, and in the absence of love, nothing compassionate or in the best sense fatherly. Where Mr. Bennet's enjoyment of everything stupid, fatuous, vulgar, boring is simply a spectator sport, Dr. Sloper makes himself a willful participant in a game played not for fun but for very high stakes. That the opponent is a callous fortunehunter cannot obscure the fact that Dr. Sloper turns the real center of interest, a plain girl passionately in love, into a football. And indeed we cannot so much look back from Dr. Sloper to Mr. Bennet as look forward to Henry James's own Gilbert Osmond in *The Portrait of a Lady*, who in a sense is Dr. Sloper plus Morris Townsend, is at once an overrefined cold-hearted man of the world and a conspiring fortunehunter.

But, however vital the relationship between Catherine and her father, the full dramatic force of *Washington Square* derives from Catherine's being menaced and closed in upon from three sides, from the convergence upon her of three people, from her own isolation in struggle, her aloneness in suffering. If the least ill-meaning of the three is the aunt, just there we see how vulnerable Catherine is, for the person who signifies help proves an instrument of harm, and a foolish ally when not a false one. James is often deliciously amusing about this romantic-minded, meddlesome fool. "You must act, my dear!" she tells Catherine. "In your situation the great thing is to act"; and, hoping for a secret marriage between Catherine and Morris, "she had a vision of the ceremony being performed in some subterranean chapel; and of the guilty couple—she liked to think of poor Catherine and her suitor as the guilty couple—being shuffled away in a fast-whirling vehicle to some obscure lodging in the suburbs, where she would pay them (in a thick veil) clandestine visits."

But if Mrs. Penniman's is the lightest and slackest of the

244 / THE POLISHED SURFACE

converging lines, it yet decidedly helps hem Catherine in. To Morris Townsend's classic role James brings nothing very distinctive: he gives Townsend the surface charm and sophistication and the play-acting patience that would captivate a girl like Catherine; he is not made, in his manner, too stagy, or in his cruelty, which is one of pure self-interest, too base. But his being a set traditional role, it is what he arouses in Catherine and instigates in her father that count most with him. As for Catherine herself, James has drawn her with a fine perception and understanding; has known to just what degree this girl can summon up, out of inarticulate helplessness, the courage to act; has made, of what can never be a matching of wits with her father, a measuring of wills. James gives us, and makes us see, the strength of Catherine's limitations,that sense and growth of character in her that is all the greater for a lack of personality and intellect, and that by the *fact* of its dullness has immense dignity. Catherine, insensibly, becomes more because of everything she is not, as her father becomes less because of everything he is; and, though carried too far, this kind of antithetical judgment can become a sentimental one, on its own terms, and, allowing for its own irony, it is a real facet of the morality of worldliness. James, incidentally, far from sentimentalizing Catherine, says of her refusing to mope in the midst of her misfortunes: "She was really too modest for consistent pathos." And if too modest for self-pity, she was equally so for resonant self-assertion. Just there the play that was made from *Washington Square* went crucially wrong: for most of the way very faithful to James, *The Heiress* had Catherine, at the end, lure Townsend into *thinking* she would have him in middle age, in order to turn the tables on him and give him a highly theatrical dismissal. But of such assertiveness, such guile, such retaliation Catherine was quite incapable, not just because something far deeper than her vanity had been bruised, but because her life had been sealed of the event. Love had burned something away in her, leaving her not vindictive but destitute.

Catherine at the end catches the light impressively if still modestly, and from a simple, partly moral, contrast between herself and the tissue of worldly values that shaped and misshaped her life. The worldly irony is that none of the worldlings, any more than Catherine herself, has really been victorious. But there is something besides worldly irony in *Washington Square;* its own severity of form, its not stressing period manners, its going beyond mere period situations, makes for a graver final effect. This is a love story of a peculiar kind; not any of those unfulfilled love stories we are familiar with—the patient Griseldas, the "She never told her love"s, the lovers frustrated by religious scruples, or social gulfs, or family feuds, or inconvenient spouses; not, either, of a parent's love in conflict with a suitor's. This is a love story in which only one person involved is capable of love, where the parent no more is than the suitor, and where love burns fiercely and lingeringly to no avail. The framework of old New York, with its period-piece overtones, holds everything in place, but what it frames is not just lightly drawn on the plane of worldly manners; it is etched in something deeper, and that provokes a strong response.

XV

EDITH WHARTON: *THE AGE OF INNOCENCE* AND *THE HOUSE OF MIRTH*

ONCE LOOKING BACK FIFTY YEARS, ONCE LOOKING out at what directly met her eye, Edith Wharton wrote two novels that today are equally notable period studies of New York society. Whatever their fictional shortcomings, they provide unsurpassed portraits of a compact social world, an established social "order," at two differing stages of its existence—*The Age of Innocence* (1920), treating of the 1870's, and *The House of Mirth* (1905), set at the turn of the century. They possess, moreover, a further interest because Mrs. Wharton herself wrote them fifteen years apart, in moods that differentiate something in her approach as well as in her subject matter. Their chronology is not hers—the earlier period was the later novel; but *their* chronology is the one to follow since it reveals how, and how much, New York society underwent change, and how, and how powerfully—even in reverse—Mrs. Wharton had recorded the changes. No other American has written with such knowledge and penetration, and at the same time such intensiveness, of a consciously operating, magisterially legislating social group. Its horizons may expand or contract at times, but its center remains fixed; its ranks may open or close, but its rules remain punitively sovereign.

The Age of Innocence is so notable for its evocation of milieu and its anatomy of a reigning caste that, before concentrating on them, it seems sensible to confess that one whole side of the novel is too fictional, and at moments even sentimental, in its appeal. The book, I suspect, has made many addicts of circulating-library fiction now rather snobbishly and now rather tearfully happy; they have reveled in a detailed picture of high society; they have sighed over Newland Archer's and Ellen Olenska's romantic passion and dabbed at their eyes over its renunciatory end. For the narrative—like so many notable ones, *Gulliver's Travels*, *Pride and Prejudice*, *Vanity Fair*—can be thoroughly enjoyed without any infusion of irony. Also, I doubt whether the Countess Olenska is entirely convincing. As a storybook figure, she is vivid and touching; as a symbol of an opposed way of life, she pulls her weight: she is gay and cosmopolitan and cultivated in a sense that old New York is not, and is far too smug to want to be. She knows that the right people in New York are the wrong people, though of course she has suffered in the past at the hands of too much sophistication as she is penalized now by too little. But she comes off a touch too noble, far more scarred by life than stained. At the end she would give herself to Newland Archer, but only in token of farewell; and she never does. To be sure, there are scruples involved for Mme Olenska, for Newland is married to her cousin. But at times it seems less Mme Olenska who draws the line than Mrs. Wharton.

But in spite of storybook touches and a rather storybook heroine, *The Age of Innocence* tells an apt and, in terms of treatment, most certainly an adroit story. Apt, because it dramatizes the point of view, indeed the whole ritualized way of life, of a definite class during a definite period. And the book is very adroit: were our principal concern one of narrative, we could profitably analyze the skill with which Mrs. Wharton creates her situations, advances her story, and combines elegance of manner with sureness of pace. She may not be quite the master of the art of narrative that we find in a different sort of New York period novel, more severe in form and economical in movement—in Henry James's *Washington Square*. But as a storyteller she has more allure, from her nostalgically photographic use of background; and she has more appeal, from her always making the social situation a human situation, and from her making the period itself a decisive element of the plot.

That *The Age of Innocence* is preeminently an appraisal of a period society is clear from the very title. It is with a particular age and what that age was aware and unaware of, capable and incapable of, tolerant and tyrannical about, that Mrs. Wharton is most concerned. Purely as fiction, she has told a romantic story against a picturesque background; but in terms of social mass and weight, the book's interests are as realistic as its implications are ironic. Mrs. Wharton is as informed about everything as an Emily Post and as informative as a Baedeker. Here we are told of a grand-style dinner party, "with a hired chef and two borrowed footmen, with Roman punch, roses from Henderson's, and menus on gilt-edged cards"—and the fact that Roman punch signified "either canvasbacks or terrapin, two soups and a hot and a cold sweet." Elsewhere we catch the atmosphere of the Welland household, of "the heavy carpets and watchful servants, the perpetually reminding tick of disciplined clocks, the perpetually renewed stack of cards and invitations on the hall table."

It is indeed such families as the Wellands—their fetishes, the social and tribal marks that bind them together, bind them legs and arms against free movement—that are challenged here. Old New York, a backdrop for a *Washington Square*, is the arena of *The Age of Innocence*. The title has its layers of ironic meaning: closest to Sir Joshua's picture is the *couleur de rose* outlook on life of the May Wellands of the period. The next layer is the period's pretense of innocence, its trick of looking the other way or in a pinch looking straight through what lies in front of it. But even beyond *appearing* innocent as a way of seeming ignorant, the age used innocence as a way of cultivating ignorance—of remaining, in its myopically well-bred fashion, as provincial and even parochial, as unenlightened and even prejudiced, as unruffled and even indifferent, as conventional and even philistine, as it could readily be. The ignorance of this old New York, where it is not dissimulation, is chiefly smugness. "Ah, no," Archer reflected in terms of his fiancée, "he did not want May to have the innocence that seals the mind against imagination and the heart against experience!"

Mrs. Wharton's intensive picture is wonderfully exact. Much of it, moreover, is done lethally for being done lovingly: in places it can be almost as wistful as it is ironic, and it is as passingly given to extenuation as ultimately to indictment. It is a very comfortable world should it not happen to be stifling. It has its own laws, and woe betide whoever breaks them; but equally its own loyalties—an *esprit de corps* if never quite a *noblesse oblige*. It has its own dexterities, the ability to make an art of trifles, or a historical fabric, a genealogical edifice, of gossip. It has a feeling for tradition, that most enriching but also most enfeebling aspect of settled societies—which is to say that it has little awareness of where a tradition boasts patina and where it merely embalms prejudice, of where it invokes generous sentiments and where it enforces narrow views. Above all, along with its brutal decrees go its graceful pretenses, as in the farewell party to Mme Olenska, a solicitously affectionate way of ushering out those whom it is set against letting in.

Such a society as this reduces life in a great city to the dimensions of an affluent, privileged village: in the same degree that it recoils from the crude, it distrusts the cosmopolitan. And such a society is as omnipresent in the unfolding of *The Age of Innocence* as it is omnipotent concerning the outcome. The triangle story of Newland Archer, May Welland, whom he marries, and Ellen Olenska, whom he gives up, dramatizes the predicament of the decently sensitive, potentially superior young man of the 1870's who is pulled two ways. At the story level, the alternatives for Archer are a pleasant conventional marriage and an exciting, liberating *grande passion*. But they mean more than the gilded provincial cage as against wide and uncramped vistas, they mean acquiescence as against inquiry, placid subsistence as against positive involvement, society as against, indeed, selfhood. It should be noted that Newland Archer must not just combat external social pressures, he must overcome his own belief in their validity. We have not here that war, so common to fiction, between the respectable world and the rebellious nature; we have rather a civil war within a divided nature; a conflict involving how far the worldly advantages Archer enjoys are an armor, and how far they are a straitjacket. In all this, Newland Archer, like others of Mrs. Wharton's characters, plainly represents something in Mrs. Wharton herself—one of her own pulled-two-ways attitudes toward an established place in society; and *The Age of Innocence,* published when she was nearly sixty, is almost the last time in her fiction that she more strongly attacked her old New York world than she defended it. Thereafter, she was to contrast this world not with an Ellen Olenska's larger and freer one, but with, instead, the social pattern that began to emerge after the Civil War, with its unblushing materialism, its parvenu vulgarians, its ruthless buccaneers. Old New York stands here in menacing relation to Newland Archer as already in *The Custom of the Country* (1913), Mrs. Wharton's Undine Spragg would stand symbolically in relation to old New York.

Old New York is, at any rate, the nearest thing to a villain in *The Age of Innocence,* for there are no villains among its characters. Ellen Olenska's behavior is little short of noble, and May Welland can be condemned only so far as the world that formed her can be. *The Age of Innocence* deals finally much less with human beings than with social products: it disparages their way of life rather than themselves, it exposes their ideals as the merest lacquering of their expediencies, it dramatizes their habits as indications of their horizons. The personal pronoun, in all this, may strut at times or declaim, but it is the collective noun that always punishes and decrees.

Newland Archer is most victimized by what is best in New York society, for it is what is virtuous in the old point of view that comes increasingly to impress and influence Ellen Olenska. Newland and she are at once each other's teacher and pupil: here, to some degree, we have another *Thaïs,* another novel—in E. M. Forster's phrase—with the shape of an hourglass; for the more Newland is liberated by Ellen's approach to life, the more is she inhibited by his, so that when he is finally ready to bolt, she seems scarcely able to. If the irony of this is effective, it is also a little factitious and pat; for where Newland needs only to be roused—in this case, by love—to gain a larger perspective, Ellen is not so easily to be exalted by love as to accept the ruinous smug morality of old New York. As she is less real than May Welland, so in the end she is less crucial. Deeply grateful Ellen may be to her New York relations who have taken her in, but unless they have taken her in in a different sense, how can her gratitude outweigh her love for Newland? (That premonitions of his guilt or regrets, should he run off with her, might subconsciously color Ellen's thoughts, Mrs. Wharton never hints.) More is involved in Ellen than doubtful characterization; there is the deterministic burden of the plot, with its *need* to keep Ellen and Newland finally apart.

The final determinant, to be sure, is neither Ellen nor Newland, but May—May with her coming child, and her riveting Newland with an appeal to decency and duty. If, simply in terms of the conveniently timed baby, the denouement seems stock, the cards seem stacked, essentially the hand *is* played out on classic lines, for May represents, in a pleasantly persuasive form, a morality not easily withstood. She stands for what Newland has been brought up to seek and cherish in a wife; she stands, too, for a certain instinctive shrewdness that goes with her official innocence: if the hand inside her velvet glove can never become a claw, the glove itself counts most because by way of it May never *shows* her hand. And just as she never shows her hand, May never raises her voice: by avoiding scenes she prevents a showdown; by not upbraiding Newland she puts him, and not herself, in the wrong. Her power resides in her pathos, her ultimate strength in her pretending to have none. This is not to be cynical about the May Wellands. What such women fight for is not just what they want, but what they truly believe in; and their judgment of what lies beyond their horizons can bespeak lack of imagination rather than want of heart, and a sense of horror rather than a show of hypocrisy. Their innocence constitutes the trump card of their worldliness: among other things, it saves them from having to scrutinize and dissect their moral dilemmas— Right for them is Right, and Wrong is Wrong, and never the twain shall meet, even to talk things over. Most matters are indeed so crystal clear for them as to deny any need for dilemmas in others; and when matters are not, an appeal can be made to Mr. and Mrs. Henry van der Luyden, exactly as with religious questions an appeal can be made to one's bishop.

For just such a personal story as this, the 1870's are perhaps the *locus classicus*, for they represent the moment when New York's tightly woven society had particular power and sway, being enough unthreatened to feel peculiarly assured, and more self-righteously than self-defensively cruel. Such a society might tolerate an occasional climber, as one would a personal pet; and behind closed doors, which is to say behind high tribal walls, could relish its own contretemps and scandals. By the 1880's the great new fortunes and the gaudy new journalism were fast altering the nature of things; the time was passing when matters were inbred and thoroughbred enough for a look or a gesture to communicate everything, even excommunication or doom.

Readers of that admirably full, honest *Diary* of George Templeton Strong, with its detailed picture of upper-class

New York life and thought from the 1840's through the 1870's, may agree with me and,—I have just discovered, with Louis Auchincloss in an introduction he has written for *The Age of Innocence*—that, though no Mme Olenska appears in Strong's life, the life itself has much to suggest at times a Newland Archer. Here we have a conventionally intelligent, cultivated man, a lawyer, with period rather than personal good taste, who serves on the boards of universities and orchestras, who represents what is most upright in society while revealing how unenlightened and even unventilated that society—and sometimes he with it —can be. In what is good about George Strong we too often feel the need of something better. His mind, not being very porous, in time grows less perceptive; his strength of character takes on, in time, aspects of intolerance. One recognizes in Strong facets of what Newland was, and senses, too, what Newland would become.

It is the individual in Newland that is never really freed —indeed, is never really formed; and for preventing this Mrs. Wharton's old New York was most dangerous and culpable. "A frivolous society," she herself once wrote, "can acquire dramatic significance only through what its frivolity destroys." And if the frivolity of champagne and dancing till dawn is not what first comes to mind for a world reigned over by Mr. and Mrs. Henry van der Luyden, in the intellectual sense that world *was* frivolous, as in the human sense shallow, and in the moral sense evasive. Rather than the cynicism of the shrugged shoulder, we find here the hypocrisy of the averted gaze. Such a society made puppets of its people; above all, by making moral appearances sovereign, it slowly diminished what might exist of genuine moral concern.

Mrs. Wharton said of George Eliot that she "vibrated to

nuances of conduct" as does an artist to subtleties of line and color; and so in a way did Mrs. Wharton herself, in terms of manners and tribal customs. In American fiction Mrs. Wharton stands unsurpassed at her best in the treatment of upper-class manners and in what they express and expose and signify, whether as a formal tradition or a worldly reading of life. In *The Age of Innocence* she provides us, moreover, with a somewhat yellowed balance sheet where, in a spidery hand, are entered the pluses and minuses, the assets and liabilities, of a way of life greatly benefiting an establishment at the cost of the individual. In such a world violence is quite alien, conflict consistently muffled. There was an assured, delicate finish to old New York's procedures—in its tactics, if nowhere else, it perfected an art. And though *The Age of Innocence* has real weaknesses as a work of fiction, as a picture of a society it possesses all the assured, delicate finish that it portrays.

It is in Mrs. Wharton's earlier novel that we confront New York society on wholly realistic terms, and find it subjected to a quite merciless scrutiny. The period of *The House of Mirth*—the opening years of the twentieth century —possesses today almost as much sense of period as does *The Age of Innocence:* we move about a New York where hansom cabs and smart C-spring barouches still vastly outnumber cars, where Sherry's is the recognized place for tea, and small apartment buildings for bachelors are called "flat-houses"; and where, indeed, there are as many months when the world of society flees the city as flourishes in it. And society itself, though distinct inroads have been made on the correctness of its manners and the roster of its membership, is still an identifiable and despotic collective force, not only for those waiting to get in or being shown the way out, but even for those who are at home in its drawing rooms. The social chronicler will find almost as much that is historical here as in *The Age of Innocence;* and we, indeed, are farther from this scene than was Mrs. Wharton, when she wrote *The Age of Innocence,* from the 1870's. But Mrs. Wharton made the seventies faintly aromatic even as she distilled the deadly nightshade lurking within them; she made them nostalgic even as she pierced beneath atmosphere to airlessness. Indeed, Mrs. Wharton made almost everything ironic by first making a good deal of it, in places, sympathetic. And in *The Age of Innocence* Mrs. Wharton did offer something not poisonous, however petrifying, and did provide, in however wry a form, the nosegay of romance and the sachet of renunciation.

But there is nothing aromatic about *The House of Mirth;* nothing even ambivalent, nothing to suggest, with the passing of the world it portrays, the possibility of a certain loss as well as gain. *The House of Mirth,* as we shall note later on, has in its storytelling a good deal that suggests the theater; but the theater comes immediately to mind in the matter of the book's stage lighting, in its insistence on a kind of hard pitiless naturalistic glare. The light, even when it envelops the whole fashionably elegant stage set, confers no radiance, kindles no charm. And when it spotlights a face or highlights a scene, it leaves nothing in shadow, it makes everything prominent. In *The Age of Innocence* Mrs. Wharton bids us distrust the glow; here we cannot for a moment avoid the glare.

In *The Age of Innocence,* moreover, Mrs. Wharton was writing of what was historical for *her;* of scenes, at most, during her childhood—scenes that her childhood prevented her from witnessing. In *The House of Mirth* she wrote of something very actual and immediate; of a world she knew from the inside, of people she perhaps knew by their real first names; of a whole code of manners and morals that she had absorbed and practiced, but had also challenged and increasingly condemned. Here, in any case, under a battery of lights and a barrage of body blows, that world was to be actively challenged, was to be unequivocally condemned. Much of the time, in reading *The Age of Innocence,* we regard society—for all we understand its sheathed force and sway—as a smug barrier, a stupid obstacle, or even a luxurious prison house. But in *The House of Mirth* we are at once conscious of it as a formidable living antagonist. In *The Age of Innocence* we are aware of society's limitations and how deadening its genteel edicts can prove; here we are soon aware of its positive faults and how destructive are its decrees. Where in *The Age of Innocence* society insists on certain personal sacrifices and caste primacies, here it engenders moral difficulties and enforces heartless laws. There is something sacred, to society itself, about the boundaries in *The Age of Innocence;* there is something callously secular about them in *The House of Mirth.* We never encounter either the aura that deceives or the aura that faintly justifies.

The lack of aura in *The House of Mirth* partly derives from its wealth of hard-earned knowledge, from Mrs. Wharton's direct view and deep-graven memories. But what counts as much here as her writing at first hand is what she is writing about. This is Lily Bart's story always; nothing happens in it that does not bear on her; indeed, the merest dinner party she does not attend, or house party she isn't invited to, concerns her all the more—and all the more menacingly—because she isn't there. But always joined to the fact that Lily in the fullest sense is the protagonist is the fact that Lily in the most crucial sense is poor. And that being true, in the most crucial sense society itself becomes the antagonist of the book; society can be the dominion wherein Lily reigns, or the ally that facilitates her reigning, or the enemy that thwarts or forbids it. Society plays no background part, ever, in this picture: even to call it foreground tends to make it seem inanimate, where it is always fiercely alive and immediate.

We are accustomed, of course, to describe vast numbers of novels as portraying the relation of the individual to society, the struggle of the individual against society, the disablement or defeat of the individual at the hands of society. But though we can scarcely find anywhere a human being more at grips with society than in *The House of Mirth*, the modern descriptive formula uses the word in a larger and looser sense than it can be used here; makes it a caption word for all the broad forces, pressures, impediments of modern life; for something with strong pinioning arms and a deep condemnatory voice, but without a face. And the "individual" that we see pitted against it is someone with seldom adequate fists or a sufficiently clamorous voice who is yet struggling to master the obstacles of life, to resist the pressures, to endure the blows, and to emerge, if not unscarred, at least intact in spirit, unwhipped in will. In novels involving a genuine individual who does combat society, he stands forth the hero; in more determinist novels where he simply struggles against his fate, he stands forth a victim. But in both instances, society is a covering word for various hostile forces, and the individual is opposed to much that is as shadowy as it is massive, and that he is powerless to strike out at because it never comes within striking distance; because it constitutes a historical force or economic imperative.

But however determinist the mood of the book, the fierce

animate opposition in *The House of Mirth* is not of this kind. There is nothing shadowy about Lily Bart's world, nothing that Lily finds it powerless to strike out at for its being beyond her reach. Here is a world that not just she— but you or I—could accurately blueprint; could provide with a history and a geography and a philosophy; and an itinerary for March or May or October; and a dinner-party menu; and a visiting list. It is self-enclosed and fully enclosed, with here and there a side-door entrance, or a back-door exit, or a secret passage. It is self-governed and tyrannically governed, with now and then a law that can be ignored, or with a suspended sentence or a show of clemency. And more important than its history or geography is its morality: its inscribed Thou Shalt Nots, its placards of Proceed at Your Peril, its unwritten laws that need not be written, so widely are they known; its uncodified reactions that cannot be codified, so much do they depend upon circumstance. Moreover, inflexible though this morality is, it contains a kind of escape clause—a kind of dissolvent of its iron laws in the form of gold.

The House of Mirth is very explicit, is almost aphoristic, about this world of Lily Bart's and the people in it. There is the extremely rich and rigid—and proper-minded and small-minded—Mrs. Gryce, who, Mrs. Wharton tells us,

> had a kind of impersonal benevolence: cases of individual need she regarded with suspicion, but she subscribed to Institutions when their annual reports showed an impressive surplus. Her domestic duties were manifold, for they extended from furtive inspections of the servants' bedrooms to unannounced descents to the cellar.

Or we have simply a picture of Mrs. Trenor, as a great weekend-party hostess, who had left the card table

clutching such a heap of bills that she had been unable to
shake hands with her guests when they bade her good night.

It is a world whose poorer but eligible members approached
"a hall table showered with square envelopes which were
opened in haste, and oblong envelopes that were allowed to
gather dust in the depths of a bronze jar"; a world in which
the rich, says Mrs. Wharton, "may not be thinking of money
but are breathing it all the time." As for the not-rich people,
the only way to keep a footing in society, Lily is told, "is to
fight it on its own terms—and above all, my dear, not
alone." And to conclude with its First, or its Eleventh,
Commandment, with the very essence of its moral code, a
woman's husband is the sole judge of her conduct; so long
as he condones it, society will.

This, then, is Lily Bart's world; and her difficulty, as a
member of it, is a lack of means, not of position; no familiar How to Succeed, but a much less common How Not to
Fail. This gives the book a special value. In *Vanity Fair,*
which probably remains the classic novel of worldly means
and ends, the heroine is an outsider and an intrigante; we
watch her knocking not at one door but at a whole succession of them, invading not one but every level of society. In
all this beautifully defined account of a shifting, many-lay-
ered society, Becky's own position is necessarily shifting
too; but hers is always in its methods an assault, in its
maneuvers a campaign; and hers is almost always a double
problem, equally economic and social. On such grounds
there consequently exists a double or two-way morality.
Society owes Becky nothing on personal terms—she is an
outsider; and nothing on humane or ethical terms—she
herself is ruthless and unprincipled.

Lily Bart, as the poor, high-principled girl *in* society—

much more tellingly than Becky as the poor unprincipled girl out of it—reveals its essential nature, since it owes her something on personal terms and on ethical terms alike. But, given Lily, the situations from the outset are double-edged in a way they never are, given Becky, in *Vanity Fair*. For, however arduous, Becky's problem, of wanting to succeed, is perfectly straightforward; and the business for her of How to Succeed—which is by all possible means, fair or foul, guile or grit, the bedroom or the drawing room, the enemy charmed or the friend betrayed—is straightforward also. Becky's problem is to know how to disarm or outwit. She doesn't always *know* how, but it remains throughout a master plan. With Lily, however, we have neither a single-minded objective nor an undivided nature; we have, instead, highly conflicting personal qualities and often opposed personal desires. Just this aggravates the problem of How Not to Fail, for always what Lily wants, without failing socially, is not to fail herself, not to compromise her finer instincts. She is very believably represented as, even after ten years in society, a beautiful woman of great poise and breeding, ease and charm. Being all this, and being impeccably placed however shakily circumstanced, she had been a triumphant debutante; so plainly desirable, so eminently marriageable as to feel no strong need to marry; so fastidious as to need to marry on society's finest terms, and with the taste to want to marry beyond those terms. She is not at all intellectual or concerned with the arts: Mrs. Wharton does not complicate Lily's desires with one form or another of dilettantism. Rather the opposite: Mrs. Wharton writes, very early in the book, that Lily

> was fond of pictures and flowers and of sentimental fiction, and she could not help thinking that the possession of such tastes ennobled her desire for worldly advantages.

What Lily wanted beyond what Society could offer was nothing opposed to worldliness, but only what might purify, freshen, brighten it. She is never torn between two ways of life; she is simply tired of the shallowness, limitedness, frequent coarse-grainedness, of one of them. She would not just have her cake, she would eat it off the finest porcelain —and opposite someone at dinner with more than just banking interests or sportsman tastes. She is a thorough-bred bored with going round and round the same dull un-deviating tracks.

Despite a situation now grown acute, Lily has not mar-ried because no one equally right in the world's eyes and in her own has appeared to claim her. In the first part of the book Mrs. Wharton introduces, with classic simplicity, the right man from both points of view—but as two men, not one. Lawrence Selden has, like Lily, every social require-ment except money; has, also, finer values and a larger outlook on life than other men in their world. Percy Gryce has hardly any attraction except money; he hasn't even a turn for worldliness; he is dull, correct, churchy, mother-ridden. Selden's lack of fortune is for Lily—and for Selden, with his knowledge of Lily—a great obstacle; Gryce's im-mense fortune is obviously a great inducement. As she herself reflects:

> There was room for her, after all, in this crowded selfish world of pleasure whence, so short a time since, her poverty had seemed to exclude her. These people . . . were glad to make a place for her in the charmed circle around which all her desires revolved. . . . Already she felt within her a steal-ing allegiance to their standards, an acceptance of their limitations, a disbelief in the things they did not believe in, a contemptuous pity for the people who were not able to live as they lived.

Yet, from some deep kind of instinct that no claim of prudence can control, Lily at the last moment throws the game away, loses Gryce. Later in the book someone says of her, apropos another such situation:

> That's Lily all over, you know: she works like a slave preparing the ground and sowing her seed; but the day she ought to be reaping the harvest she oversleeps herself or goes off on a picnic.

And since, in one way or another, Lily keeps throwing the game away, this quotation may count as a key to what is hurtful, unworldly, "unwise," in her outlook. For, after she loses Gryce and at the same time regretfully shuts the door on Selden, too aware of what her background has trained her to need, her situation becomes critical. She has debts which the well-off aunt she lives with will do little about; she has fears that her youthful bloom and beauty are beginning to wane; she has a sense of how society, loyal and kind so long as her worth is not impaired, can quickly grow indifferent, callous, even hostile, toward its defenseless members. Now, except for Selden, Lily has for salvation only a rich, climbing Jew whom she finds impossible. Meanwhile, certain married men in her set, from her not realizing in her high-mindedness that she is playing with fire, get her into trouble with their wives. One of these men traps her into coming to his house and gets her into trouble with Selden, who chances to see her leaving it; another man is the cause of a brutal public insult on his wife's part toward Lily.

For all her perfect understanding of the rules of her world, and the machinations, she has infringed those rules and let herself be outmaneuvered; and, if not quite an outcast, is now close to social ruin. She still, however, has the weapons to avert ruin, to turn defeat into victory, into marriage with one of the husbands, or with the rich, now reasonably eligible Jew. No doubt it is a half-portion, yet still served up on the best china. But, between what is sordid in the method she must pursue, and second-rate in the future it entails, she refuses to act. Thereafter, she is driven into employments increasingly unpalatable or dubious; and when desperate and finally ready to make use of a slightly questionable weapon, she finds—after a last scene with Selden—that she cannot stoop to using it; and moves from an exalted moment to an accidentally tragic end.

What gives *The House of Mirth* unusual seriousness and scope is that, while showing its heroine in conflict with society, Mrs. Wharton shows her equally in conflict with herself. Mrs. Wharton has not been content, by indicting society alone, to suggest that for Lily circumstance is fate. She has created a heroine who, far from being an essential puppet, is again and again in a position to direct her life; and for whom in the end, because she knows the likely consequences of her decisions, character also is fate. If there is always here a determinist force at work, there is yet more than a mere illusion of free will. It is, in fact, because determinism imposes one kind of penalty, and free will interposes another, because society ordains an outcome that the self can neither accept nor circumvent, that Lily is overwhelmed.

Her defeat constitutes, to be sure, a moral victory: in old-fashioned language, though all is lost, honor is not. Honor, indeed, has proved so consistently persuasive as to ensure her defeat. It remains something more, in the telling, than a conventional heroinely quality: we feel it a mobilizing force in Lily from being for her something not so much abstractly ethical as concretely fastidious. Moral sense counts less here than personal sensibility, than a horror of anything coarse or tarnished. This squeamishness, this need for worldly substance in an unflawed form, is the most convincing element in Lily's moral strength. For, again and again, integrity has *inclination* for its ally— though all other claims of self-interest may be against it. On the other hand, in the later, painful stages of Lily's story, integrity has, along with all else, strong disinclination against it; and Lily's actions begin to seem fictional and come to raise doubts. And the final moral victory seems highly theatrical, all too *exalté*. Lily's greatest weakness as a character is that she never succumbs to weakness.

The scene with Selden, at the very moment when we should feel Lily and her story most powerfully, notably weakens them. Doubtless some of the trouble lies in its grandiloquently "period" presentation. But any scene so crucial must have in it so strong a ring of truth as to withstand the shifts of fashion and the wear of time. This scene, at least for me, decidedly has not. Worse, it stresses what has begun to seem questionable in earlier scenes. Lily, physically, is real enough for us—we can accept her beauty, move inside her finely bred personality, grasp her hatred of the cheap and shoddy, understand her rejections, costly though she knows them to be. But against this Mrs. Wharton badly overuses coincidence, ranging from chance encounters that do not matter to single-and-double ironies of fate that matter far too much; and she subjects Lily to the same dilemma—a luxurious life she craves at the cost of a marriage she cringes from—over and over again. As a result, along with feeling that in some part circumstance, and in some part character, is fate here, we cannot but think that in some part contrivance is fate as well.

Moreover, there is quite lacking in Lily what I feel would have been part of so divided and overdelicate a nature—a neurotic element. Exquisite sensibilities and hothouse-bred reactions seldom argue un-neurotic natures. Mrs. Wharton does not sufficiently allow, in a woman so fastidious as Lily, for the slow cumulative effect of being worn down—and hence for a certain falling off in character. In the face of being so battered and beset, would not Lily's excessive squeamishness recoil from the whole world of fatiguing jobs in unaired rooms among distasteful people, followed at night by bad meals in squalid boarding-house basements? Could such squeamishness *endure* a hideous day-long, night-intensified, no-end-in-sight ordeal in preference to a merely second-rate rich man? Would it cleave to what, after all, were almost academic scruples—the more so as, say in the matter of Mrs. Dorset's letters to Selden, Lily was obliged to use them, not to ruin Mrs. Dorset but simply to rehabilitate herself? Would somebody who has always led a parasitic life of one kind, and has been driven into a menial and outcast one, so heroically reject a parasitic life of another kind? Lily is pure worldling, with no hint of the rebel in her, or the eccentric, or the artist, or the self-dramatizing romantic; with no real inner resources or enlightened values; and any qualities that made her queasy with a Sim Rosedale would have quite nauseated and prostrated her in a life of squalor and smells. In a novel of worldliness, fundamental "worldly" factors simply cannot be ignored.

In spite of a symbolically significant heroine, and of many effective scenes and passages, Mrs. Wharton fails with Lily in conflict with herself. But with Lily in conflict with society Mrs. Wharton's success is tremendous. And this conflict is the true thematic stuff of the book, and remains in the end quite independent of the plot. Indeed, in

The House of Mirth theme and plot do not—which becomes a serious weakness—really travel together. Plot increasingly takes the highroad, full of stagy scenery, and rather loses its way; but theme keeps sure-footedly to the lowroad and makes of its journey a masterly guidebook. However much may seem trumped up in terms of story, in terms of society almost everything seems true—so much so as to provide our finest study of an entrenched, moneyed, self-serving New York world. As a realistic portrait of such a world, *The House of Mirth* reflects the period but in some degree also transcends it, to indicate the fundamentals that govern such a world almost always. In certain traditional societies, or in certain superior ages, an element of *noblesse oblige* may confer something finer or higher-principled. But far oftener, *noblesse oblige* is no match whatever for *sauve-qui-peut;* self-respect loses out to self-interest, and certainly to self-preservation.

The picture Mrs. Wharton draws here, compared to that in *The Age of Innocence,* adds a new ruthlessness to the old rigidity; something corrupt to what was earlier cramping; something hard and callous to what was protective and smug. Something almost impersonally respectable closed in on Newland Archer; something all too personally disreputable closes in on Lily Bart. In *The Age of Innocence* hypocrisy still serves conventionally pious ends, still strives for outward harmony; in *The House of Mirth* it would merely hoodwink or conceal. If, in *The Age of Innocence,* gentility strangled self-attainment, it also policed behavior. Dullness presides over the New York society of the 1870's; by 1900, the great thing is to escape from dullness at all costs. Ministering to this is a greater tolerance of divorce, a much greater atmosphere of sexual intrigue, a slow reluctant acceptance, as against the old stubborn resistance, of outsiders. *The House of Mirth* chronicles the exact moment when carriages are giving way to cars, when society is beginning to live on freer terms, at a faster tempo. It seems, in retrospect, a moment when almost every change was for the worse. Society, if now less stuffy, is far more shallow. If its social rounds are more varied, they are all variations of expensive pleasure; and society, going now to many more places on the map, sees much fewer sights. If it talks less moralistic cant, this is from a frank absorption in materialistic values. Frivolousness, furthermore, has made these people more impervious to many aspects of culture than prudery had made their parents.

There are partial exceptions—people who can be carelessly kind or carefully solicitous; who can display good nature, and value and return affection. And people have impressive social gifts, can bestow a compliment as perfectly as they can administer a snub. But beyond a rather expert malice in many of them, there is something noticeably two-faced; and in their self-regardful, materialist-appraising way, they exhibit a variation on Wilde's famous remark—they know the price of everything and the value of everybody.

They know the precise value, as shifting in itself as a Wall Street stock, of Lily Bart. They know what, in the great beckoning bloom of her debutante days, she was, and what, ten years older and still unmarried, she has become. They know when she treads slippery ground, and when she has slipped and just saved herself, and when she has slipped and fallen. Rosedale, the shrewd determined climber, is perhaps the best barometer of all, from having always to be aware of atmospheric pressures and shifting winds. And one whole side of Lily knows, just as expertly, the stock fluctuations of everyone in society, herself not least.

As a study of manners in the amplest and ablest sense— a study that reflects the values and unearths the motives of a large cast of characters—*The House of Mirth* is a tremendous exposé; an indictment of a whole high-placed selfish world, and hence of all high-placed selfish worldliness. Mrs. Wharton's unsoftened, unstinted realism proclaims the strength of her moral feeling. As a novelist she too often turns theatrical, but that may proceed from working with a novelist's tools and refusing to be bloodlessly tractarian. But if her drama falters, her documentation superbly holds. Her situations may come off contrived; but the basis for them, the nature of them, is almost always valid.

Moreover, the *nature* of the indictment has an inherent moral drama beyond the ability of plot contrivance to spoil or annul. For the whole picture acquires a peculiar ugliness, from representing action on society's part toward a member of it who must fight on unequal terms. A Newland Archer, with his comfortable fortune, does fight on equal terms, and if he gives in to society, he is giving in, no less, to something in himself. But, even if we grant all Lily's initial advantages, all her queenly airs too, and star-part assumptions at times, she is victimized by these people from being in a position to be victimized; and just as they exact small chores of her, they exact sacrifices: she must not just play the game, she must play *theirs*. They will forgive her on only one condition: not that she'll never do it again, but that she'll never have to do it again—that a good enough marriage will carry her to their own level. They don't quite stack the cards against her, as Mrs. Wharton's plotting does; rather, if Lily draws a magnificent hand and throws it away, that is too bad: after all, she is a very experienced player and quite aware of the size of the stakes. Their assumptions of worldly awareness in Lily save them from being really wicked.

And Lily, one whole side of whom was aware, and scarcely demurred, and had enough honesty to recognize that side and acknowledge it, is their victim from where her attitudes coincide with theirs rather than from where they diverge. Her tragedy lies in what a shallow frivolous society made of her early, not in what it did to her late. It made of her a dependent, not just in needing money but in needing a life of elegant moneyed ease; she shrank equally from a cramped and dingy home as from a crude or dreary husband. Thanks to her sensibilities, Lily was a perfectionist of a kind; but her sensibilities were subdued to her worldly tastes; and what followed, however selfish society's behavior, followed as much from Lily's refusal to make sacrifices as from society's to make allowances. What Mrs. Wharton intended as Lily's growth through suffering is better blueprinted than portrayed. Mrs. Wharton was plainly in no mood for a happy ending, was plainly too determined a determinist; but there can be florid unhappy endings too, and this is one.

The weakness of Lily in relation to herself, the contrivances of Mrs. Wharton in respect of her story, are for me very serious flaws in *The House of Mirth*. But the book, at the same time, is an unassailably trenchant social indictment. Indeed, had Mrs. Wharton's method succeeded with Lily to the extent that it did with the life Lily was bred to, we should have had a great novel. What we have instead is great social criticism, given at least the concreteness and strong character interest that a novel alone can provide.

XVI

THE LETTERS AND LIFE OF
HENRY ADAMS

HENRY ADAMS STANDS SO DECIDEDLY IN THE FORE-
front of American historians and autobiographers that it
perhaps needs be stressed that he stands decidedly first
among American letter writers. Moreover, it is Adams the
letter writer who most vividly reveals Henry Adams the
man, the possessor of a particular temperament, the product of a particular society—a society that was in one sense
to help create his values, in another, to help make them
crumble. The *man* is fairly remote from us in the scholar
and the historian, the man is posed very formally for us in
the autobiographer and the man of thought; on the other
hand, the man comes brilliantly alive in the letter writer,
where he is constantly the man of the world. If, again, in
his letters he makes us think of another man of the world
who was also a great social letter writer—Horace Walpole
—it is not least because Henry Adams thought so himself.
Not only did Adams find Walpole and his eighteenth-

century world congenial and absorbing enough to make a dinner companion of them when he dined alone, but, as a young man, Adams could confess that without hoping to become a Walpole, he would like to think that in aftertimes his letters too might be read and quoted as "a memorial of manners and habits," in his case, "of the time of the great Secession of 1860." And "what surprises me most," Adams remarks of Walpole some ten years later, "is that he is so extremely like ourselves; he might be a letter writer of today . . . until," Adams adds, "I trip over a sword!"

Now, clearly, what attracted Adams to Walpole was not the man himself, for in all sorts of important ways they crucially differed—though more than we might imagine, they could be strangely alike, or allied. What attracted Adams is the world they both inhabit, and the worldly events they both chronicle, and the worldly tone they both display in their chronicling. "If we didn't know these people," Adams says in 1869 of Walpole's cast of characters, "then we know some one for all the world like them! How little the world was changed in a century!"

The fact of the matter, of course, is that the world had changed tremendously in a century. Things are as far apart as *The Vicar of Wakefield* and Zola; as early Mozart and late Wagner; as the sedan chair and the transcontinental railroad; as the reign of the aristocracy and the rule of the middle class; as thirteen discontented colonies and some thirty-odd United States. The world between 1769 and 1869 had passed through momentous revolutions—American and French, agrarian and industrial, mechanical and sociological. Malthus and Darwin had invaded the scene; medicine and science had transformed it. Most people, looking back a century from 1870, would have an all-too-complacent sense of spectacular distance.

And yet one can quite understand how a Henry Adams might remark "How little the world has changed in a century!" For the great point involved is how little the two men's way of looking at things—and what they looked at—differed. At bottom Adams' comment is not one of fact but of attitude, of *nil admirari*, and of encountering nothing that really could surprise one. But in a far more literal sense, Adams could feel how little the world he encountered in Walpole's letters differed from the world he looked out on from his Washington window. For what each man means by "the world" is almost identical, is the world of politics seen from the inside and the world of society lived at its very center; is a world of forms and punctilios that conceal much more than they show and that make, accordingly, for a great hive of gossip, for looking through keyholes and feeling for cracks; a world of bland treacheries and bizarre alliances and astounding coalitions, a world with moments of fairyland and more frequent moments of farce; a world, above all, of merciless anecdote and mandarin innuendo, its surface all gloss, its underside all grime.

If I so extensively compare two men who lived an eon and an ocean apart, it is to make the essential point that in Adams' case they really didn't—that he was in temperament very much an eighteenth-century man, that he was most often in his sympathies both aristocratic and English. At least two very important qualities distinguish Adams from a social chronicler of genius like Walpole: Adams had a first-rate mind where Walpole, by any significant standards, had no mind at all; and Adams had generally what Walpole wholly lacked, a masculine outlook. But the very fact that Adams far surpassed so distinguished a dilettante worldling is what lends particular interest to his so often resembling him. The magnificence of Adams' letters *as* letters, as light thrown on a whole age and society, remains in the end their high and absolute merit. But they have an additional value, as an accumulative, unwitting self-portrait of someone not just a great letter writer, but of someone who might have been, and in his letters reveals why he failed to be, a great man.

However different the nineteenth century might otherwise seem, it still offered its letter writers decided eighteenth-century opportunities and rewards. If the eighteenth century's Walpole was the son of a tremendous prime minister, the nineteenth century's Adams was the grandson and great-grandson of Presidents. When young, Adams too had his own form of the classic Grand Tour, to become thereafter a member of a wellborn and well-connected circle, and to move very rarely outside it. He professed, as had Walpole, a high-minded Roman-style republicanism, which with him too was a kind of mist-shrouded ideal, a kind of ultrapatrician illusion. Adams took an eighteenth-century pleasure in the company of clever women who possessed the attributes of great ladies; he took an eighteenth-century interest in the minor forms no less than the monuments of culture—in objets d'art no less than paintings, in country houses as well as cathedrals. Adams too, within his own constricted social world, became the friend of party politicians as well as of distinguished statesmen, and became, just so, as shruggingly cynical of what his friends were up to as any worldling under the Georges. In high Horatian eighteenth-century strain Adams professed to live apart from society; yet, with eighteenth-century finesse, he contrived to be intimately, indeed confidentially, in touch with it. All this helped imbue his letters with peculiar, particular, delightful eighteenth-century overtones and effects. He shared one thing further with that supreme era of social letter writers: however much he might disparage whom he was writing about, whomever he was writing to he made every effort to please.

Sometimes this was simply by being playful: he wishes, he says, that he could offer news

> either that I was dead, or born again, or had lost my grand-mother, or was left an orphan, or was elected King of Manchuria. On the contrary, nothing has happened. Almost every one *else* has died, as usual, or threatened to die, and whole batches of Kings have been *elected* in Manchuria; but I am sitting here in Washington just as you left me ten years ago.

Adams had that quality among great letter writers not only of making something of nothing, but of almost wishing for nothing to show what could be made of it. And he had always a certain sophisticated fancifulness, or whimsicality of phrase. He describes the great Temple of Aesculapius as a sort of "Greek Carlsbad." He writes from his summer home in Massachusetts that "the mosquitoes are so thick that on hot, sunny days they cast an agreeable flickering shade." He speaks of a coming marriage (echoing Lady Mary Montagu) as "meant for wear rather than show." He had also the gift of creating something wild and amusing out of what in itself might be grisly:

> Old Levi P. Morton, who is hovering in or about his nineties, was in the Bernay R.R. accident the other day, and crawled out from the dead bodies through an upper window; got a cab nearby, drove two hours, caught another train, and got to Paris at 11 o'clock, while his daughters were turning over all the corpses on the field to find him.

And Adams adds by way of postscript:

> The man knew better than to be killed and leave his daughters ten millions apiece. No King Lear about *him!*

In no very different style, Adams describes his fiancée to one of his closest English friends:

> Imprimis, and to begin with, the young woman calls herself Marian Hooper and belongs to a sort of clan, as all Bostonians do . . . She is 28 years old. She knows her own mind uncommon well. She does not talk *very* American. Her manners are quiet. She reads German—also Latin—also, I fear, a little Greek, but *very* little. She talks garrulously, but on the whole pretty sensibly. She is very open to instruction. *We* shall improve her. She dresses badly. She decidedly has humor and will appreciate *our* wit. She has enough money to be quite independent. She rules me as only American women rule men, and I cower before her.

A little more acidly, indeed with a touch of the snobbish dowager, Adams describes his first White House call on President and Mrs. Grant:

> At last Mrs. Grant strolled in. She squints like an isosceles triangle but is not much more vulgar than some duchesses. Her sense of dignity did not allow her to talk to me, but occasionally she condescended to throw me a constrained remark . . . I flattered myself that it was I who showed them how they ought to behave. One feels such an irresistible desire . . . to tell this kind of individual to put themselves at their ease and talk just as though they were at home.

Twenty-five years pass, and Adams goes again to the White House, this time to dine with the socially far more acceptable Theodore Roosevelts: they, indeed, are his good friends.

> We waited twenty minutes in the hideous red drawing room before Theodore and Edith came down, and we went into dinner immediately with as much chaff and informality as though Theodore were still a civil service commissioner . . . Edith was very bright and gay, but as usual Theodore absorbed the conversation, and if he *tried* me ten years ago,

he crushes me now. To say that I had enjoyed it would be, to you, a gratuitous piece of deceit. The dinner was indifferent, very badly served, and, for some reason, nothing to drink but a glass of sherry and some apollinaris.

It is almost possible to say of Adams, here, that whether or not he enjoyed the dinner party is beside the point. What is clear is that he immensely enjoyed *not* enjoying it. After all, to the social chronicler, the more gaffes and solecisms and contretemps on any occasion, the better; to a sort of drama critic of the social scene, the staging, the lighting, the performances of the actors make all the brighter copy for not being quite right in themselves.

On the public and political side also, even on the side of large events, Adams can be lightly mocking, can mingle froth with bile. Though himself keeping, with a certain insistent disdain, outside the arena, he is decidedly pleased with how well he knows all the gladiators, and no less pleased with having a commanding view of the show, which he describes with a kind of cynical gusto.

Mr. J. P. Morgan gets practically the whole loan, and the small thieves are furious. My view . . . is always to encourage the big thieves and to force the pace. Let's get there quick! I'm for Morgan, McKinley and the Trusts. They will bring us to ruin quicker than we could do ourselves.

Like Horace Walpole again, Adams is very wishful of ruin —only to show considerable fright when anything real starts threatening him.

But it is time to move on from the eighteenth-century worldling in Adams to the nineteenth-century man of intellect and the child of a far more complex age. The nature of the great world may have changed rather little in a century;

but something disenchanting—and democratizing—had intervened. Talleyrand's pre-French Revolution *douceur de la vie,* where it had not vanished, had survived precariously; and where men a century before, with their modishly skeptical minds, were not too often confronted with taxing and vexing new forces and hypotheses, Adams, with his own inquiring nature, was now constantly *assaulted* by them. Where men a century before basked in that short sunny interregnum between the reign of superstition and the reign of smoke, Adams came to manhood in a century whose geology could be as menacing as its munitions, and whose new ways of writing history seemed almost as radical as its new ways of making it. There was also a side of Henry Adams that not just responded to this but went forth to meet it. The ambivalences, the contrarieties, the ironies of life held and fascinated him; and where a mere accomplished worldling could see only the masks and false faces of politics and society, Adams saw into the true, or at any rate trenchant, forces behind them.

The lights of Adams' searching curiosity play all over the letters from the far parts of the world where he went to satisfy it, where, often with considerable discomfort, he went poking and rambling about, and looked into corners and questioned. To grasp their range, we must read the letters from Japan or from Samoa as a whole; short quotations can only garble general reactions, and even pith must be sacrificed, here, to picturesqueness. But let us linger for a moment with Adams in Samoa:

> Another generation will leave behind . . . the finest part of the old Samoan world. The young chiefs are inferior to the old ones. Gunpowder and missionaries have destroyed the life of the nobles. In former times . . . chiefs fought only with chiefs. The idea of being killed by a common man was

sacrilege. The introduction of fire-arms has changed all this, and now, as one of the chiefs said with a voice of horror, any hunchback, behind a tree, can kill the greatest chief in Samoa.

He calls the Samoans "the least imaginative people I ever met":

> They are pure Greek fauns. Their intellectual existence is made up of concrete facts. As LaFarge says, they have no thoughts. They are not in the least voluptuous; they have no longings and very brief passions; they live a matter-of-fact existence that would scare a New England spinster. Even their dances—proper or improper—always represent facts . . . Old Samasoni, the American pilot here for many years . . . tells us that the worst dance he ever saw here was a literal reproduction of the marriage ceremony, and that the man went through the entire form, which is long and highly peculiar, and ended with the consummation—openly before the whole village, delighted with the fun—but that neither actors nor spectators showed a sign of emotion or passion, but went through it as though it had been a cricket match.

In his earlier days Adams had brought to his letters, as to so much else, the sense of political and social curiosity, of intellectual and moral inquiry, that bespeaks the dedicated student of the world at large rather than the cosmopolitan spectator of a world of capitals. To the austere, republican, crusading family strain, the young Henry added a touch of what is good and enriching in Hamlet. And yet, as the letters—which are the truest index to the personal life—reveal, there came as time passed, there came increasingly, a touch of what was bad and debilitating in Hamlet, and hardly anything at all of the old true Adams strain. There was in Henry Adams on his mother's side—as he was swift to point out at the very beginning of the *Education*—the

Boston rich mercantile strain, what he called the State Street side. If the Adamses had put at birth a sword, or a torch, or the tablets of the law in Henry's hands, the Brookses had put in his mouth a gold spoon. He spent much of his life pretending to gag on the spoon, as on so much else; but in truth he was not to suffer from gagging on it, he was to suffer from being unable to do without it. It was the golden apple, the apple of *inner* discord, in his life. In terms of intellectual distinction, in terms of Henry Adams the serious and great historian, the paternal strain was to prevail. But with the *man* it did not; with Henry Adams the man, it was the State Street side, in the sensitive and cultivated forms it had the means to create, that would predominate.

The tragedy of Henry Adams' marriage—his wife's suicide when he was forty-seven and at the height of his intellectual career—helps account, perhaps, for the character of his later life, for what Paul Elmer More called his "sentimental nihilism"; for what we might call—while saying nothing much different—his half-rueful, half-malicious pleasure in watching the best-laid plans, or the world itself, go smash. The great austere Adams tradition—which he had at the outset cherished, partly because it was a fine tradition and partly because it was a family product—had lost its hold on the nation; but in any vital sense it had also lost its hold on Henry himself. We have no right to demand a militant nature of someone with a speculative mind. Yet, however much Adams may have been deterred from the life of the arena by temperament, surely he was drawn *toward* it, for a time, by a consciousness of his Adams heritage and by an ambition all his own. But something—family pride of a sort, and the very background of family Presidents— made any rough-and-tumble seeking out of high office extremely repugnant. Clearly Adams tended to see himself as an heir-apparent; the possessor of the gold spoon expected his political career to be served up to him on a silver platter. But the rough-and-tumble political world was not so deferential or obliging; denied the rewards of office, Henry Adams never, in any crusading sense, endured the rigors of opposition. His were, at first, privately acidulous avowals, and then disgruntled dissents, and eventually mere cynical rejections. The world's senates and the world's stock exchanges, Adams muttered, were dominated by rascals; and what could any gentleman or any wise man do but sit back and sniff and shudder? Despite the cultivated voice of Boston and Henry Adams, we are rather close at times to the tone and temper of Baltimore and Henry Mencken. They apply to people the same kind of facetiously derisive epithets; they even inveigh against the same liberal and labor causes. John Adams and John Quincy Adams, surveying the triumph of vulgar materialistic democratic forces, would, in their way, have shuddered as did Henry Adams in his; but might they not have shuddered a little, too, at what Henry was doing, or not doing, and at what he winked as well as shuddered at?

If Henry Adams was Hamlet in that he lacked the resolution to help avenge the murder of his grandfather's and his great-grandfather's dreams; if he was Hamlet in that he, in the *Education,* like the Prince of Denmark in his soliloquies, had a fine gift for dramatizing himself; if he was Hamlet in possessing a reflective and humorous nature veined with sensibility and streaked with cruelty and disgust, and masculine in its thinking and feminine in its emotions—if he was Hamlet in all these things, he was Hamlet in one thing more: in relishing his place in life, and the privileged, princely atmosphere of courts. Adams might be the retired scholar, but on how high and high-handed a level of retirement: it was not merely as a scholar that he seldom went out in Washington but had everybody come to him; it was as a personage, almost a potentate. That he saw no one in Washington is of course a ridiculous myth: he saw whomever he wanted to, and on his own terms. And elsewhere, any such contention would come close to nonsense; year after year Henry Adams crossed to Europe on luxury liners and for months on end moved about Europe at least as much prince as Hamlet—in a succession of splendid hotels and restaurants and country houses, and in an atmosphere not always so conspicuous for seriousness of thought or loftiness of purpose as for sumptuousness of living and haughtiness of tone; an atmosphere, no doubt, of cultivation and elegance, but also of the great world as it had come to be, and of the new worldlings who had come forth to be part of it.

There was a savor of the English gentry about it, a certain smack of established Boston, but these sureties of aristocratic or republican breeding went hand in hand with the high-mucky-mucks and panjandrums of the Republican Party in the age of Mark Hanna, with the enlightened tone of Pennsylvania's ruthless political boss, Senator Cameron. A great many of Adams' companions were very rich. Henry White was to marry a Vanderbilt, John Hay had married a fortune, and his daughter now married a Whitney; and Adams, thanks to his quite handsome inheritance, could always hold up his end. To be sure, even when in 1900 a million-dollar fortune yielded him more than $50,000 a year (perhaps $150,000 in our money), Adams "humorously complained." He had, moreover, as Ernest Samuels tells us in his splendid biography, "an expert knowledge of stocks and bonds." On this head, all the sniffs at vulgar moneymaking from somebody whose money had been made *for* him, and not really very far back, by a merchant grandfather, turn a little tiresome. And in view of his annual London and Paris visits, there is something not just tiresome but a little fraudulent about his remarking—to quote just one of many examples—that "of all parts of the world I know, the rottenest are Paris and London."

It is not that, in all this, one would cut Adams off from the cosmopolitan life and the international scene that he was heir to; but that this cut *him* off from so much else. The drawback to all highbred sensibility is its tendency toward the snobbish and squeamish; the drawback to all traditionary forms and values is their tendency toward petrification. At his best Adams was a great individual, and in the letters there is something notably individualizing, too. But more and more in the letters, we begin to encounter, for all their sharp comments and vivid phrases, certain small prejudices and fixed postures; the *tones* of dissent that cloak the gestures of acquiescence, the air of criticism that would diminish the refusal to act. A distinguished intellectual is not to be summarily condemned because so many of his best friends are millionaire pillars of the Republican Party during one of its most dubious eras. But it can't help making us wonder how many real artists and intellectuals who lacked social credentials were part of Adams's circle, were the people he saw and not simply people he wrote to. It can't help making us ask how much the worldling Brahmin in him was stopped by surfaces and appearances from appreciating what had decided value and depth. The two American writers whom Adams saw in later years are surely those we might have supposed he did: Henry James and Edith Wharton. This is unexceptionable; but what of other writers? His very first comment on Kipling has nothing to do with his merits as a writer or a man: "I imagine Kipling," Adams wrote to Mrs. Cameron, "to be rather a bohemian and wanderer of the second or third social order." His superbly described meetings with a Robert Louis Stevenson who looked, said Adams, "like an insane stork," acknowledge Stevenson's kindness, but they harp on the messiness of his Samoan ménage, on what Adams calls its "dirt and discomfort." John Jay Chapman was for Adams only "the most ordinary, conventional, simple-minded of cranks," a comment that squares nicely with Adams' brother-in-law assessing Chapman as "just his grandmother and nothing more." A further drawback to being part of a tight gilded circle is that, with something like the Dreyfus case, Adams becomes an anti-Dreyfusard; moreover, for being pro-Dreyfus, the great scholar Gabriel Monod puts himself beyond the pale and is dubbed by Adams "my idiot friend." And when in 1899 Dreyfus was sent back to France for retrial, Adams writes: "To my regret they have brought Dreifuss [sic] home, and ceased to talk about him, which makes life dull. I hope they soon begin to bait somebody else, to make it lively again." Even accepted as banter, this sounds nasty. In terms, again, of literary taste, Mallarmé and Verlaine get short shrift; in terms of paintings, Adams could write in 1895, when the Impressionists were still fairly easy to come by, that the Paris dealers "offer no good pictures."

Obviously, a man's personal merits and shortcomings are one thing, and his values as an artist or thinker another. Balzac was not the less truthful delineator of the great world because of his ardent royalism, or Jane Austen less truthful for her personal provincial snobberies, or Proust for a snobbishness almost pathological. An insistence on telling the truth, a compulsive artistic probity, went into all such writers' work. But it seems to me that, over the years, something comparably vital went out of Henry Adams' responses to the life about him. The *History* remains a great monument; both the *Education* and the *Mont-Saint-Michel* have distinction and importance. But the truth is, and the letters are our guide to it, that in the end Henry Adams failed of a certain sense of contemporary responsibility. Consider his habit, in his letters, of disparaging the powers that be—the cynical tone, the *Schadenfreude* that discolors the criticism, the readiness to blame everything on democratic vulgarians or "Jew bankers" (the anti-Semitism was so intense and rabble-like that when stocks went down, Mr. Samuels tells us, Adams "eagerly gorged himself on the filth of the anti-Semite press"). Such disparagement comes to sound like a glib, mindless justification of his own passivity and withdrawal. Cynicism is always a moral evasion, an inward malaise. In terms of Adams' *personal* emotions, of lostness and perhaps inner deadness and unfulfillment, much that could be ascribed to his wife's death or his frustrating love for Mrs. Cameron can be by so much forgiven. But on that score there is no excusing the callous, irresponsible shoulder shrugs about the public life of the day or the growls that are all too often whines. All this becomes habitual, mechanical—a fixed attitude in Adams, as John Hay described it to Henry Cabot Lodge, of "Whatever is, is wrong." And Hay wrote to Adams himself, in that jocular tone wherewith we maneuver to tell our friends the truth, that his chronic complaints were "the sentiments of a scholar and a gentleman who has had a better time all his life than he deserved, and now whines because it is over." This indeed, and only the more in coming from an intimate friend, is a summary judgment.

The *Education*, unlike the letters, is pretty much a full-dress performance, a careful, skillful, resourceful—and in places rather artful—apologia; a document of disillusionment, a confession of failure. It remains an extremely impressive indictment of the more and more corrupt, and corrupting, forces in the public life in which Adams came to manhood and first sought and later refused to do battle. He had, I think, the right to refuse; with his endowments as a man of thought, it might even have been wrong to become a man of action. But he fought hardly more with the pen than the sword. The mass of cynically disgruntled private letters is surely no offset to the fine public responses to current issues which simply never got written; while, as a kind of monumental abdication speech, the *Education* so laces the sense of futility with a sense of self-pity, so elevates Adams' failure as to suggest something sordid about success, that we may wonder whether he was abdicating the throne of duty from never having occupied the throne of power.

Yet, beyond all their other merits, the letters of Henry Adams constitute an outstanding document of worldliness, revealing the defeat, by a too acute social sense and a too rarefied sensibility, of a final human largeness of spirit. If all this in the great letter writer as worldling induces a final comparison with Horace Walpole, it is to make the point that Walpole found perfect fulfillment in the role. His particular era, his special niche, his temperament and talent —indeed, his decided limitations—blend into something single and whole, never at the expense of anything greater. Walpole was saved a thinker's perturbations; for him, the darker side of things stopped with Gothic dungeons and country-house calamities. In a different way, another eighteenth-century figure with whom Adams was at certain points allied—I mean Gibbon—perfectly fulfilled himself also. Gibbon's reputation, much like Adams', rests on a voluminous great work of history and on an autobiography. And Gibbon's autobiography is something of a full-dress performance too, and perhaps on one score more acceptable: for being as self-congratulatory about success as is Adams' for being so self-pitying—and, for that matter, self-congratulatory—about failure. What is more important, the scholar in Gibbon had the upper hand over the worldling; whatever his dips and darts into society, Gibbon led a life of supremely unruffled retirement.

Adams, despite superb achievements, can hardly be thought to have fulfilled himself, or even to have altogether nobly failed. I think his failure was on more vulnerable grounds, and from less inevitable causes, and after less determined struggle, than he supposed. It represented a kind of moral valetudinarianism. In the end, what proved harmful to Adams was not despairingly drawing the blinds, but so often peeping gleefully out the window at degrading sights, only to chuckle and turn away. Some of the trouble too must have sprung from his seignorial spurning of favor and acclaim, from his feeling that he was beyond ambition and above contrivance, from such things as making a rather showy ritual of anonymity, with his books to begin with and then with his being buried "without an inscription"—while sharing the most famous cemetery memorial in the United States! About it all there persists a sense of being a kind of law unto oneself, a sacred cow at very luxuriant pasture.

For the whole man, the soundest comparison is perhaps with Matthew Arnold. Arnold had, Adams himself remarked, "the most honest mind I have ever met"; it was a mind, moreover, much concerned with the same cultural, social, political problems as was Adams' own. In moral inheritance, too, Dr. Arnold's son might boast something as sober as could the grandson of John Quincy Adams. And all his life Arnold, like Adams, moved in a world of society and politics, of scholars and public men, and often among the cosmopolitan and wellborn. Nor did tragic death spare Arnold either, who saw son after son taken from him. But, as I have said elsewhere, there was one vital difference between the two men: Arnold had always a living to make. With Arnold, indeed, a *lack* of leisure offers as good a reason for peevishness as any that Adams might put forth. But it was certainly not the pack on his back that made Arnold the finer man; it was that his nature was fed by deeper and purer springs. In Arnold, as in Dr. Johnson, worldliness was always tributary to humanism. And Arnold was not only, like Adams, responsive to the currents of culture, he was roused by them; he again and again spoke out.

Yet, if what is largely absent from Adams' other writings is all too dominant in his letters, it would be quite wrong to put a final emphasis on the letters for what they "reveal." Rather, it is in every way right to conclude with the greatness of the letters as a thing in itself, untouched by the faults in the letter writer. Furthermore, the man of the world is, even late in life, very often absent, replaced by the scholar, the traveler, the thinker, the affectionate uncle or friend. And if the man of the world *is* oftener present, or constantly dancing in and out of the text, or very much its master of ceremonies, he carries us with marvelous verve from country house to country house, from capital to capital, even from crisis to crisis, serving up, with *sauce diable,* what will one day be history; portraying at every season, with its attendant colors and lights, the much changing, never changing way of the world. Doubtless what the letters reveal about Adams is part of the price paid for what they are; but what they are, as I said at the outset, is the best thing of their kind in American literature.

AUTHOR'S NOTE

As the subtitle of this book indicates, the approach to the writings I have dealt with is based on a theme—on the delineation, dissection, appraisal of worldliness, its forms and procedures, its ambitions and values. I have not, however, in any way sought to deal comprehensively with so many-sided a literature; a number of—often important—writers are not represented. But I have tried, in a mingling of periods, milieus, and genres, to provide my theme with a good many variations. Nor have I been so restrictive as to look on these writings for worldliness alone; as all of them have literary or artistic virtues, all of them have induced me to pass aesthetic judgments. Nevertheless, the theme that channels the book has usually put decided limits on additional forms of assessment, and I should be the first to agree that there are other and very different ways of approaching these works. A fair number of them, after all, are masterpieces.

Thanks are due to *The Atlantic Monthly, Encounter, The Michigan Quarterly Review,* and *The Kenyon Review,* in which portions of this book first appeared; to Random House for an earlier appearance of "The Tribe of La-Rochefoucauld," and to Alfred A. Knopf, Inc., for an earlier appearance of "Byron's *Don Juan.*" I have also, in a few essays, drawn on material used previously. I would, as often before, particularly thank Herbert Weinstock for both specific comments and wise general help.

A NOTE ABOUT THE AUTHOR

Louis Kronenberger was born in Cincinnati, Ohio, on December 9, 1904. After attending the University of Cincinnati, he entered the book-publishing business in New York. He later became an editor of *Fortune*, and from 1938 to 1961 was drama critic of *Time*. He has been a visiting professor at Columbia, Harvard, and Stanford universities, and Professor of Theatre Arts at Brandeis University, of which he was for a time also librarian. His numerous books include *The Grand Manner* (1929), *Kings and Desperate Men* (1942), *Grand Right and Left* (1952), *The Thread of Laughter* (1952), *Company Manners* (1954), *The Republic of Letters* (1955), *Marlborough's Duchess* (1958), *The Cart and the Horse* (1964), and several anthologies, including *The Pleasure of Their Company* (1946). Well known for his affinity with the eighteenth century, Mr. Kronenberger has edited works of Jane Austen, Byron, Defoe, and Pope and has contributed widely to periodicals.

A NOTE ON THE TYPE

This book was set in a typeface called Primer, designed by Rudolph Ruzicka for the Mergenthaler Linotype Company and first made available in 1949. Primer, a modified modern face based on Century broadface, has the virtue of great legibility and was designed especially for today's methods of composition and printing.

Primer is Ruzicka's third typeface. In 1940 he designed Fairfield, and in 1947 Fairfield Medium, both for the Mergenthaler Linotype Company.

Typography by Anthea Lingeman. Composed, printed, and bound by Kingsport Press, Inc., Kingsport, Tennessee.